FIELDS OF PROTEST

Social Movements, Protest, and Contention

Series Editor: Bert Klandermans, Free University, Amsterdam

Associate Editors: Sidney G. Tarrow, Cornell University
Verta A. Taylor, The Ohio State University

FIELDS OF PROTEST

Women's Movements in India

Raka Ray

Social Movements, Protest, and Contention
Volume 8

University of Minnesota Press
Minneapolis • London

Published by the University of Minnesota Press
111 Third Avenue South, Suite 290
Minneapolis, MN 55401-2520
http://www.upress.umn.edu

Library of Congress Cataloging-in-Publication Data

Ray, Raka.
       Fields of protest : women's movements in India / Raka Ray.
       p.   cm. — (Social movements, protest, and contention ; v. 8)
       ISBN 0-8166-3131-X (hc : alk. paper). — ISBN 0-8166-3132-8
(pbk. : alk. paper)
       1. Women's movement—India—History.   2. Women—Suffrage—
India—History.   3. Women in politics—India.   I. Title.   II. Series.
HQ1236.5.I4R39   1999
305.42'0954—dc21   98-30623

Printed in the United States of America on acid-free paper

The University of Minnesota is an equal-opportunity educator and employer.

10 09 08 07 06 05 04 03   10 9 8 7 6 5 4 3 2

To my parents, with love and gratitude

Contents

Acknowledgments

This is a book about women who are trying to make a difference, and it is to these women that I owe the biggest debt. It is difficult to acknowledge adequately the activists in Bombay and Calcutta who, despite their busy lives, generously shared their time and their thoughts with me. I would particularly like to thank Sonal Shukla, Madhushree Datta, and Bonani Biswas for their friendship, advice, and generosity. Flavia Agnes, Vibhuti Patel, and Nirmala Banerjee were invaluable resource persons and advisers at various stages of this project.

Conducting this research would not have been possible without the generous support of the American Institute for Indian Studies, fellowship and graduate assistant support from the University of Wisconsin, and grants from the Office of the Chancellor at the University of California, Berkeley.

This book grew out of my dissertation, and I feel deeply fortunate to have been able to work with Erik Olin Wright and Charles Camic at the University of Wisconsin–Madison, who were unfailingly generous with their time, ideas, advice, and encouragement. Gay Seidman, Pamela Oliver, Joe Elder, and Linda Gordon provided me with wonderfully constructive comments and criticisms. At Berkeley, Peter Evans, Nancy Chodorow, Neil Fligstein, Barrie Thorne, Arlie Hochschild, Kim Voss, Rachel Schurman, Michael Goldman, Kris Barker, Ashok Bardhan, and Karen Booth read various parts of the manuscript, helped me clarify my ideas and question others, and generally kept me on track. I am also indebted to my research assistants in India—Latika and Suparna—for the hours they put into this project, and to Lissa Bell, Rhonda Evans, and particularly Anna Korteweg in Berkeley.

I owe the greatest debts to Seemin Qayum and Michael Burawoy—Seemin, both for her friendship and for critically engaging every idea and word in this book, and Michael, for critiquing and encouraging me every step of the way, serving by example as a reminder of why I chose a life in the academy.

Finally, I'd like to thank family and friends for making my life so much easier in their individual ways during the writing of this book—particularly Isha, Jitendra, Vanessa, Kris, Rachel, Sukirat (on his annual visits), and above all Ashok.

Political Parties and Women's Organizations in India

AAWAZ-E-NISWAN (VOICE OF WOMEN). A Muslim women's group in Bombay, briefly associated with (but not affiliated with) the CPI.

ALL INDIA DEMOCRATIC WOMEN'S ASSOCIATION, OR AIDWA. The national women's front of the CPI(M). Its branch in Calcutta is referred to as Paschim Banga Ganatantrik Mahila Samiti (West Bengal Democratic Women's Association), or PBGMS; also called simply "the Samiti" by its members. Its branch in Bombay is referred to as Janwadi Mahila Sanghatana, or JMS.

ALL INDIA WOMEN'S CONFERENCE, OR AIWC. The oldest national women's organization in India. It is autonomous but has historically been associated with the Congress Party.

BHARATIYA JANATA PARTY, OR BJP. The Hindu nationalist political party. It won federal elections in 1998.

COMMUNIST PARTY OF INDIA, OR CPI. A major Communist party in India. It has not been strong enough to win any state electorally.

COMMUNIST PARTY OF INDIA (MARXIST), OR CPI(M). The most powerful Communist party in India today. It heads the Left Front coalition government in the state of West Bengal.

COMMUNIST PARTY OF INDIA (MARXIST-LENINIST), OR CPI(ML). A party comprising Maoist groups of varying sizes. Once strong in West Bengal, its pockets of influence are now restricted to Andhra Pradesh and Bihar.

CONGRESS (I). The party that has controlled the central government for most of post-Independence India. The "I" stands for Indira Gandhi, who led a breakaway faction of the original Congress.

CONGRESS OF INDIAN TRADE UNIONS, OR CITU. The CPI(M)-affiliated trade union. The women's wing is the All India Co-ordinating Council for Working Women, or AICCWW.

FORUM AGAINST OPPRESSION OF WOMEN, OR FORUM. The dominant autonomous women's organization in Bombay.

MAHILA DAKSHATA SAMITI. The women's wing of the Janata Dal party.

NARI NIRJATAN PRATIRADH MANCHA (FORUM AGAINST OPPRESSION OF WOMEN), OR NNPM. One of Calcutta's autonomous women's groups, which started out as an umbrella organization but then dissolved. Although NNPM considers itself autonomous, some of its members are affiliated with the CPI(ML).

NATIONAL FEDERATION OF INDIAN WOMEN, OR NFIW. The national women's front of the CPI. It is referred to in Calcutta as PBMS (for Paschim Banga Mahila Samiti).

SACHETANA (SELF-AWARENESS). One of Calcutta's few autonomous women's organizations.

SHETKARI SANGHATANA. An organization for farmers, powerful in Maharashtra.

SHIV SENA. A right-wing nativist organization in Maharashtra, gaining increasing popularity and power. At present, it is part of the state government.

SHRAMIK SANGHATANA (WORKERS ORGANIZATION). A powerful tribal organization in rural Maharashtra.

STREE KRUTI (WOMEN'S ACTIONS). CPI(ML)-linked women's organization in Bombay.

STREE MUKTI SANGHATANA (ORGANIZATION FOR WOMEN'S LIBERATION). One of the best-known Maharashtrian women's organizations. It is affiliated with the Shramik Sanghatana.

STREE UVACH. Autonomous group in Bombay composed primarily of native Marathi speakers.

WOMEN'S CENTRE. An offshoot of FORUM. It is an autonomous organization that women can go to for individual support.

WOMEN IN MEDIA. A group affiliated with the Bombay Union of Journalists. It is semiautonomous.

Chapter 1

Women's Movements and Political Fields

A pivotal scene in the recent controversial Indian film *Bandit Queen* shows the protagonist, a lower-caste young woman, being repeatedly and gruesomely raped. A few scenes later, now the acknowledged queen of the bandits and driven to avenge the hideous crimes committed against her, she is seen leading raids on villages, plundering and looting the rich. She returns to the scene of her victimization and, with the help of her enthusiastic band of robbers, rounds up and kills many of the men in the village who had so savagely wronged her.

Bandit Queen is based loosely on the life of Phoolan Devi, a scheduled caste woman who did indeed become the queen of the Chambal Valley robbers in central India during the 1970s and early 1980s.[1] She eventually surrendered herself, as legend has it, when she realized that too many of her people were being killed in the police hunt for her. Shortly after her release from prison, she began to contemplate running for political office, and as she did so, she called for a ban on the film. While originally interested in having a film made about her life, Phoolan Devi strongly objected to the final product on the grounds that it dwelled for too long on her multiple rapes. She asked the people of India whether they would want to see their own mothers and sisters raped repeatedly on screen. No matter how sympathetic the portrayal, Phoolan Devi, as a woman running for political office, needed to be seen as the legendary (and pure) savior of her people, not as a multiply violated (and therefore impure) woman.[2]

This story captures the mythic polarization of "the Indian Woman" in popular imagination. Phoolan Devi is indeed seen to possess only two

I

choices. Victim or heroine, witch or goddess, housewife or prime minister—these are the dual images that persist in our minds about Indian women. Coverage of Indian news, while minimal in the West, fluctuates between the heroic and the horrifying. Thus readers of newspapers such as the *New York Times* and viewers of television programs such as *Sixty Minutes* are confronted with accounts of apparently socially sanctioned individual acts of cruelty against women, such as the story of eleven-year-old Amina, sold by her parents to an old man in the Middle East, interspersed with stories of individual women's triumphs in the face of oppression, such as celebrated Indian policewoman Kiran Bedi, who was formally invited to the White House. As Mohanty (1991:56) argues, a potent image has been constructed, even in feminist scholarship, of an "average third world woman" who "leads an essentially truncated life based on her feminine gender (read: sexually constrained) and her being 'third world' (read: ignorant, poor, uneducated, tradition-bound, domestic, family-oriented, victimized, etc.)." In the popular imagination, therefore, there do not appear to be spaces for the millions of ordinary Indian women who live, love, and work inside and outside the home, struggling singly and collectively, with varying degrees of success, to survive—and sometimes remake—the family, home, and social life. This book is first and foremost about some of these anonymous and unsung women. It is especially about those women—who are neither the always privileged and powerful Indira Gandhi nor the ultimate-victim-turned-avenging-queen Phoolan Devi—who are collectively trying to make life better for themselves and for other women.

Toward the denouement of *Bandit Queen,* local authorities are seen agonizing over the consequences of the capture of Phoolan Devi. If she were to be caught, would all hell break loose? Would her people rise up in protest because their leader was being taken away from them? It is clear from the film that Phoolan Devi is now not only the leader of bandits but also the leader of a movement, which, although unstructured, demands a better lot for her people. What is not clear is how such a movement came to be, how she came to lead it, or how the movement was powerful enough to leave authorities nervous about revenge. As I watched the film, I found myself trying to fill the elusive narrative gaps between her being raped and her emergence as the bandit queen, and between her emergence as the bandit queen and her becoming a leader of her people. I imagined the nascent movement, the precarious building of alliances, the everyday negotiations and risky strategizing that Phoolan Devi must have engaged in to prove her leadership capabilities, the little successes that added to her legitimacy, and the language and images she used to appeal to her people.

In the United States Phoolan Devi is seen both as a triumphant feminist hero (as evidenced by the nature of the questions I have received about her at talks and conferences) and as a peculiar, exotic, and irrational phenomenon. I think she is unmistakably part of a larger political movement and is most usefully understood in that light. Her election as a member of Parliament should be seen as a testament to the high degree of organization and mobilization of the lower castes in her district. Understanding Phoolan Devi requires that we examine the political and cultural circumstances under which lower castes in her district have been able to organize. But this organization and mobilization are invisible in the *Bandit Queen*. Like much of the scholarly and popular literature and imagery about the third world, *Bandit Queen* leaves matters of strategy, rationality, and organizing and mobilizing to our imagination. All we know is that a lower-caste woman mysteriously rose to become a leader of her people.

This book explores the political and cultural circumstances, absent in the story of Phoolan Devi's individual transformation to queen of the bandits and leader of her people, under which groups of women organize to create and sustain movements to fight for their rights and their self-worth. In order to understand the historical, cultural, and political specificity of the construction of social movements and of the agency and practice of actors, I compare activist women and the women's movements in two of India's most important cities, Bombay and Calcutta. I use the comparison to examine closely the circumstances under which movement issues, styles, and strategies come to be selected by participants and to understand concretely the making of each social movement. The comparison is particularly useful because of the differences between the movements of Calcutta and Bombay. They are two cities in the same country, yet the ways in which activists engage women's issues, the nature of the issues, and indeed the activists' understandings of what constitutes a legitimate women's movement are fundamentally different. By exploring these differences I hope to bring to light fresh understandings of the motivations and circumstances under which activists create and sustain movements.

Calcutta and Bombay

The Indian women's movement has a long and rich history linked to the social reform movements of the nineteenth century and the political challenge to British colonialism in the twentieth, with the first all-India women's organizations being formed in the 1920s.[3] The beginnings of the contemporary women's movement are usually traced to the early 1970s, when women were particularly active in radical protests against the Indian state.[4] The first new groups comprised women from Maoist movements in Hyderabad (Progressive Organization of Women) and Maharashtra (Purogami Stree Sanghatana and Stree Mukti Sanghatana), while women's issues were given national legitimacy by a report on the status of women published in 1974 and by the United Nations Declaration of 1975 as International Women's Year. Driven underground, along with other political organizations between 1975 and 1977, with Prime Minister Indira Gandhi's declaration of a state of emergency, the women's movement really exploded on the Indian political scene after 1977. Today the movement exists in highly decentralized form with hundreds of organizations in both urban and rural areas throughout the country, including the women's fronts of socialist and communist parties, independent trade unions, women's wings of mass organizations such as Shetkari Sanghatana in Maharashtra and Chhatra Yuva Sangharsh Vahini in Bihar, and smaller autonomous counseling centers and agitational groups.

Together and singly these groups have fought for the rights of *dalit* women (*dalit*, meaning "oppressed," refers to the lowest castes in the Hindu hierarchy), maintenance after divorce for Muslim women, and equal inheritance rights for Christian women. They have fought against alcohol abuse by husbands, domestic violence, sexual assault, the forced prostitution of children, the destruction of the environment, and the portrayal of women in the media. They have tried to unionize domestic workers; demanded equal wages and employment, maternity leaves, and working women's hostels; and struggled for legal reforms of every kind. While the range of issues with which the women's movement has been concerned nationally is vast, not all issues or all parts of the movement are equally visible in the media and in feminist discourse.

As a child growing up in Calcutta, I was well aware that the city had the reputation of being politically tempestuous—a city where young men and women alike burned with political passions. Returning to India on various visits, as an undergraduate and graduate student, increasingly concerned with feminist theory and practice, I found a rich and vibrant women's movement flourishing in many parts of India. Yet Calcutta was conspicuous by its absence in both academic literature and public discussion about Indian women's movements. Urban women's movements were visible in Bombay and Delhi, as well as in Hyderabad and Bangalore, but not in Calcutta. I was puzzled: this did not fit with the Calcutta I knew. The seeds of this project can be found, then, in an exploration of the *apparent* absence of a strong women's movement in Calcutta.

As I began to investigate this puzzle, it was quickly obvious that the explanation for Calcutta's absence from the publicly acknowledged realm of feminism lay in the issues women tend to organize around, rather than in the absence of organizing. In Calcutta there is an emphasis on issues of literacy, employment, wage discrimination, water, electricity, and the participation of women in general democratic struggles—issues that have alternatively been described as economistic or of "pragmatic interest" to women (Molyneux, 1985). In Bombay, on the other hand, issues such as violence against women, sexual harassment, safe contraception, and amniocentesis are at the forefront, issues that have come to be defined as explicitly "feminist" or of "strategic interest" to women (Molyneux, 1985). To the international feminist community, Bombay stands out as an example of the Indian women's movement at its strongest (Omvedt, 1986b, 1987) precisely because issues of "strategic interest" have come to be defined as *the* authentic gender issues.[5] There are clearly differences of both style and content between the Calcutta and Bombay movements, but what Molyneux identified as the divide separating pragmatic and strategic interests has also served to color the general public's perceptions and the particular feminist perceptions of those movements. It is this perception of Calcutta's failure to conform to the "feminist" model that has written Calcutta out of the women's movement in India. By working toward an understanding of why and how women organize in Calcutta in ways different from women in Bombay, I hope to expand the notion of "legitimate" feminist issues and thus write Calcutta back into the annals of the Indian women's movement.

If the explanation for Calcutta's absence in the international feminist community can be attributed to its movement's adoption of issues that are not considered authentically "gendered," how do we explain the absence of these authentically gendered issues from Calcutta but not from Bombay? Why should movements look dissimilar in two of India's major metropolises? Why, given the plethora of grievances, do women in these two cities choose to be vocal about different types of issues? What are the constellations of factors that make movements put forward certain demands rather than others?

Part of what makes these questions interesting is that the two cities are, in many ways, quite similar. Bombay (a city on India's west coast) and Calcutta (a city on India's east coast) were both key sites of British colonial rule and are crucial to both the political and commercial life of contemporary India. Calcutta, which was the capital of British India for more than two hundred years, lies on a mineral-rich jute, iron, and steel belt. Bombay's access to the Deccan Plateau allowed it to become the home of the Indian cotton textile industry. More than in other cities and regions of India, British influence pervaded all aspects of life in the two cities and created a distinct class of Western-educated white-collar workers, clerical workers, and civil servants. While Bombay is a more prosperous city than Calcutta today, both cities retain their preeminence in independent India.

The similarity of the two cities extends to the social and political history of women. Women in Calcutta and Bombay have a history of active participation in political life, from the social reform movements of the nineteenth century to the struggle for Indian independence. Indeed, women from both West Bengal (of which Calcutta is the capital) and Maharashtra (of which Bombay is the capital) have a history of militancy against invading kings, corrupt landlords, and the British. Legends about women martyrs who ran guns and threw bombs to kill British soldiers and officials abound. Similarly today, women in Maharashtra and West Bengal have significantly higher rates of voting than in many other states. Yet, despite these and other structural similarities (which I will further explore in chapter 2), the issues and goals adopted by the women's movements in Calcutta and Bombay are strikingly dissimilar.

In her rich and important book *Two Faces of Protest: Contrasting Modes of Women's Activism in India,* political scientist Amrita Basu compares rural women's activism in Maharashtra and West Bengal, arguing that a combination of socioeconomic and political factors lends itself to a greater level of women's militancy in rural Maharashtra than in rural West Bengal. The socioeconomic factors referred to are mainly a higher level of capitalist development in Maharashtra and the nature of the caste structures in the two regions, while the political factors involve both the logic of electoral participation in parliamentary democracies and what may be termed political will. While many of her insights are relevant for this study of urban women's movements, the two cities that form the focus of my study are far more similar to each other than are the rural areas surrounding them. Thus the comparison of these two particular cities enables me to hold socioeconomic factors largely constant and to argue, therefore, that it is not demographic, economic, and other social indicators that will help us understand why the women's movement in Calcutta focuses on different issues or looks different from the women's movement in Bombay, but rather political logics, specifically the political fields within which the movements are embedded.

Political Fields

> *To think in terms of field is to think relationally.*
> —Pierre Bourdieu

A field can be thought of as a structured, unequal, and socially constructed environment *within* which organizations are embedded and *to* which organizations and activists constantly respond.[6] Organizations are not autonomous or free agents, but rather they inherit a field and its accompanying social relations, and when they act, they act in response to it and within it. In

Pierre Bourdieu's use of the term, fields are understood both as configurations of forces and as sites of struggle to maintain or transform those forces (Bourdieu and Wacquant, 1992:101). This dual nature of fields makes it particularly relevant for the analysis of social movements.

In the literature on social movements, discussions about political environments are usually limited to a social movement's political opportunity structure—that is, those dimensions of a political system that affect the mobilization, trajectory, and chances for success of a particular social movement organization (McAdam, 1982; Tilly, 1978; Tarrow, 1989, 1994; Kriesi, 1995). Useful as this concept is, it has been limited by the excessively utilitarian focus of the dominant paradigm of social movements (especially in the U.S. sociological literature)—that is, resource mobilization.[7] It is only recently that attempts are being made to recognize that culture may exert independent effects on a social movement organization (notably Katzenstein, 1989; Meyer and Staggenborg, 1996; Taylor, 1996; and Johnston and Klandermans, 1995), or even that culture should be considered an integral part of an organization's political opportunity structure (Gamson and Meyer, 1996). The concept of field adds to these attempts to provide a corrective to the overly resource-oriented paradigm of the political process model by recognizing the crucial and explanatory power of cultural factors and by insisting that action is relational.

While Bourdieu's use of the concept of field is promising and exciting, his unwillingness to be more explicit about specific definitions and characteristics of fields inhibits further analysis. While agreeing with his claim about the impossibility of specifying a priori boundaries of a particular field, I suggest that we can specify at least two analytically distinct factors according to which fields vary—distribution of power and political culture. By *distribution of power* I mean the pattern of concentration or dispersal of forces within the field. By *political culture* I mean the acceptable and legitimate ways of doing politics in a given field, what some have called the prevailing climate (Brand, 1990; Gamson and Meyer, 1996) and others have called collectively shared understandings (Fligstein and McAdam, 1997). Thus an organization's actions are governed both by the distribution of power in a field and by the acceptable ways of transacting everyday business that marks the field.

The *political field* includes such actors as the state, political parties, and social movement organizations, who are connected to each other in both friendly and antagonistic ways, some of whose elements are more powerful than others, and all of whom are tied together by a particular culture. The stakes in this field are both the definition and elaboration of the "legitimate principle of the division of the social world," on the one hand, and control over the "use of objectified instruments of power," on the other (Bourdieu, 1991:181). In other words, the stakes in the political field are both symbolic and material.

Within political fields may lie smaller or even more localized political subfields. There may also be critical or oppositional subfields, which I call *protest fields*. Protest fields consist of groups and networks that oppose those who have the power in the formal political arena and may or may not share the logic of politics in the larger political field, although they are constrained by it. Thus social movements that are oppositional to the state or the present government are embedded in a protest field, which is in turn embedded in the wider political field.

I choose to use the terms "political fields" and "protest fields," and not "social movement fields," "social movement industry," or "social movement family," because protest movements are affected by the cultures, histories, and institutions of politics in general, not just by other social movements. The concept of social movement family, as used by della Porta and Rucht (1995), refers to a set of *movements* of a similar type, such as the family of left-libertarian movements. Social movement industry, as used by McCarthy and Zald (1977), refers to a set of *organizations* oriented toward the same goal. The concept of field is closer to that of social movement sector, as used by Garner and Zald (1985): it refers to all parties—including the media, pressure groups, and the church—that might affect a particular social movement organization. The division between political institutions and social movements has been too sharply drawn in the literature. Instead, as this study demonstrates, they must be linked both theoretically and analytically if our understanding of people's agency and mobilization is to be furthered.

Political Culture

The term "political culture" has a long and complex history.[8] I use the term to refer to the acceptable and legitimate ways of doing politics in a given society, strongly influenced by but not reducible to the complex web of class, gender, race, religion, and other relations that order society. Even as I define political culture in this way, I want to be clear that I do not mean to imply that culture is a monolithic, or seamless, whole. I see it rather in Raymond Williams's terms—as a contested terrain, with insiders and outsiders, dominant and subordinate, countercultural and oppositional forms. Defined this way, political culture becomes both a constraint and an enabler of social movements, something that limits the possibilities of discourse and action and is itself a target for change and, at times, rupture.

The dominant discourse within a political culture defines what politics is, who legitimate actors are, and what can or cannot be put on the political agenda.[9] In some political cultures, for example, mothers are highly respected political actors; in others they are not. In some political cultures, issues framed in terms of individual liberty would be immediately apprehended; in others such a framing would be unintelligible. Dominant discourses do not, however, go unchallenged but are, rather, periodically contested (and in some cases, transformed) through written works and public debates on radio and on television, in protest rallies and in the classroom, and through public actions and guerrilla theater.

Political cultures can be characterized in a variety of ways, but for understanding the effects of political fields, the most important criterion is, I would argue, their degree of homogeneity. Heterogeneous political cultures tend to be flexible, allow the coexistence of multiple and oppositional discourses, and more readily incorporate new ideas. Homogeneous cultures, on the other hand, tend to have one dominant discourse; are rigid, monolithic, and intolerant of difference; and are more difficult to change by a movement. Political cultures can range from the most homogeneous to the most heterogeneous.

In order to be effective, social movements attempt to represent their issues in such a way as to fit the understanding or experiences of at least some people in the society (Tarrow, 1992; Morris and Mueller, 1992; Snow and Benford, 1988; McAdam, 1994). Social movement theorists refer to these representations as "framing" processes. Although there are struggles that test and push the boundaries of culture, it is obviously easier for a social movement to be effective when its framing of issues, attribution of blame, and suggestions for resolution and change are culturally resonant (Snow and Benford, 1988; Snow et al., 1986; McAdam, 1994). A social movement organization confronting a hegemonic political culture has less freedom and must find some way of working with the dominant discourse. When faced with a heterogeneous political culture, however, social movement activists have more room to maneuver and can more easily find, amid the oppositional discourses, an alternative and meaningful way to frame their issues.

In our investigation of fields, then, we must consider the culture that simultaneously permits a particular configuration of a field and is itself configured by it. The political culture of a particular city or country shapes the kinds and the content of issues that can be put on the agenda by the political players in the field, as well as how such issues will be defined and resolved.

Distribution of Power

By *distribution of power* I mean the pattern of concentration or dispersal of forces in the field. This pattern determines the degree of access an organization has to policy decisions, its capacity to implement policies, and the availability of allies, factors that analysts have considered important features of an organization's political opportunity structure (Tarrow, 1989; Rucht, 1996). Fields can be concentrated or dispersed, depending on the strength and numbers of individual actors, as well as the asymmetries between them.

Resource mobilization theorists have detailed at length the sorts of resources that make an organization strong, but they do not emphasize the relational aspects of power.[10] Power in a field is, after all, not just about the possession of resources. It is in some sense the ability to influence others in the field that is the surest yardstick of power. Thus an organization's power can be judged not only by its access to resources, but also by its ability to create alliances with other actors in the field and by its ability to influence the state, usually the preeminent force in a political field.

Organizations, then, can be more or less powerful. Fields can have a concentration of power or more dispersed power depending upon the organizations within them. Some political fields are marked by several organizations able to mobilize equivalent amounts of resources and influence to push forward their interests, such as in a relatively egalitarian, pluralist political system. These fields have a low concentration of power. Others are dominated by one or a few organizations, who control the majority of mobilizable resources and are able to influence others. These fields have a high concentration of power.

Preexisting hegemonic groups within the same movement powerfully affect the survival chances of, and selection of issues and tactics by, newer organizations, since the field tends to be structured such that it favors incumbents (Fligstein and McAdam, 1997; Conell and Voss, 1990). Thus, when a field has a concentration of power, it is more difficult for newer groups to break into it or to carve out spaces for themselves. That is, the initial cost of entry is much higher. For more dispersed fields, the gaps between the agents are smaller and the corresponding importance of any one agent is lower. Both exit and entry are easier in dispersed fields.

Characterizing Fields

> *The limits of the field are situated at the point where the effects of the field cease.*
>
> —Pierre Bourdieu

Fields can be characterized on the basis of the two factors we have discussed. A field that has both a homogeneous political culture *and* a concentration of power can be thought of as *hegemonic* (figure 1.1, cell 4). That is, its reach is more powerful, it is more monolithic and less tolerant of diversity, and the dominant groups within it are more dominant. As I will argue in this book, Calcutta's political field is hegemonic. A field that has a more heterogeneous culture and a dispersion of power can be thought of as *fragmented* (figure 1.1, cell 1). This means that the nature of dominance in the field is tenuous and always partial, and a multiplicity of organizations and ideologies can co-exist. Such a characterization more accurately describes Bombay's political field. While these two cells are the focus of this book, they are not the only two possible scenarios. A field with multiple cultures, on the one hand, and a concentration of power, on the other, can be thought of as *segmented*. Apartheid South Africa is an example of such a field. A field with no domi-nant group but a homogeneous political culture can be thought of as *plural-ist*. That is, within it, organizations of more or less equal power coexist, al-though all share the same political culture, the same understanding of how politics is to be done. Modern Italy is an example of such a field.[11]

Figure 1.1. A typology of political fields.

		CULTURE	
		Heterogeneous	*Homogeneous*
	Dispersed	Fragmented	Pluralist
POWER			
	Concentrated	Segmented	Hegemonic

My argument, then, is that the differences in the two women's move-ments emerge from their being embedded in two kinds of political fields. In Calcutta, the women's movement inhabits a hegemonic field with a concen-tration of power and a homogeneous culture, and in Bombay it inhabits a dispersed, heterogeneous, and fluid field. In this book the strategies and out-comes of women's movements will be analyzed in terms of their embedded-ness in fields, thus granting greater analytical weight to external rather than internal movement dynamics. While the actions of movement actors are un-deniably important in determining the actual shape and substance of a movement, the range of possibilities of actions and outcomes, and indeed the very understanding of gender politics, I suggest, are structured by the political field.[12]

Looking at social movements and their organizations through the lens of political fields offers us an approach that is sensitive to the particular his-tories and cultures of social movements in different parts of the world. This approach argues against excessive structuralism (women's movements vary with levels of development) and an excessive individualism (women's movements are led and defined by certain exceptional women). It also argues against an ahistorical reliance on cultural attributes while taking the dynamic aspects of culture seriously. Finally, by acknowledging the potent effects of already existing organizations and political cultures, the concept of political fields enables us to gauge the weight of history on the present.[13] The history of past movements is crystallized in the present structuring of a field, for past winners and losers, past events and their memory, all play a part in fashioning its contours and circumscribing its possibilities.

Women's Movements and Political Fields

We have long known that women's movements do not occur in a vacuum and that they have often emerged out of generalized political instability and protest—circumstances that have both encouraged and constrained them. In the United States, the nineteenth-century movement to abolish slavery and the Civil Rights and anti–Vietnam War protests of the 1960s were each soon followed by cycles of women's protest and organization (Davis, 1983; DuBois, 1978; Evans, 1980; Rowbotham et al., 1979). The recent collapse of communism in the former Soviet Union and Eastern Europe has drastically changed the context of women's organizing in those countries (Basu, 1995; Ferree, 1995; Molyneux, 1996). In the third world in particular, almost without exception, women's movements have arisen in conjunction either with nationalist movements, such as the Indian, Palestinian, and South African struggles for freedom (Jayawardena, 1986; Abdo, 1994; Seidman, 1995), or with struggles against authoritarianism, especially in Latin America (Alvarez, 1990; Jaquette, 1989). As the editors of a recent volume about feminist organizations note, "Feminist organizations are outcomes of situationally and historically specific processes. In each time and place, feminism reflects its history and prior developments, as well as present opportunities and constraints" (Ferree and Martin, 1995:2). Using the frame of political fields brings definition and analytical clarity to specificities of time and place.

Throughout the book, we will see how the fields in Calcutta and Bombay structure both the rhetoric of their two women's movements and the possibilities for action. We will also see how individual activists understand and work around the fields that their organizations inhabit by allying with some groups and not with others, by magnifying rhetoric around certain key issues and downplaying others, and by advocating certain tactics and bypassing others. Beyond the two particular cases, this book will also use the lens of political fields to rethink three issues in the debates on gender and politics: the role of the state, the question of autonomy of organization, and the concept of women's interests.

The Role of the State in Feminist Organizing

Feminist activists have always had a highly ambivalent relationship to the state. On the one hand, the state is seen as fundamentally patriarchal, an institution that systematically promotes the interests of men over women.[14] On the other hand, the state serves as the guarantor of women's civil and human rights. It creates and changes laws about wages, inheritance, marriage, divorce, eligibility for the armed forces, and other issues crucial to the quality of women's lives. The state is potentially, after all, one of the strongest institutions in any political field. While some scholars maintain that the state unqualifiedly and unconditionally acts on behalf of men (MacKinnon, 1983) and that women are used as pawns in strategic games played between male elites and the state (Mani, 1989; Pathak and Rajan, 1989), others maintain that while indeed state institutions are deeply gendered, the state can be "both friend and foe" and women's organizations should work with it, either from within or from outside (Jenson, 1987b).[15]

In the third world especially, argue Alexander and Mohanty (1996), feminism cannot escape state intervention. State institutions attempt to control, survey, and discipline women's lives and to facilitate the movement of transnational capital within its borders. State modernization and development policies marginalize women and make them invisible (Kannabiran and Kannabiran, 1996; Kabeer, 1994), and in some countries like Thailand and the Philippines, whose economies benefit substantially from the sex trade, the state is an "active agent" in structuring exploitation (Heng, 1996:32). The issue of working with, or against, the state is thus even more complicated in third world countries.

Women's groups in India battle with this issue constantly. Given the nature of the state, should they pursue legal reforms, push for state enforcement of already existing laws, or remain as ever-vigilant watchdogs to prevent erosion of hard-won women's rights? Some groups unconditionally favor working with the state and are even willing to serve on state-created advisory bodies, believing that, ultimately, effective reform can only come through the state. Others are unconditionally opposed to the state because they believe that, in the end, it serves the interests of patriarchy and therefore it is a mistake to rely on the state for legislation in the interests of women. Indeed, some believe that the co-optation of women's issues by the state is one of the major problems faced by the women's movement in India today. These activists argue further that while the state has responded to some of the demands of women's movements, each new piece of legislation has afforded the state—not women—more power. Finally, there are others who are more instrumental in their dealings with the state, picking and choosing their issues as well as the branches of the state with which to interact.

This last pragmatist view is the one I will argue for in this book. When the state is seen through the lens of political fields, it will become clear that there is little that is intrinsic to it. States and their component parts undoubtedly embody several sets of interests, only some of which intentionally or unintentionally serve women well. However, the precise sets of interests that dominate at a particular moment are not given a priori, but rather are formed out of struggle and negotiation within a political field. Thus at any given point, a women's organization pushing for change must be aware of the power of the state vis-à-vis the other political players in the field's distribution of power. It must also pay attention to the political culture within which the state operates. Being located in a field in which there is a plurality of women's organizations of roughly the same size, all jostling for power, where the very definition of "woman" is contested, is singularly different from being located in a field dominated by a powerful and benevolent corporatist state, where discussions of women's issues have been foreclosed.

Organizing Women

The tension between autonomous women's organizations and politically affiliated women's organizations is one of historic proportions, particularly in the third world. In the United States, feminist debates about the ideal form of organizing have focused on the relative merits of "collective" versus "bureaucratic" forms of organizing.[16] The debate between autonomous and affiliated organizing includes some of the issues raised by the collectivist-bureaucratic debate but raises, in addition, problems of political loyalty and the role of men in women's organizations. In particular, the struggles between women working within the parties of the left and women organizing autonomously have been of decisive importance in the ideological debates that have rocked the women's movements of the 1970s and 1980s in Europe and the third world. This book attempts to move beyond the assumptions typically made by and about both types of groups, as well as the accusations hurled back and forth about which organization truly represents women's interests.

The parallel and sometimes converging histories of feminism and the left have often been fraught with tension and contradictory outcomes. In the early part of this century, for example, the ruling progressive or left parties in Mexico and Chile were hesitant to grant women the right to vote, fearing that women's involvement with the church would lead them to vote for parties connected to the church rather than to the left (Alvarez, 1990). A wealth of documentation by feminists in the United States and Britain testifies to the apparently untenable marriage between the organized left and feminism.[17] Yet the left continues to be the natural ally of women's movements. Various studies of Western Europe have shown that strong socialist parties and labor unions have acted as potential organizational vehicles for implementing feminist policies (Klein, 1984; Lovenduski, 1986; Hellman, 1987; Segal, 1991). Socialism, some claim, has always held out a promissory note to women (Kruks, Rapp, and Young, 1989) and women in socialist countries from China to Nicaragua have had high hopes and expectations of their revolutionary governments. While it is true, as Moghadam (1994b) points out, that feminism was on much better terms with socialism in the early twentieth century than it is today, the left, in many countries and with varying degrees of success, has been in alliance with the contemporary women's movement.

Autonomous women's organizations and activism have drawn three sorts of criticism from many who are affiliated with conventional left parties and governments. First, in the context of party organizations, opponents do not see women in a structurally similar position to workers—that is, in terms of the capital/labor relationship of exploitation—and thus do not believe that organizational structures for women should be parallel to that of workers (Beall et al., 1989). Second, some critics maintain that even while accusing the left of ignoring or "engineering" the women's movement, autonomous feminists have not enabled the participation of the masses of women, and, moreover, that autonomous groups are incapable of mobilizing the masses. India-based feminist scholar and activist Gail Omvedt (1986a) argues further that few autonomous women's organizations have a genuine interest in including poor and working women, since they tend to have a middle-class membership.

Finally, some who oppose autonomous organizing argue that rather than be marginalized by maintaining ideological purity, it is better to ally with a popular left party and thereby reach more women (Wierenga, 1985). It is this concern that has led many feminist organizations in Europe to work with social democratic parties (Lovenduski, 1986).

Over the past few decades, however, critiques of the organized left's relationship to women's issues have led to increased support for women's independent organizing. First, supporters accuse left parties of systematically ignoring women's issues. Ideologically bound to a narrow vision of women, the communist left is seen to be incapable of overcoming the "natural" division of labor between men and women (Molyneux, 1981). Since many consider the critique of the division of labor to be essential to feminism, it follows that it is not possible to be a feminist within a traditional party structure. Some scholars consider those who choose to remain within that structure, such as women in trade unions, as less feminist (DuBois, 1978), since only autonomous organizing allows women to be active participants in their own destiny (Gelb, 1989).

Proponents of autonomy see left parties as hierarchical and nondemocratic. They favor more egalitarian, participatory approaches over the principles of democratic centralism, which are seen as fundamentally unequal. If democratic centralist organizing lends itself to the goals of the left movement—the capture of the state or political power—these goals negate the very aims of autonomous feminist groups (Jayawardena and Kelkar, 1989).

Since the leadership of the left worldwide is predominantly male, critics accuse it of viewing women as pawns to be used strategically. Thus it is threatened by feminist demands and makes only halfhearted attempts to bring women into the fold (I. Sen, 1989). Further, because women are used strategically, their issues may be dropped when expedient, as Stacey (1983) and Gilmartin (1989) have made evident in their studies of Chinese communists.[18]

Those favoring autonomous organizing conclude that the only way women's interests can truly be represented is through separation from male-dominated institutions, such as most political parties and trade unions. Not only are men blind to many women's issues, they are sufficiently threatened by some, such as the issue of sexual violence, to deliberately marginalize or deny them. The apparent advantages of political affiliation are offset by significant losses in the identity, autonomy, and distinctiveness of the women's movement. The resources and privileges associated with political parties, it is thought, will corrupt and compromise the movement's demands.

In reviewing the history of this conflict from the vantage point of the mid-1990s, a few scholars of the women's movement in the United States and Europe have reflected that, on the one hand, the two forms of organizing are in fact complementary and, on the other, that little effective action occurs without interaction with existing political institutions and organizations (Threlfall, 1996; Ferree and Martin, 1995). Thus while it appears that the two positions are being increasingly reconciled, this book questions the very premise of this debate, since it is based on an analysis of organizational characteristics that appear to exist entirely free of context. By analyzing both autonomous and affiliated women's organizations in Bombay and Calcutta, I will show that both the *decision* to organize autonomously or not and the *effects* of the type of organizing can only be judged within the context of the localized political field.

"Women's Interests"

> *"Women" en masse rarely present themselves, unqualified, before the thrones of power.*
>
> —Denise Riley

> *For an actor to elaborate expectations and to evaluate the possibilities and the limits of the action presupposes a capacity to define himself and his environment. This process of "constructing" an action system I call collective identity.*
>
> —Alberto Melucci

From the very first wave of feminism in the nineteenth century, feminist theory has fluctuated between conceptualizing women as different from or the same as men. Indeed, the history of feminism seems to be a history of engagement with that question.[19] And it is a question that is often answered one way or another for both strategic and ideological purposes. The question has certain logical corollaries, as well. If women are to be considered different from or equal to men, then are their interests different or the same? What does this equality/difference mean for organizing women? Further, if women as a group are found to have no authentic interests, then how are they to be organized? These questions have not been adequately answered in the literature, since their consideration is often overly general and theoretical.

In a now classic article, Molyneux (1985) argued that in fact "women's interests" was not a particularly useful term. "Women" as a group have many interests, only some of which are gender interests. Gender interests can be seen as that subset of human interests that women have in common and that "may develop by virtue of their social positioning through gender attributes." While Molyneux's work in third world countries has led to a deeper understanding of the varying role of gender interests in women's lives, interests in her framework are fixed, even if they are prioritized differently at different moments. Further, Molyneux's formulation of the differences between strategic and practical gender interests (see chapter 2), where strategic interests can only be formulated after practical interests are met, is not, as we will see, a distinction that can be sustained.

Sonia Alvarez's (1990) otherwise pathbreaking book on the politics of gender in the transition to democracy in Brazil considers only those movements giving expression to women's gender interests. Since politically affiliated organizations were not primarily organized to advance women's specific concerns, they are excluded from her analysis. Moreover, women's movements are defined as those which make claims on "cultural and political systems on the basis of women's historically ascribed gender roles" (23). This definition leaves out changes in the economic system that are considered of primary importance to poor women, as well as any movement that attempts to give women more control over their lives by providing them with training and employment. The narrowing of the definition of what constitutes women's movements and their authentic interests and the accompanying belief that only autonomous groups can be the legitimate vehicles for these interests thus result in throwing out a range of actions taken by women, particularly poor women, to increase the control they have over their lives.

Postmodern feminist theory approaches the question of interests from another direction, arguing that a fixed, already determined subject is not necessary for a feminist politics and argues further that identities and the interests that spring from them must be recognized as "contradictory, partial and strategic" (Haraway 1990:197). This statement makes three claims. First, the same person can hold contradictory interests and embody contradictory identities. Second, individuals do not have one primary identity, but rather identity consists of many constantly shifting strands that together make up a person's subjectivity, and the a priori primacy of any of them cannot or should not be assumed. Third, these partial, contradictory strands of identity (and their interests) are pragmatically deployed. Postmodern theory argues further that these partial and contradictory identities are continually and socially constructed and therefore shift with various social configurations. The question then becomes, "What possibilities of mobilization are produced on the basis of existing configurations of discourse and power?" (Butler, 1992:13).

Recent scholarship in the field of social movements helps ground these insights about the constructed nature of identities. Theorists of collective action have argued that not only do existing configurations of discourse and power shape the possibilities of mobilization but, in addition, mobilization constructs and creates collective identity (Melucci, 1985, 1988; Fantasia, 1988; Taylor and Whittier, 1992, 1995). Thus, through participation and interaction in social movement communities, identities are negotiated and sustained (Fantasia, 1988; Taylor and Whittier, 1992, 1995). Particular political fields can then be seen to enable certain mobilizations and therefore to promote the salience of specific identities.

Postmodernist theories tend to stress the ways in which the subject (and her interests) are constructed through different discourses. This book gives more weight to the constitution of the collective subject (and her interests) through her participation in a matrix of political possibilities. Women have many sets of shifting interests, some of which they share with men, some of which conflict with men's. They inhabit a class, a race, a nation, and a religion and are daughters, mothers, lovers, wives, and sisters. They are also soldiers, communists, prime ministers, street cleaners, and prostitutes, and thus they have interests that sometimes coincide and sometimes clash. Clearly, these identities do shift, but they do not do so in a random or continuously fluctuating manner. We may not be able to tell a priori which aspect of a woman's identity will assert itself as primary, but we can, if we pay close attention to the construction of the political field, understand the process by which certain identities become salient.

Conclusion and Direction

Neither hapless victims nor blazing heroines, the activists in India's women's movements organize and strategize within constraints, as do activists in all social movements. They struggle against rape, domestic abuse, and environmental destruction, and they struggle for the right to work for equal wages and the right to better health, education, and inheritance. They use legal means, direct confrontation, press and media campaigns, popular education, and street theater to wage war against various aspects of male domination.

Some issues and tactics bring them more success, others less. At some moments they are seen as heroines, at others, as embittered destroyers of families. Sometimes they truly succeed in creating dramatic changes in the lives of women; at other times they bring unwanted publicity to hitherto anonymous victims. What is it that enables these women to struggle successfully over some issues and fail in regard to others? What is it that provokes them to be seen as heroines or witches? Under what circumstances are their causes seen as legitimate and when are they not? And how do these activists themselves decide on issues with which to become involved? How, in other words, do these women's movements daily negotiate their survival? These are the sorts of questions that this book will address for the cities of Calcutta and Bombay.

Chapter 2 examines the social, economic, and political conditions of women in Calcutta and Bombay, arguing empirically that neither social nor economic differences nor the background of the activists themselves can explain differences in the women's movements and in the interests of women activists in the two cities. Rather, it is because of differences in the nature of the political fields of Calcutta and Bombay that the two movements have developed as they have. The chapter mediates between alternative hypotheses regarding the differences between the two movements and introduces readers to the lived experiences of Bombay's and Calcutta's women.

I argue that Calcutta has a hegemonic field with a homogeneous political culture and a concentrated distribution of power, while Bombay has a fragmented field with a heterogeneous political culture and a dispersed distribution of power. This means that in Calcutta, dominant organizations tend to occupy most of the political space, leaving little room for subordinate groups to establish themselves. The dominant political force in Calcutta is the governing Communist Party of India (Marxist), or the CPI(M). In Bombay, on the other hand, there is no ultimately powerful organization, and it is easier for multiple groups to coexist. Bombay's politics, particularly in the protest field, is dominated by coalitions that form and dissolve according to the need of the hour.

This difference in the constitution of the fields sets up two very different dynamics for the women's movements in the two cities. Chapters 3 through 5 take us into the women's movement in Calcutta, and chapters 6 through 8 into the women's movement in Bombay. In chapters 3 and 6, I outline the development of the two political fields, paying special attention to their political cultures and the concentration of power within them. I further elaborate the nature of the fields and their effects on the women's movements.

In chapters 4 and 5 and chapters 7 and 8, I focus on two groups in each city, one hegemonic and one subordinate, in order to demonstrate the effects of political fields on the goals and strategies of social movement groups. The organizations I discuss are the CPI(M)-affiliated Paschim Banga Ganatantrik Mahila Samiti (PBGMS) and the autonomous Sachetana in Calcutta; and in Bombay, the autonomous Forum Against Oppression of Women (FAOW, or simply the Forum) and the CPI(M)-affiliated Janwadi Mahila Sanghatana (JMS). I deliberately choose an autonomous and an affiliated organization in each city to call into question assumptions about form of organization and the attainment of feminist goals. For each city, I first discuss the effects of its political culture on the two groups and then the effects of the distribution of power.

Chapters 3 through 8 as a whole explore the motivations and strategies of women activists in both cities and situate them in specific and local fields so that we can better understand why certain issues could be successful in one city and fail in another, or why certain battles could be undertaken by one group and ignored by another. I move back and forth between the possibilities created by specific fields and the activists' assessments of those possibilities. For it is through this constant interaction that social movements are made or broken.

It is my hope that, through this book, the mystique around the tortured and heroic Indian woman will be replaced by an appreciation for the difficult tasks that ordinary women engage with in the process of building a collective movement. It is also my hope that this study can provide useful lessons for women's movements internationally. The last chapter of this book addresses itself to that question.

Chapter 2

From Lived Experiences to Political Action

One Saturday, in the midst of my fieldwork in India, I attended a monthly meeting at the Women's Centre in Bombay, coordinated by Lata, one of the Centre's full-time workers. At this meeting were various women who had received help from the Centre: Meena, a middle-class woman, who said she had known little about the injustices of the world until she got married; Mariamma, who sells flowers at Dadar train station and whose husband had tried to burn her; and Sita, whose husband, deciding that education was making his wife uppity, delivered to her an ultimatum on the day of her college examination: "If you leave the house, you can never come back." These women and others told me that the Women's Centre had given them *himmat* (courage), the feeling that they weren't alone, the feeling that something could be salvaged out of their lives.

The scheduled topic of the day was women's control over their bodies, and Lata encouraged them to open up by asking the women questions about their childhood. Amid much laughter and some shaking of heads, the women spoke about how naive they had been before marriage, about the humiliation of menstrual taboos, and about their concern for their daughters. Vimla said: "My daughter asks me questions about sex. She learns from her girlfriends. She asked me, Is there such a thing as an abortion pill? I told her what I learned here, that there were a lot of problems associated with it. It isn't so simple."

A month later I was in Calcutta at a well-publicized children's immunization camp organized by the Paschim Banga Ganatantrik Mahila Samiti (PBGMS, the West Bengal Democratic Women's Organization) in a *bustee* (slum) inhabited by "untouchables." There, surrounded by injections and serums, doctors and nurses, were more than 100 children with their mothers. One doctor told me that he expected to immunize between 100 and 150 children that morning. The two grassroots activists from the *bustee*, who were largely responsible for bringing the women there, told me that the Samiti had helped them so much, it was only fair that they reciprocate and bring women to this event. The Samiti had brought them electricity, safe drinking water, and clean streets, they said. As she efficiently held up children for the doctor to inoculate and assured mothers that the injections would help rather than hurt their children, Shanti explained to me that she had tried to convince the women that bringing their children there, no matter how scared of the needle they were, was important because it would ensure their survival. But, she added, it was difficult to convince them that these things were important, for "all women want is a job and money to meet their expenses. We try to explain to them that it isn't that simple."

Movement Issues

In the course of my conversations with activists like Lata and Shanti in both Calcutta and Bombay, I asked, "What are the three most important issues facing women today?" This question was meant to get not at the issues the women's movements dealt with per se, but rather at activists' perceptions of the crucial issues that touched women's lives. The short answer to this question in Calcutta was likely to be "jobs," and in Bombay, "freedom from violence." Table 2.1 details the responses of thirty women's activists in each city to the question.[1]

What we have in this table is a fairly comprehensive list of issues that women's movements have engaged with around the world. Some of these issues are more easily called feminist—especially those that challenge women's subordination directly—and correspond roughly to Molyneux's (1985) definition of "strategic gender interests." Others have to do with conditions of human misery, the alleviation of which will profoundly help women, but which are not often recognized as "gender interests." I am less interested here in the extent to which these issues are or are not explicitly gendered and more interested in how the activists have constructed women's needs.

It is immediately evident from the table that there are significant differences between Calcutta and Bombay in the issues considered important for women. In Calcutta, the predominant women's issues are employment and poverty, literacy and skill acquisition, and women's own ideology, which is seen as holding them back. In fact, employment is twice as likely and literacy six times as likely to be mentioned in Calcutta as in Bombay. Calcutta's movement appears to cater to women's practical gender interests. In Bombay, on the other hand, violence against women vastly overshadows other issues, but is followed by fundamentalism, employment and poverty, and concerns about the family. Violence is six times as likely and family issues four times as likely to be mentioned as important in Bombay as in Calcutta. Bombay's movement appears to cater to women's strategic gender interests.

Table 2.1. Issues Important to Women in Calcutta and Bombay

(Percentage by City and Response Ratio)

Issue	Calcutta	Bombay	Ratio[a]
Employment and poverty	75.9	34.5	2:1
Violence against women	10.3	65.5	1:6
Consciousness	44.8	13.8	3:1
Literacy and skill acquisition	41.4	6.9	6:1
Family-related issues	6.9	27.6	1:4
Religious fundamentalism	0.0	37.9	
Low social status	27.6	6.9	4:1
Consumer issues	13.8	17.2	1:1
System	10.3	0.0	
Ecology	0.0	6.9	
State co-optation	0.0	3.4	

Note: Each of 29 respondents in each city was asked to list (but not to rank) three of the most important issues facing women in India today. Thus, for example, 75.9 percent of the 29 women in the Calcutta sample listed employment as one of the three most important issues facing women today. Conversely, 24.1 percent of the 29 women did not mention employment as one of the three most important issues.
[a] Ratio of women in Calcutta to women in Bombay citing the issue as important.

In short, in Bombay, women's activists are more clearly in tune with the second wave of feminist activity in the United States and Western European nations in that violence against women in its many manifestations is a primary focus. Bombay's movement also explicitly challenges the sexual division of labor and patriarchal power on many fronts (including the family), and is thus considered by feminists in the West as a sign of feminism's arrival in India. Calcutta's activists, on the other hand, tend to challenge the state and economy more than they challenge men (and the family), and they focus on basic needs such as poverty, literacy, and the availability of jobs. Because of prevalent narrow conceptions of "feminism," the concerns of

Calcutta's movement are often taken as proof that feminism has not really arrived in that city.

How can these differences be explained? While it is clear that there is no direct relationship between oppression and social protest, it is rare that there are social movements without real grievances.[2] There would, after all, be no need for a movement focused on affordable child care if child care were free, no call for stricter punishment of rapists if there were no rape, and no demand for working women's hostels if single women did not work outside the home. Molyneux (1985) has argued that strategic interests can only be formulated after practical interests are met. Is it possible, then, that women's practical gender interests have been met in Bombay but not in Calcutta? Does the women's movement simply reflect possible differences in socioeconomic welfare? Is there, in short, a *constraint from below*?

As we take a closer look at Calcutta and Bombay in the next section of this chapter, we shall see that, in fact, their women share similar levels of poverty, inequality, and violence. They share, as well, characteristics that distinguish them from other major cities in India; for example, both have traditions of social reform around gender issues and high levels of political participation by both men and women. What differentiates Calcutta from Bombay is the divergence in the histories of their political fields. These fields in which the women's movements are embedded constitute a *constraint from above*.

The Social, the Cultural, and the Demographic

The social and economic account that follows serves a dual purpose. On the one hand, it provides information to enable the reader to better situate and understand the dynamics of the two women's movements. On the other, it explores the lived experiences of the women of Bombay and Calcutta, paying particular attention to demographics, levels of poverty and violence, possible cultural differences, and histories of political participation. It does so in order to judge their relevance to the question at hand: Is there any feature of the lived experiences of women in Calcutta and Bombay that might lead to differences in the issues adopted by their women's movements? Two caveats should accompany what follows: First, what I will argue is not that the lived experiences of women in Calcutta and Bombay are identical, but only that the differences between them are not significant enough to account for the differences in the women's movements. Second, the states of Maharashtra and West Bengal are more dissimilar along macroeconomic lines than are the cities of Bombay and Calcutta.

Demographic Factors

Chafetz and Dworkin (1986) contend that family size, increased age at marriage, and a surplus of women in the population are, among other factors, important demographic variables that determine levels of feminist activity. These factors are important not only because they are linked to increased labor force participation (which I will discuss in the subsequent section) but also because they are good indications of how much free time and energy a woman might have to expend on political or other activities. At the very least, we need to examine whether any of these factors plausibly explain why women in Bombay might have more of an interest in dealing with issues of reproductive control and sexuality than do women in Calcutta, or why women in Calcutta might have more of an interest in literacy. As table 2.2 shows, the differences in demographic characteristics of women in Bombay and Calcutta, while not absent, are minimal. What can we infer about women's lives in these two cities from interrogating this demographic data?

India is one of the few countries in the world where the ratio of women to men is on the decline. This is a more significant statistic than it sounds, because a low sex ratio is usually an indicator of women's low status.[3] In urban areas such as Calcutta and Bombay, both industrial centers that attract large pools of male migrants in search of work, the ratio is particularly low. Thus in Calcutta, there are 829 women to every 1,000 men, and in Bombay, 827. Marital status, household size and type (that is, whether nuclear or extended), and age often shape a woman's concerns, the restrictions placed on her, and how she spends her time. It can be hypothesized that having fewer children or spending a larger portion of one's life outside the family would enable a woman to have and demand greater control over both reproduction and sexuality, and the women's movement would then have to cater to those demands. However, most of an Indian woman's life is spent in marriage, since, although the minimum age for a woman to be legally married in India is 18, women are usually married before that. In 1971, the mean marriage age for women in Maharashtra was 17.54 and rose to 18.76 in 1981. In West Bengal during this time the mean marriage age rose from 17.92 to 19.26.

A woman's life changes drastically after marriage in India, and, moreover, India is a country where the incidence of nonmarriage is low.[4] Throughout India women are expected to devote themselves to childbearing and childrearing in early adulthood, and thus they enter the labor force, if at all, far later than men. While urban Indian men reach the peak of their labor force participation between the ages of 25 and 29, urban women do so between the ages of 40 and 44, thus leaving less time for the

Table 2.2. Demographic Characteristics of Women in Calcutta and Bombay

	Calcutta	Bombay
Ratio of women per 1,000 men[a]	829	827
Mean marriage age[b]	19.26	18.76
Household size[c]	4.56	4.81
Female headed households (in percent)[c]	8.9	9.2
Female literacy (in percent)[d]	79.2	75.27
Female college graduates (in percent)[e]	6.28	6.33
Infant mortality (per 1,000 live births)[e]	40	38
Age distribution:[e]		
15–29	34.42	34.83
30–44	19.97	21.69
45–59	13.75	12.76
60 and older	9.55	5.61
Marital status:[e]		
Never married, widowed, or divorced (in percent)	58.18	55.19
Currently married (in percent)	41.82	44.81

[a] Government of India, *Census of India*, provisional tables, 1991.

[b] Government of India, Ministry of Social Welfare, *Handbook on Social Welfare Statistics*, 1986. Mean age at marriage for all Maharashtra and West Bengal.

[c] Government of India, Ministry of Planning, *Sarvekshana*, national sample survey, 43rd round, 1990. Figures refer to all urban households in Maharashtra and West Bengal.

[d] Centre for Monitoring the Indian Economy, *India's Social Sectors* (Bombay: CMIE, 1996).

[e] Government of India, Ministry of Planning, *Sarvekshana*, national sample survey, 38th round, 1988.

acquisition of skills and, correspondingly, fewer opportunities to move to better jobs (N. Banerjee, 1992). Given the patrilineal and patrilocal arrangements prevalent in most of India, a woman's marriage means that she leaves her natal home forever and becomes part of her husband's family. A newly married woman is thus at the lowest end of the totem pole, and has usually to wait until the birth of a son to begin to wield some power within the family. This constellation of a woman's fortunes within marriage and in the labor force holds true for women in both Bombay and Calcutta.

Commonly, the husband's parents live with the couple, making the wife responsible for their daily welfare. Between 1987 and 1989, average household size for urban households in Maharashtra increased from 4.7 to 4.81 and in urban West Bengal from 4.3 to 4.56 (NSSO, 1990). The larger the family, the more work women have to do and the less discretionary time they have on their hands. As can be seen from table 2.2, there is not much difference in the age composition of women below 60 in Calcutta and Bombay. There is approximately the same proportion of women in their childbearing years, so one can speculate that the kinds of household tasks women have to perform in the two cities are similar.[5]

The last significant demographic factor that must be mentioned, because of its particular relevance for women's movements, is education. Freeman (1975) and others have argued that in the United States, the contrast between available opportunities and the numbers of college-educated women led to feelings of relative deprivation among that population (Chafetz and Dworkin, 1986:55). While the figures for the proportion of women college graduates in Calcutta and Bombay are close to one another (at about 6 percent; see table 2.2), the numbers are simply not great enough to warrant a tremendous surge of relative deprivation. Manisha Desai's (1990:199) study of the women's movement in India shows, moreover, that personal experiences of frustration with jobs or opportunities have not been a factor in attracting college-educated women to the Indian women's movement.

What we have, then, from this quick glance at the demographics, is a fairly similar picture for women in Calcutta and Bombay. Men outnumber women in the population as a whole. Women tend to marry young, bear more than two children, and spend most of their lives taking care of their families. While they are more literate than their counterparts in the villages, few of them have college degrees.

Labor Force Participation

Efforts to link women's employment and emancipation have a long history in both liberal and Marxist social science. Women who are in the workforce are often found to have more progressive attitudes in general (Klein, 1984; Safa, 1990).[6] Increased access to resources have been found to add to a woman's ability to control her own destiny, or at the very least her ability to leave a particularly oppressive situation. At the same time, it is being increasingly recognized that the fact of labor force participation is perhaps not as important as are the conditions of work.[7]

The most significant aspect of women's labor force participation in Bombay and Calcutta is its relative absence. While female labor force rates throughout India are low, they are lower still in urban areas. The recorded female labor force participation rates in Calcutta and Bombay are, for example, 7.04 percent and 11.55 percent, respectively (GOI, 1991). In 1981, the corresponding figures were 6.1 and 8.97 percent. It must be borne in mind, of course, that male labor force participation rates in 1981 and 1991 were

54.14 percent and 53.66 percent in Calcutta and 55.45 percent and 54.94 percent in Bombay (GOI, 1981b, 1991).

Calcutta's 1991 female labor force participation rate of 7.04 percent is a substantial increase over the 1971 rate, when Calcutta had the lowest formal-sector labor force participation rate for women of all the major metropolitan cities (at 4.7 percent). Poverty, high male unemployment, and an increase in jobs in certain sectors have contributed to this increase in labor force partici-pation. In her study of 114 Calcutta households, Hilary Standing (1985) found that the majority of women worked in the informal sector, doing in-formal piece-rate work on a subcontractual basis, and were severely under-counted in official statistics.[8]

Women in Calcutta were once employed in substantial numbers in manufacturing—particularly in jute and textiles—in the early part of this century. Today there are few women left in jute manufacture, once the largest employer of female labor (Standing, 1991). In a recent study of women workers in export industries in Calcutta, however, Nirmala Banerjee (1991) found that the number of women employed in the garment industry was increasing, although men still controlled the skilled and well-paid jobs. She found further that contrary to popular stereotype, women expressed great interest in accepting factory work despite deeply rooted cultural barri-ers against women working with heavy tools.

Maharashtra is one of India's most urbanized and industrialized states, and Maharashtrian women have a long history of working in Bombay's in-dustries, particularly around the industrial belts of Thane-Belapur, Kurla, Mulund, and, more recently, the export processing zone in Santa Cruz (Ramanamma and Bambawale, 1987).[9] In Maharashtra, as well, however, women's employment in industry has been on the decline over the course of the twentieth century.[10]

Pore's (1991) survey of women workers in the garment and electronic industries in the Bombay-Pune industrial belt concluded that, irrespective of the state of economic development and pattern of industrialization, most women workers in industry are employed in low-income, low-skilled, and low-productivity jobs. The majority of women she interviewed had not re-ceived any promotions nor did they expect any. More than 85 percent of these women had joined the labor force for economic reasons; neither age nor marital status made any difference in their motivation. These findings for Bombay are similar to both Nirmala Banerjee's (1991) and Hilary Standing's (1991) for Calcutta.

As in many other developing and advanced capitalist countries, the service sector provides the bulk of jobs for women in both Calcutta (over

70 percent in 1981) and Bombay (50 percent in 1981). A large proportion of women work in domestic service as cooks, launderers, and child-care providers.[11] Their incomes have increased significantly in the past few years both because of increased demand for these services as more middle-class women go to work and because of the changing nature of domestic workers. Today, Calcutta's domestic workers are increasingly young women who commute into the city each morning, in contrast to the historic pattern of domestic workers who lived with and were entirely dependent on their individual employers. The shared commute and daily contact has resulted in a greater degree of consciousness and an increasing uniformity in the prices they demand for their services (N. Banerjee, 1992). Other poor women in Calcutta are self-employed vendors, ragpickers, and low-level workers in printing presses, leather, and other industries.

Poor women in Bombay also work primarily as domestic workers, vendors, and construction workers. Many of the women who live in squatter settlements are migrants who left their villages in search of work because of famine or drought. A survey of six thousand pavement-dweller families found that women comprised 27 percent of all wage earners but only 6 percent of all skilled workers (SPARC, 1987).

Increased participation in the labor force often contributes to conflict over the household division of labor between husband and wife. Poor women face this conflict acutely and, as several studies show (Savara, 1986; Mitter, 1986), simply work twice as hard, often for both practical and ideological reasons. While they readily complain about the amount of work they have to do, few expect any help from their husbands. In urban middle-class India, however, the availability of domestic workers mediates this relationship. While the wife is still responsible for the management of the household and often the cooking, neither she nor her husband actually do much of the remaining household chores.

In conclusion, women in both cities, as indeed in most parts of the third world, work because they have to. Few women work in spite of their husband's opposition (Debi, 1988), and the domestic division of labor is relatively unchanged. Indeed, the experience of working women seems by and large the same in both cities. The state of Maharashtra has a longer history of women's employment than does West Bengal, and while labor force participation rates are low in both Calcutta and Bombay, they are slightly higher in Bombay. Yet in Calcutta, the city where there is less female labor force participation, activists consider economic and employment-related issues to be more important.

Poverty

Despite the plethora of social and economic development programs and initiatives, there has existed in India, at least since the 1960s, an increasing sense of poverty and deprivation. While it is true that the incidence of rural poverty declined with some rapidity in many states during the 1980s, the same cannot be said of urban poverty in Maharashtra or West Bengal. This affects women particularly, as economist Nirmala Banerjee, among others, has shown, since women are disproportionately represented in poor households. Further, the percentage of poor women in both urban India as a whole and in each state is consistently higher than the percentage of poor men (N. Banerjee, 1992). In Bombay, 51 percent of the population live in slums; in Calcutta, 49 percent (table 2.3). The availability of basic facilities such as water, electricity, and adequate sanitation, most of which fall within the purview of women's responsibilities, continues to be tenuous for at least half, if not more, of the residents of Calcutta and Bombay, since only 59 percent of households in urban Maharashtra and 57 percent of households in urban West Bengal have all three amenities (CMIE, 1996). Given the irregularity in earnings of large sections of the population, best estimates of income are gathered from accounts of monthly expenditures. As table 2.3 indicates, the household monthly per capita expenditure in Calcutta is a little lower than in Bombay (Rs 311.76 versus 268.67), although a greater proportion of Bombay residents (73 percent as opposed to 68 percent in Calcutta) live below the mean. Table 2.3 paints a picture of two cities with considerable poverty and low employment, where people spend the largest proportion of their income on food and shelter. The data also enable us to

Table 2.3. Economic Characteristics of Calcutta and Bombay

	Calcutta	Bombay
Population[a]	10,916,272	12,571,720
Male workforce participation rate[a]	54.24%	55.45%
Female workforce paticipation rate[a]	7.04%	11.55%
Mean monthly per capita expenditure in urban households[b]	Rs 268.67	Rs 311.76
Families below mean expenditure[b]	68.1%	72.9%
Slum Population[c]	49.34%	51.03%

[a] Government of India, *Census of India,* provisional tables, 1991.
[b] Government of India, Ministry of Planning, *Sarvekshana,* national sample survey, 43rd round, 1990. Figures refer to all urban households in Maharashtra and West Bengal.
[c] Chandan Sengupta, "Bombay versus Calcutta," 1987.

conclude that while the disparities between those who have and those who have not are profound and the costs of daily living are high, the overall situation is essentially the same in Calcutta and in Bombay. The problems of poverty are overwhelmingly present in the lives of women in both cities, as indeed in the lives of most Indian women. On these grounds, there is little difference between the two metropolises.

Violence against Women

Violence against women, in particular domestic violence, assumes distinctive forms in India. In the early 1980s, a spate of suspicious deaths of young married women in the middle and lower middle classes surfaced in the media. It became clear that these were young women who were either being murdered by their husbands or were being driven to commit suicide by their wretched married lives. The standard form these deaths took was burning as a result of kerosene being poured over the woman's body. These murders came to be dubbed "dowry deaths" or "bride burning" by the media, since they frequently occurred when the bride's family was unable to meet the continuous dowry demands made on it by the groom's family after marriage. So prevalent did the phenomenon appear to be that eventually the courts ruled that there would be investigations in the cases of all women who died within seven years of marriage.

Indian newspapers daily file reports of women dying from burns under suspicious circumstances. Here is a typical entry from the *Statesman*:

Woman Dies from Burns

By a Staff Reporter

Mrs. Dola Dey (22), a resident of Kalighat Road in South Calcutta who had been admitted to SSKM Hospital with severe burn injuries on Monday, died in the evening, according to a spokesman of the hospital. Police sources stated that the woman had tried to commit suicide by setting herself on fire. Her three unmarried sisters-in-law and one brother-in-law were arrested in the case. Dola, married for five years and with a son, had had strained relations with her in-laws, police sources alleged. She had left for her parental residence a few days ago. When, on Monday, she came to the residence of her in-laws to take her son she was not allowed to do so. At this, she had poured kerosene on her body and set fire to it, the police alleged.

Because the statistics are notoriously unreliable, it is difficult to make a determination about levels of violence against women in Calcutta and Bombay. There is reason to believe that the incidence of rape is somewhat higher in Bombay than in Calcutta, although there is ambiguity in the official accounts.

In looking through various sources for statistics on crimes against women, I found that *Crime in India,* the official publication of the National Crime Records Bureau of the national government, reported in 1988 that rape accounted for .6 percent of all crimes reported. It reported that there were, in 1986, 31 rapes in Calcutta and 102 in Bombay. I found, too, that in the pages of *Sunday* magazine, Calcutta was declared a relatively rape-free city in 1980 (*Sunday,* July 27, 1980). A more recent article in the *Times of India* (July 24, 1990), on the other hand, reported that "atrocities" against women were on the rise in West Bengal and that there were perhaps as many as two rapes a day being reported to the state government. Yet another estimates that there were on average .63 rapes per 100,000 of population in Maharashtra in 1978–79 and .97 per 100,000 in West Bengal. Thus, while the actual number of rapes was greater in Maharashtra, there were more rapes proportional to the population in West Bengal (Desai and Krishnaraj, 1987). The disparity between these official reports is clearly enormous, but it may be safely said that rape is certainly not an unknown crime against women in either of the cities.

Perhaps violence against women is lower in Calcutta than in Bombay, but in neither city is it negligible or "low" per se. "Bride burning" has caught the imagination of the press in both cities and is surely reprehensible enough in and of itself to guarantee its place high on the agendas of the women's movements in both cities. In the light of the more egregious forms of violence, wife battering has not been given the attention it deserves, but it is certainly common in both the cities and the villages of India. Suffice it to say that in both Bombay and Calcutta there is enough violence to keep women's organizations and courts overflowing with clients.

Religion and Caste

While India is a predominantly Hindu country, there is a multiplicity of "minority" religions; both the formal legal system and informal custom carry within them particular codifications of religious beliefs. India inherited its legal system from the British and with it the British colonial strategy of governing each community by a different set of laws. Personal laws in India are based on religion, and they define and regulate relationships in the family—marriage, divorce, custody, and adoption, as well as inheritance and property rights. All other laws are common to all of India's citizens. There is as yet no uniform or common civil code under which all Indian women have equal rights. Thus Hindu, Muslim, Christian, Sikh, and Zoroastrian women are subjected to different laws on matters that relate to marriage, children, and inheritance.[12] While Hindu law has recently been changed, the personal laws of minority communities remain largely untouched, in great part, analysts suspect, to retain the votes of minority men. Thus, for example, Christian women are still faced with an 1869 divorce law under which a man can get a divorce on the grounds of adultery, but a woman must prove, in addition to adultery, a second ground, such as desertion or cruelty (Agnes, 1994). And a notorious 1986 Act of Parliament reinforced the divorced Muslim woman's lack of right to maintenance.[13]

Despite recent changes in Hindu laws, they remain, on many levels, antiwoman. The Hindu Succession Act ensures male coparcenary rights, for example, which means that a male, by birth, becomes a partner in ancestral property (Flavia, 1994). In patrilineal Hindu India, a woman cannot be a coparcener. Furthermore, Hindu law continues to uphold the father as the natural guardian of "legitimate" children, thus denying a wife either the right to adopt or to give her child up for adoption. In Muslim, Christian, and Hindu communities, men inherit property and valuable assets and women tend to inherit jewelry and gifts, which they take with them into their marriages. Yet (except for Muslim women) they have no absolute right to a share of their husband's property when he dies. These laws are each in their own way deeply misogynist and codify religious strictures that hold that women are to be kept dependent and controlled. While they may be administered at state and local levels, they are federal laws, and as such the ultimate court of appeal is the Indian Supreme Court.

As the majority of women in both Maharashtra and West Bengal are Hindu, they are subjected to the principles of Hindu orthodoxy as interpreted today. This similarity overrides other smaller distinctions, such as Maharashtra's long-standing tradition of independent women soldiers and warriors or Bengali worship of Kali, the most dynamic and potent of all goddesses.

However, and this is the second point to be noted, there are caste differences in the application of Hindu orthodoxy: it is more closely followed in middle- and upper-caste communities than in lower-caste communities. Upward caste mobility within Hinduism carries with it increased female seclusion as one of its signifiers. Thus, in her study of rural women's activism in Maharashtra and West Bengal, Basu (1992) suggests that the caste structure in West Bengal is more malleable and permits greater levels of upward mobility, unlike the caste system in Maharashtra. *Adivasis* (literally, "original inhabitants," tribes who remain outside of the Hindu caste system) and *dalits* (the lowest castes) of Maharashtra have more egalitarian sexual norms and are less assimilated into the rigid codes of Hinduism. The assumption here is that structurally, where there are more members of low and unassimilated castes, there will be a greater likelihood of sexual egalitarianism and freedom.

In examining the caste structures of West Bengal and Maharashtra, we find that there are certain differences as well as striking parallels. Maharashtra does have a dominant caste, the middle-caste Marathas, whereas Bengal does not. The three upper castes of Brahmin, Vaidya, and Kayastha jointly dominate Bengal politics and culture. It is also true that in West Bengal, where there is no one dominant caste, there have been fewer caste-based uprisings than in Maharashtra. Thus, while there are differences in which caste is dominant in Calcutta and Bombay, in both cities the dominant castes are from the middle to upper ranks of the caste hierarchy. Moreover, in the cities of Calcutta and Bombay, the proportions of scheduled caste populations are quite similar. In 1981 the percentage of scheduled caste population to total population was 4.84 (5.1 percent women) in Bombay and 4.54 (4.23 percent women) in Calcutta (GOI, 1981a; GOI, 1981c), thus the inhabitants of Bombay, unlike those in the rural regions of Amrita Basu's study, do not tend to come from the castes lowest in the hierarchy.

Interestingly, in both Maharashtra and West Bengal there is an absence of an indigenous trading or entrepreneurial caste or class. Educated Bengalis and Maharashtrians tend to work in similar government or private-sector service and clerical occupations, while Marwaris (a trading caste from Rajasthan) in Bengal and Marwaris and Gujaratis in Maharashtra control industrial and trading activities. Thus in both places, economic agitations often take the shape of hostility to nonnative people. Once again, there is no consistent pattern to the differences that might actually explain why women in Calcutta and Bombay would have different interests.

Activism and Activists

History has taught us that participation in social movements previous to participation in the women's movement is crucial in the formation of the interests and capacities of the latter. Davis (1983) and DuBois (1978), for example, show how the demands, discourses, and tactics used by suffragists in the United States, such as Elizabeth Cady Stanton, Susan B. Anthony, and the Grimke sisters, were strongly influenced by their experiences in the struggle to abolish slavery. While some have argued that the struggle for Indian independence had a similar effect on the Indian women's movement

(Ray, 1988; Omvedt, 1979), others have questioned the validity of this assumption (Sarkar, 1992; Jayawardena, 1986).

Women from Maharashtra and West Bengal were, in comparison to women from other Indian states, particularly active in the social reform movements of the nineteenth century, as well as in India's struggle for freedom. While male social reformers such as Raja Rammohan Roy in Bengal and Jyotiba Phule in Maharashtra are better known, extraordinary Maharashtrian women, such as Pandita Ramabai and Ramabai Ranade, campaigned for women's education and for a better life for widows. In Bengal, Swarnakumari Devi, Kadambini Ganguly, and Abala Bose struggled with similar issues. Women from Bengal and Maharashtra were also at the forefront of the fight for female suffrage (Ray, 1988; Bala and Sharma, 1986).

While the social reform movement was led by men, with the impetus ultimately resistance to the British rather than the liberation or emancipation of women, as a result of their campaigns, widow remarriage was allowed, child marriage at least legislated against, and education for women initiated. While it is undeniable that it remained in large part an upper-caste movement led by an educated male intelligentsia, willing to extend female space but not to give up control over their women, it did lay the foundations for women to act on their own and push for further reforms.[14] By the late 1880s, women began to graduate from universities and medical schools. These were the women who led the next, more radical, round of reform, which then provided the legitimacy for the creation of the All India Women's Conference (AIWC) in the 1920s.

When the Indian National Congress (INC) was formed in 1885, women were allowed to become members. Ten participants from Bombay and Bengal attended its sessions in 1889. Women were to participate in all forms of agitation against the British. They fasted, they burned foreign goods, they marched, and they threw bombs. Of the eighty thousand arrested during the satyagraha, seventeen thousand were women (Jayawardena, 1986:100). While women all over India responded to Mahatma Gandhi's call to participate in the nationalist struggle, the response was particularly strong in Gujarat, Maharashtra, and Bengal. Previous to the civil disobedience movement of the 1930s, the participation of women had been limited to the ranks of the elite. Bombay-born Madam Bhikaiji Cama, for example, garnered support for the independence movement in Europe and unfurled the first (improvised) Indian flag at a socialist conference in 1907. Once the civil disobedience movement started, thousands of women sold khaddar (handspun cloth popularized by Mahatma Gandhi in resistance to cloth spun in British mills), picketed and boycotted shops that sold foreign goods, organized meetings, and attended demonstrations (Pearson, 1981; Desai and Krishnaraj, 1987). In Bombay, led by Kamaladevi Chattapadhay and Sarojini Naidu, women participated in large numbers in breaking the salt laws by manufacturing salt illegally.

Bengali women in the late 1920s and 1930s were energized not so much by Gandhi as by the Bengali revolutionary leader Subhas Chandra Bose. Because women were largely instrumental in decision making with regard to household consumption, Bose targeted women to spearhead the boycott movement (Sarkar, 1987a). While women like Lotika Ghosh and Basanti Devi were major organizers of the noncooperation and civil disobedience movements, Bengali women participated in what were called "terrorist activities" more so than women in Maharashtra. This was, of course, in large part because Bengal was the center for these activities. Among others, Kalpana Dutt ran guns and manufactured explosives, Suhasini lived with a comrade (pretending to be his wife) so that she could provide shelter for those who were fleeing from the British, Bina Dass attempted to shoot the governor at her college convocation, and two schoolgirls, Shanti and Suniti Ghosh, assassinated the district magistrate of Comilla (Sarkar, 1987a; Kaur, 1985; Bala and Sharma, 1986).

Today, women from Maharashtra and West Bengal remain more politicized than women in many other parts of the country. They have significantly higher rates of voting than women in many states (Desai and Krishnaraj, 1987), and a high level of organizational involvement. Activists who work at the grassroots levels of the women's movement tend to come from working and lower middle classes, while the leadership in both cities tends to come from the elite—albeit an elite indelibly marked by its colonial past. It was the ambition of Lord Macaulay (one of the most powerful members of the legislative council of the East India Company's government in Bengal and author of the infamous Minute on Education) that the British create, through the spread of English education, "a class of persons, Indian in blood and color, but English in taste, in opinions, in morals and intellect" (quoted in S. Banerjee, 1989). By the end of the nineteenth century there was in both Calcutta and Bombay a middle class consisting of professionals who were products of an English colonial education system. Separated from the popular classes and castes in every way, this new class was infused with Anglophone ideas and values. Calcutta's westernized elite came from the ranks of middle-class and rich upper-caste Bengalis, and Bombay's westernized elite came from native upper-caste Maharashtrians and Parsees, but not from the ranks of the rich traders, the Gujaratis (Ramanna, 1989; Kosambi, personal communication, 1990). In both Bengal and Maharashtra, English education served as the central means of upward mobility for the middle classes. The products of this education system and their children were to become the intellectual and political leaders of India (Basu, 1992:109), particularly in Bengal, as we shall see. While there are major activists from other religions, castes, and classes in the women's movement, the leadership of the movements of both cities is drawn by and large—with certain striking exceptions, such as the renowned activist Flavia, who is of Christian origin—from a similar pool of highly educated, upper-caste, secular Hindus.

An examination of the lives and histories of women in Bombay and Calcutta, then, reveals that while the two cities are not identical along every dimension, they do not differ in ways that the theories about women's movements consider significant. However, many of the facets of women's lives to which I have alluded do mark women in Bombay and Calcutta as singular in India. The primacy of both cities in colonial India, their early industrialization, their tradition of social reform, the histories of political participation and struggles of both men and women, and the nature of their elites all contribute to the particular configuration of the women's movement in both cities.

It is evident that women in both cities face enormous problems in their daily existence. Yet, as we have seen, not all of these problems have become movement issues in the two cities. It is undeniable that women's lived experiences significantly influence the nature of their involvement in social movements and politics; however, the structures and contingencies of political fields substantially determine the nature of the public demands and protests, as well as the visible activism of those movements. Public demands are fundamentally political in nature, and it is in the different organization of politics in the two cities that the explanations can be found. Specifically, the key to the divergences between the movements may be sought in the formation of two very different political fields within the last twenty years.

The Political

Indian democracy is based on a federal, multiparty, parliamentary system. Each of its twenty-five linguistically organized states has considerable autonomy with regard to taxation, law and order, education, and certain other areas of civil life.[15] The party governing at the federal level for most of the period of this study (1977–94), the Congress (I), is also the party most closely identified with the struggle for Indian independence. Other major national parties include the centrist Janata Dal (a successor to the Janata Party); the right-wing Bharatiya Janata Party, or BJP; and to a lesser extent the two communist parties, the Communist Party of India, or CPI, and the

Communist Party of India (Marxist), or CPI(M). Many other political parties have regional strengths and have little influence outside of particular states, but they combine with the major parties to form potentially governable coalitions. The strongest regional oppositional parties are powerful in areas outside the Hindi belt, which has historically been controlled by the Congress Party.

The most powerful player at the level of India's national field has been, without doubt, the Congress Party. It was the party of nationalism, democracy, and secularism; the party of Mahatma Gandhi; and the party of the first prime minister, Jawaharlal Nehru, and his daughter Indira Gandhi. It was, until the people could no longer be silent in the face of its failed promises, the party that transcended all divides. Up to the mid-1960s, the Congress was the central pillar of India's democratic order.

As the Congress increasingly failed to deliver on its programs of social and economic development, the Indian state faced its first major crises in the late sixties, exemplified by the Naxalite upsurge (1967–72). Starting with a tribal uprising in Naxalbari, in northern Bengal, and spreading to a number of rural areas around the country in the next three years, Naxalism has appropriately been called the "child of the crisis years of 1965–69 when India's economy, political leadership and military prowess failed badly" (Rudolph and Rudolph, 1987:391). It was also a product of rank-and-file discontent within the CPI(M), a worldwide radicalization of youth, and the image of China as the revolutionary center of the world (Vanaik, 1990:182). By the early 1970s, the crisis was severe. Poverty, corruption, and unemployment were rampant. The war with Pakistan in 1971 was a severe drain on India's resources, and OPEC's oil prices pushed India into an inflation that affected industrial areas, in particular Calcutta and Bombay (Calman, 1992). Youth, worker, and peasant protests began to escalate. Opposition to Prime Minister Indira Gandhi began to grow, spearheaded by the Gandhian socialist Jayaprakash Narayan (popularly called J. P.). Led by the socialist trade union leader, George Fernandes, 1.7 million workers participated in a railway strike, during which thousands of strikers were arrested. There were massive student demonstrations in Bihar, as well. The entire country seemed to be responding to J. P.'s call for a "total revolution."

What followed proved to be a defining moment both for India's political field at the national level and for various subfields at the local and state levels. In June 1975, the Allahabad High Court found Indira Gandhi guilty of engaging in fraudulent and corrupt election practices in the 1972 elections. Realizing that her grip over the country was slipping, Indira Gandhi declared an "Emergency" in which she took all powers into her hands.

Opposition state governments were dismissed, the freedoms of speech and organization were severely curtailed (under the newly passed forty-second amendment to the constitution), and more than one hundred thousand people were rounded up, arrested, and imprisoned without trial. The Emergency was relaxed by Gandhi in 1977, and elections, which she apparently expected to win, were held. She was resoundingly defeated by the opposition united under the newly formed Janata Party, founded by disaffected former Congress Party members. While this victory meant that for the first time Indians could place their faith in another party, it was short-lived, as Gandhi triumphantly returned to power in 1980.

The Communist Parties and the Growth of the Nonparty Sector

The National Emergency (1975–77) formed a watershed in Indian politics because it resulted in significant shifts in regional political opportunity structures. It was particularly crucial for the parliamentary left, which had enjoyed only regional pockets of support, particularly in West Bengal, Kerala, Bihar, Tamil Nadu, and Andhra Pradesh, and on a smaller scale in Maharashtra, at the time of Independence (1947). While the Communist Party of India had been hostile to the Congress Party in the period immediately following Independence, the latter's decision to keep India nonaligned and to promote state capitalism with the help of the Soviet Union ultimately won CPI support. In the early 1950s, the right wing of the CPI stressed the importance of electoral participation rather than extraparliamentary means to achieve socialist goals. Their first electoral victory in 1957 in the state assembly elections in the South Indian state of Kerala went a long way toward confirming that belief.

With the intensification of the Sino-Soviet conflict, however, the left and right wings of the CPI split. The right, retaining the name CPI, saw the Congress as representing the nationalist anti-imperialist bourgeoisie and remained close to the Soviet Union. The left, forming itself into the Communist Party of India–Marxist, saw the Congress as representing big bourgeoisie collaborating with foreign capital and was briefly supported by China. China, however, soon shifted its support away from the CPI(M) and to the Naxalite Communist Party of India–Marxist-Leninist, or CPI(ML), which was formed by a faction of left CPI(M) members (Vanaik, 1990).

Two facts about these splits are important for our purpose. First, while the CPI emerged as stronger nationally immediately after the split, the CPI(M) was stronger in West Bengal. In fact, when the split came, the leftists held a party congress in Calcutta while the rightists held a parallel congress in Bombay. Thus in the pre-Emergency years, the CPI(M) had gained strength in West Bengal while the CPI remained strong in Maharashtra. Second, the CPI continued to ally with Indira Gandhi's Congress during the Emergency while the CPI(M) strongly condemned both the Congress and its undemocratic actions.[16] Through the period of the Emergency, CPI(M) newspapers in Calcutta, which continued to brave censorship and arrest and to criticize the government strongly, built the reputation of being a bulwark against fascism.[17] Thus, at the end of the Emergency the CPI was thoroughly discredited, while the CPI(M) was considered responsible and prodemocracy. Given their regional strengths, the elections of 1977 brought a victorious CPI(M) to power in Calcutta and left a vacuum in Bombay.

At the end of the Emergency there was an explosion of political activity that restructured the political fields in many parts of India, in terms of both political culture and the distribution of power. While Maoist and Trotskyist groups continued to proliferate around the country, many new organizations—popularly called "nonparty political formations"—were also formed in this period. Some of these were based on socialist and others on Gandhian principles. What these new organizations had in common was a deep distrust of the institutions of political parties and parliamentary democracy—a distrust that had been fueled by the suppression of democratic rights and liberties during the Emergency. According to Calman (1992), "Movement politics became an alternative to party politics." These groups chose not to work with the state, believing that social transformation was somehow possible without confronting it. In the words of one of the philosophical leaders of this new type of organization, the transformation of the state was to be achieved through the transformation of civil society, not the other way around (Kothari, 1986).

Some of these organizations were formed in rural areas and involved tribal rights, ecology, literacy, and the people's science movement, for example. Others were urban—civil liberties organizations, progressive writers associations, and women's groups. Of all the groups that were radicalized and mobilized at the end of the Emergency, the people's science groups and civil liberties and women's organizations emerged as the strongest. These were groups that injected new ideas about organizing political and social life into the fields in which they were able to put down roots, most notably in Bombay, thus filling the vacuum created in the wake of the Emergency.

In other words, after 1977, both the structure of political opportunities and the political cultures shifted in different directions in the two cities, thus enabling the creation of two different political fields. At the time of this study the political vacuum had allowed autonomous groups to flourish in Bombay, but similar groups had not found the political space to do so in

Calcutta. There it was the CPI(M), emphatically not a nonparty political formation, that had established itself firmly, controlling access to Calcutta's political field. The political fields in Calcutta and Bombay were shaped both by national events and by regional specificities (about which I will say more in chapters 3 and 6).

Thus at the same time that the new women's movement was being born in India in the late 1970s and the party system was losing legitimacy in other parts of the country, the CPI(M) was swept into power in Calcutta and has been there ever since. In Calcutta, women's interests became predominantly organized through the ruling CPI(M)—a parliamentary communist party. In Bombay, women's interests became primarily organized through a new type of association—the autonomous women's organizations. It is this conjuncture of movement and electoral politics that has created two different political fields in Calcutta and Bombay.[18]

The Organization of Women's Movements in Calcutta and Bombay

The predominance of party-affiliated women's organizations in Calcutta and of autonomous organizations in Bombay can be documented by an overview of the coverage of women's groups in the media. An examination of the leading newspapers in both cities over a ten-year period revealed that of the articles mentioning women's groups in Bombay, 28 percent referred only to autonomous groups, 21.4 percent referred to both autonomous and politically affiliated organizations together, and only 7 percent made sole mention of Bombay's politically affiliated organizations. Of the articles covering women's groups in Calcutta, on the other hand, 63 percent referred solely to party-affiliated groups, and 3 percent alluded to a mixture of Calcutta's politically affiliated and autonomous groups. The *only* sole mentions of autonomous groups in Calcutta were of the old established social-work organizations.[19]

My argument so far has been that the dissimilarities in movement demands made by women activists in Bombay and Calcutta cannot be explained by differences in any objective lived experiences—the constraint from below. Rather, these must be attributed to differences in the political fields in which these movements are embedded—the constraint from above. Bombay and Calcutta have over time developed different political fields such that in Calcutta, politically affiliated organizations have the most legitimacy and power in both mainstream and oppositional politics, while in Bombay, politically autonomous organizations have legitimacy and power in the protest field. This has, I argue, profound effects on the kinds of issues activists can mobilize around, on the success of particular issues and tactics, and, ultimately, on the possibilities of the women's movements in both cities. While the next few chapters will address the fields in more detail, here I take another look at the issues cited by activists in each city as important (table 2.1), but I do so by breaking down the responses by type of organization within each city (table 2.4), in order to examine the possibility that it is the organizational affiliation of activists rather than the political field that determines which issues are considered important. Table 2.4 thus includes the responses of activists in a variety of autonomous and affiliated organizations; the affiliated organizations include only those formally affiliated to the active center-left and left parties.[20]

Table 2.4. Top Three Issues for Women's Organizations in Bombay and Calcutta, in Order of Frequency

	Calcutta	Bombay
Affiliated	Employment and poverty	Employment and poverty
	Ideology	Fundamentalism
	Literacy	Consumer issues
Autonomous	Employment and poverty	Violence
	Ideology	Fundamentalism
	Literacy	Family

In the literature on international women's movements, politically affiliated women's groups (particularly groups on the left) are seen as having a tendency to focus on general issues of poverty and inequality, including gender concerns when convenient, but often subordinating the "strategic" interests of women to the larger interests of class.

Politically autonomous groups, on the other hand, are considered to be more explicitly feminist. They do not have to subordinate women's interests to those of the party or for political expediency, and are thus able to focus on issues most threatening to men and patriarchal institutions, above all issues of the body, sexuality, and violence (Kruks, Rapp, and Young, 1989; Alvarez, 1990; Molyneux, 1989). But, as table 2.4 shows, such distinctions are quite often simplistic. The autonomous feminist groups in Calcutta do not behave entirely like the equivalent groups in Bombay; nor do the politically affiliated groups in the two cities behave similarly, even in the case of organizations affiliated to left-wing political parties.

Assumptions commonly made about party-affiliated women's groups are, however, borne out by those groups in Calcutta, with their focus on work, poverty, literacy, and ideology, while assumptions about autonomous groups are confirmed by those groups in Bombay, with their emphasis on violence against women. The real surprise lies in the responses of activists in autonomous groups in Calcutta. The first three issues they cite are exactly the same as the issues cited by Calcutta's politically affiliated groups and are entirely different from Bombay's autonomous groups. Here we see autonomous women's organizations in one city emphasizing the importance of employment and literacy, while in another city they emphasize violence, religious fundamentalism, and the family. We also have politically affiliated groups in Bombay whose agenda appears to be a combination of Bombay's autonomous and Calcutta's affiliated groups.

What this table demonstrates above all are the effects of fields. It makes manifest that the outcome of one or another form of organizing can only be evaluated within the context of the localized political field. Some fields will be more receptive to autonomous organizing and others less. Some fields will impel party-affiliated organizations to be rigid about women's issues and others will not. There are clearly trade-offs involved in choosing one form of organizing over another. A focus on fields allows us to avoid simplistic and one-dimensional conclusions about the kinds of organizations and activism that best represent and promote women's interests. For it is the nature of the field, as we can see, that shapes the effects of organization type, be it autonomous or affiliated; the type of organization does not necessarily have independent effects.

If the divergences in the two women's movements are better explained by differences in political fields than by differences in lived experiences, we need to ask how the two fields are structured and how they affect the organizations and movements within their influence. The next section of the book demonstrates that the women's movement in Calcutta exists in a hegemonic field, dominated organizationally by the Communist Party and a strong and traditional left political culture. The women's movement in Bombay, on the other hand, exists in a more open, contested field, with a more porous political culture and a lower concentration of power. I turn now to a closer look at the two political fields and then to an examination of the strategies and actions of the organizations within them.

Chapter 3

Calcutta: A Hegemonic Political Field

Writing against the versions of Calcutta offered to tourists by the *Lonely Planet Guide,* John Hutnyk describes an alternative tour popular among backpacking young travelers from the West. This tour includes, among other things, "a visit to the College Street bookshops near Calcutta University, possible participation in a Communist rally, coffee in the India Coffee House, lunch at a small Bengali food co-op, curiosity shops, various film houses, dance halls and cultural venues." The tour also includes a view of the statue of Lenin, which "overlooks one of the busiest intersections of the city" (Hutnyk, 1996:133). This is certainly an unusual tour, not easily available in most cities around the world. While often synonymous with poverty and charity, aptly captured in the title of Hutnyk's book, *The Rumour of Calcutta: Tourism, Charity, and the Poverty of Representation,* Calcutta is also synonymous with vivid intellectual culture and deeply rooted left-wing politics. Calcutta is a city much written about, mourned and yet passionately loved, partly because people find there a humanity in circumstances usually bereft of it.

I begin this discussion of Calcutta's political field with an account of a literacy campaign launched by the CPI(M) and its women's wing, the Paschim Banga Ganatantrik Mahila Samiti (PBGMS, or the Samiti), because this campaign captures both the concern about the fate of humanity that is typical of Calcutta and the strength of the CPI(M), the organization that undertook this campaign and that has come to be seen as the representative of Calcutta's politics. The contours of this campaign make a vivid contrast with the gender-specific amniocentesis campaign in Bombay (see chapter 6).

The PBGMS Literacy Campaign: Making Girls "Whole Human Beings"

Without literacy we are not human. We are like frogs in a well. To get rid of the superstitions that hurt us, it is important to be able to read and understand. Further, we must learn in our mother tongue so that we can retain the knowledge.

—PBGMS member

The campaign to increase male and female literacy is considered one of the major concerns and successes of the PBGMS. In West Bengal, as in other Indian states, female literacy (30.3 percent) lags considerably behind male literacy (50.5 percent) (GOI, 1981b). Spurred on by the designation of the year 1992 by the South Asian Association for Regional Co-operation as the Year of the Girl Child, the CPI(M) government launched a massive campaign aimed at adult and child literacy. In 1993, the district of Burdwan was declared the first 100 percent literate district in West Bengal.

Literacy was chosen by the CPI(M) as a critical organizing issue because it was considered "a basic need" of the people. But why was it simultaneously considered a "women's issue"? The answer is best expressed by teacher and veteran PBGMS member Mrinalini Dasgupta in her presentation to the Committee on the Girl Child.

> Today's girl child is tomorrow's mother, housewife, citizen, teacher, doctor, worker, laborer, and peasant. To protect tomorrow's daughters we must educate the mothers, ensure they are healthy and financially secure, and so on. . . . Women are their own worst enemies. Women's religiosity, superstition, and illiteracy have caused their doom. . . . If we can educate today's five- to sixteen-year-old girls within and outside of schools, *if we can make them conscious, if we can make them aware that they are wholly human beings, not "just girls," but humans who can participate in sports, music, and dance and in public arenas with independence and competence, who can create and control their own lives in a beautiful way,* then we will have accomplished something in this decade of the girl child. (Mrinalini Dasgupta in *Eksathe*, 1991; emphasis added)

Here, illiteracy has tragic economic and human consequences. Making girls wholly human, enabling them to realize their personhood by opening them up to the world of ideas, is a theme familiar to liberal-feminist thought, and to Marxism, as well. Women should be made independent and competent human beings, as should men. That, according to Mrinalini Dasgupta, is what is to be accomplished, and that is what literacy will help achieve.

Women were, however, not the original targets of the literacy program. The idea of launching a literacy program was initially debated and discussed at the upper echelons of the CPI(M) and then put forward to both men and women, along with other projects and ideas. The response was overwhelming, particularly from women. It was not, as one activist said, that women understood that they could not do without literacy and asked the PBGMS for these programs. It was simply that it was women who turned up in large numbers to the literacy camps that were initially established. Women came forward and said they wanted to be able to educate their children or that they were tired of constantly having to rely on men. For many others, the chance to attend evening classes provided a welcome respite from their daily rounds of household chores.

The initial demand, then, did not come from the constituency of women, but when reports filtered back from the local committees that women were the most committed to the project, the party and PBGMS leadership began to target them specifically. This was not, then, a demand that initially came from the grass roots, although some claim that this indeed had been the case. Literacy became a women's issue because women responded to it.

The stated goal of the literacy program was not simply to teach people how to read, write, and add and subtract, but to make them aware of their political, economic, and social rights and to provide a forum for participation and discussion (*Sanghatan o Sangbad,* January 1990). PBGMS publications such as *Eksathe* and *Sanghatan o Sangbad* provided detailed information about the implementation of the literacy project. The specific aim was to make all PBGMS members literate within the next five years.[1]

Workers at local levels did not participate in the formulation of this goal. They were provided with detailed instructions as to its implementation and were expected to report to their committees about any problems they encountered. Ideally, these problems would be discussed, and programs and policies would be modified accordingly. Once targets were set and the camps set in motion, workers at the grassroots level discovered that many more centers were needed specifically for women, not only because many more of the interested illiterate were women, but also because many neighborhoods frowned upon men and women in the same classroom. They found further that child care had to be provided for and class times had to be changed to work around women's daily schedules. They tracked down women who showed initial interest and then dropped out and frequently found that their husbands had refused to let them attend the classes. In such cases, according to a grassroots activist, on verifying that the woman herself was indeed still interested in learning, they attempted to negotiate with the husband. They tried to convince him that the money she would earn in the long term because of her increased skills would benefit the entire family. "Sometimes they are persuaded by us," said the activist. "*But often they agree because they don't dare fight us*" (P11; emphasis added).[2] It is party pressure or the fear of a powerful party that ensures that husbands will not stand in the way of their wives' participation in the literacy program. This telling fact explains why the CPI(M) has succeeded, at least according to initial reports, where so many other organizations have failed.

What then, does this campaign tell us about Calcutta's political field? It gives us an idea of issues that are most easily considered politically legitimate and the language in which they must be couched. Literacy is an issue that enjoys unquestioned legitimacy within this political culture. To make it possible for women to think along rational scientific lines, to equip them with skills that enable them to find work, to rid them of the superstition that weighs them down, to teach women to take their rightful political place alongside men—few in Calcutta would deem this issue unfit for selection.

It tells us further that we have, in Calcutta, a large, powerful, democratic-centralist organization that makes decisions at the top, provides a service to its constituents, and judges its success or failure by their response. While the original idea may have been ideologically motivated (although not in gender-specific terms), decisions to invest energy into it were governed by the degree to which it was popularly received. *In this field, an issue becomes a woman's issue largely because women respond to it.*

The PBGMS-CPI(M) members also knew, given their numerical strength, that this was a campaign they had the capacity to successfully conduct. Of all the political forces in the state, theirs was the only one with the organization, reach, and capacity to undertake a campaign of this size, and they did so with considerable fanfare. This campaign is thus in many ways a perfect indicator of both the culture and the distribution of power in Calcutta's political field.

While chapters 4 and 5 draw out the consequences of Calcutta's field for the hegemonic and nonhegemonic groups within it, here I explore in some detail the nature of Calcutta's political field and how it was constituted. I argue that, as indicated by the literacy campaign, Calcutta's political field is powerful and characterized by a monolithic left political culture, on the one hand, and a concentration of power on the other. What are the implications for the women's movement of the CPI(M) being both the most powerful actor in the field and controlling the state? And what are the implications for the women's movement of a monolithic, impermeable political culture?

Calcutta: A Field with Concentrated Power and a Homogeneous Culture

Calcutta, as Partha Chatterjee has noted, fits everybody's stereotype of the third world city, with its wretched poverty and reputedly volatile political climate (Chatterjee, 1990:27). In the early part of this century, it was home to revolutionary nationalist groups (as opposed to Gandhian nonviolent groups), and in the 1960s and 1970s it exploded with the Naxalbari and student agitations. Since 1977, Calcutta has been governed by the Communist Party of India (Marxist), making the CPI(M) the longest-serving democratically elected communist party in the world. The presence of this party has indelibly marked Calcutta's political field, at once keeping alive Calcutta's reputation as a city of extremes and tempering the politics of protest in the city. It is also the force that has ultimately molded the women's movement in that state. How did the CPI(M) come to be such a power in West Bengal?

For many reasons, the Congress has not enjoyed great support in West Bengal, even though it did dominate politics in the state through the 1950s. In the pre-Independence period, the "father" of the Congress-led struggle for Indian freedom, Mahatma Gandhi, was less popular in Bengal than in the rest of India, since he effectively put an end to Bengali preeminence in the nationalist movement. Gandhi was resented not only because he removed the Bengali hero, Netaji Subhas Chandra Bose, from power within the Congress, but because he was seen to continue the domination of the Hindi heartland in Indian politics (Kohli, 1984). Even within Congress ranks, the leadership in Bengal was more left oriented and critical of Gandhi than elsewhere (Vanaik, 1990) and more suspicious of the official Congress. That the Congress managed to stay in power for so many years in Bengal is usually attributed to the ability of two men: B. C. Roy as chief minister and Atulya Ghosh in control of the Congress Party machine (Chatterjee, 1982). Together they ensured unbroken Congress rule in Bengal until 1966.

While the Congress did represent a wide coalition of interests and promised to bring equality through peaceful means, its strategy of building its electoral base through alliances with influential elites prevented it from making inroads into the districts and reaching out to peasants and agricultural laborers. Neither did it have much influence with the small yet growing sections of the industrial proletariat. It remained a party dominated by the rural rich and a party whose greatest strength lay in the Hindi heartland. Twenty years of Congress rule at the federal level did nothing to lessen the resentment of Bengalis over the neglect of their once great city, and they increasingly tended to attribute the political, economic, and cultural decline of Calcutta to discrimination by the federal government.

The undivided Communist Party of India was founded by M. N. Roy, a Bengali, in Tashkent in 1921, and it became a significant presence in the countryside in the 1930s (Mallick, 1993).[3] Today the CPI(M) is the most powerful force on the Indian left, having first emerged as a dominant force in the Bengali political landscape long before it was elected to power, briefly in 1967 and 1969 and finally in 1977. The earliest Bengali Communists were "terrorists" who had been expelled by the British in pre-Independence India or who had gone abroad to secure money and weapons for their fight against the British. There they came in contact with the Comintern in Mexico and in Moscow. These Communists were joined by Bengali intellectuals who had been attracted to Marxism in Oxford or Cambridge, such as the present chief minister, Jyoti Basu, and veteran leader and women's activist Renu Chakravarty (Franda, 1971). Active in the countryside throughout the post-Independence period, the party began to gain visible strength in the late 1950s and the 1960s (Custers, 1987).

Various reasons have been offered for the emergence and strength of the CPI(M), some pointing to the particular nature of the urban Bengali elite, the upper-caste *bhadralok* who constitute the bulk of the urban Bengali population in and around Calcutta,[4] and others to the absence of an indigenous bourgeoisie and to Bengali nationalism (Chatterjee, 1982).

The *bhadralok* were an elite with few ties to the land, a phenomenon exacerbated by the partition of India, when Bengal was divided into two: West Bengal and East Pakistan (now Bangladesh). Two things happened with this division. First, the old elite classes lost their property in East Pakistan, and second, there was an influx of Hindu refugees from East Pakistan far greater than the state of West Bengal could handle.[5] These refugees and the new generations of urban youth, no longer linked to land but educated nevertheless, formed the leadership and cadre of the communist movement. These refugees were also integrated into a new kind of workforce, unlike the traditional peasant-based working class in Bengal, in that it was formed of educated people with middle-class aspirations. Further, as we have already seen in chapter 2, there was an absence of an indigenous bourgeoisie in Bengal. None of the big business houses were Bengali owned, and few of the top managers were Bengali.[6] Thus, unlike the situation in many other parts of the country, the elite were not involved in major conflicts relating to land rights, and there was an educated refugee population and a nonindigenous (largely Marwari) elite against whom all Bengalis could unite, lending a regionalist cast to anticapitalist sentiment. The CPI(M) in West Bengal was not just a communist party, but had also, as many analysts have noted, developed into the representative of regional patriotism.

Like the economy of most of the country (see chapter 2), West Bengal's economy was in shambles by the 1960s, with chronic malnutrition, drought, deaths from starvation in the countryside, and a total lack of adequate water, sewerage, and sanitary facilities in the slums of Calcutta. Calcutta became known as the cholera capital of the world (S. Banerjee, 1984:32). Significantly, 78 percent of the unemployed were literate and more than 5 percent had college degrees. By 1966, the first generation of such nationalist leaders as B. C. Roy had passed away and Congress had begun to disintegrate into multiple factions. It was at this point that West Bengal elected the first coalition of left parties under the banner of the United Front government in 1967. This ushered in a period, which has been labeled a "decade of chaos," that was only to subside when the Left Front finally came to power in 1977 (Kohli, 1990:274).

The first United Front government of 1967 was dominated by the CPI in coalition with the CPI(M) and a breakaway faction of the Congress. The major problem facing the new government was a demand for land, and they set about distributing surplus land among the landless. In the meantime, in May 1967, a peasant uprising started in northern Bengal in a little place called Naxalbari. Under the leadership of Charu Mazumdar, a group of CPI(M) dissidents decided to guide and participate in this uprising. This was the beginning of the Naxalite movement, and it was to have a tremendous impact on the future of Bengal's politics.[7] It was also a movement that was to become simultaneously synonymous with hope and terror, liberation and repression, throughout the country. The Naxalite analysis of the Indian economy claimed that it was still semifeudal and semicolonial (Vanaik, 1990). Unlike the CPI(M), they did not believe that India had become a bourgeois democracy, and thus their strategy was armed struggle in key areas, with the intention of setting off spontaneous uprisings of peasants and landless rural laborers. While the CPI(M) was deeply divided over the conflict, its leadership chose to expel the leaders of the Naxalbari movement from its ranks. This soon led to fierce clashes between the CPI(M) and the Naxalites on the streets of Calcutta during the ensuing months. Eventually, in November of that tumultuous year, 1967, president's rule was imposed on the state and the government was removed.

The second United Front government, elected in 1969, lasted only a few months. Clashes between the Communist Party of India (Marxist-Leninist), formed by the leaders of the Naxalite movement in April of that year, and the police, as well as between the CPI(ML) and the CPI(M), continued, and West Bengal became essentially a battlefield (S. Banerjee, 1984: 187). Unable to deal with the pressures of the Congress to its right and the

Naxalites to its left, the United Front government fell once more. This time, the Congress was elected back to power in a midterm poll by a middle class tired of the continuing violence. During this period and in the period immediately after, there was escalating state violence against both the CPI(M) and the CPI(ML), although certainly the bulk of state repression fell on the Naxalites. Between 1971 through the end of Indira Gandhi's Emergency in 1977, the Congress governed the state, while the CPI(ML) became increasingly fragmented under the onslaught of state violence and internal discord. The CPI(M) distanced itself from both the Congress and the CPI(ML) and began to focus its energies on organizing from the base. To the people of Calcutta, the early resentment against the Congress, together with the more recent memory of further Congress state repression in the late 1960s and early 1970s—its manipulation of the elected governments of West Bengal and the excesses of the Emergency—culminated in a deep distrust and dislike of that party. Increasingly people looked to the CPI(M).

In 1977, in the post-Emergency rejection of the Congress, the CPI(M) came to power as the dominant partner in the Left Front Coalition, as can be seen by the CPI(M) share of legislative seats.[8] The reconfigured CPI(M) that came to power this time had no revolutionary proclivities. Reformist in aims if not in language, the party focused on consolidating itself as a ruling organization. It underplayed class antagonisms while strongly claiming to be true to its communist philosophy (Nossiter, 1988). It encouraged private investment in order to allow the state economy to grow and created a broad-based inclusive government as a means of incorporating all strata of society (Kohli, 1984). The CPI(M) that won the 1977 elections was marked by a determination to stay in power, and it has done so. Now in its fifth elected five-year term, the party is increasingly similar to its competitors, but it has nonetheless indelibly marked Calcutta's political field. And Calcutta is no longer the chaotic, violence-prone city of the past.

Distribution of Power

Even though the Indian system of government is parliamentary, there are regional differences in the strength of party politics. Calcutta's political field is marked by the dominance of party politics, and nonparty political formations and autonomous interest groups do not have much space to exist. Thus workers, students, farmers, and other sectors of the population are organized not through independent organizations or lobbies, but through the various political parties in West Bengal. Specifically, the political field in Calcutta has been controlled over the past two decades by the highly dominant, largely regional CPI(M). In chapter 1, I defined a concentrated field as one where one or a handful of organizations prevail. In particular, I referred to control over available political and economic resources and the ability to make alliances. In this section I substantiate my claim that Calcutta has a concentrated political field by elaborating on key ways in which the CPI(M) has created and maintained its grip over Calcutta's politics in general and the women's movement in particular.

While the political regime in West Bengal is limited in its power because it is a regional government, its mode of operation is as corporatist as it could be under the circumstances. The CPI(M) operates in West Bengal with the help of its front organizations—the trade union, the Centre of Indian Trade Unions (CITU); the student and youth wings, the Student Federation of India (SFI) and the Democratic Youth Federation of India (DYFI); the peasant organization, the All India Kisan Sabha (AIKS); and the women's wing, the All India Democratic Women's Association, known in West Bengal as Paschim Banga Ganatantrik Mahila Samiti (PBGMS). The most influential writers and cultural figures, as well as the teachers' unions, are also affiliated to the CPI(M).

The CITU, affiliated to the CPI(M), is the dominant labor organization, but at the expense of relinquishing certain critical workers' rights. In the period immediately preceding the 1975 Emergency, the CITU was at the height of its power. Strikes, for example, caused 75 percent of the workdays lost, as opposed to 25 percent caused by management lockouts. In 1976, the peak Emergency year, lockouts accounted for 90 percent of workdays lost (Ramaswamy, 1988). Since the CPI(M) electoral victory in 1977, however, worker conflict has been subdued. Shortly after the CPI(M) was elected to power, Chief Minister Jyoti Basu called on the CITU to pledge not to strike and to curtail their demands for higher wages. According to analyst E. A. Ramaswamy (1988:177), there is in West Bengal a nexus between "a radical political party wanting to moderate conflict on being voted to power and a large trade union whose ideological commitment to militancy is restrained by the party which is considered supreme." The party leadership is well aware that the CPI(M) did not come to power solely on the strength of the workers, and thus it has been able to impose constraints on CITU action. The CPI(M) has, in a classical social democratic move, broadened its class coalition and can afford to lose some working-class votes.[9] Precisely because it is part of the state, the CPI(M) as a party has gained in power at the expense of its front organizations.

The CPI(M) is a highly organized, centralized, and efficient cadre-based party. In the tradition of other successful left parties, it has one foot in the state and one foot in civil society (Maguire, 1995:200). While core membership tends to be middle class (its cadres in the city are generally drawn from white-collar workers, university students and faculty, and other *bhadralok* elements), membership in its front organizations comes from a wider range of people (Kohli, 1984). This cadre is known statewide for its discipline, and people are quick to criticize the slightest slip in the cadre behavior. Party membership is little over one hundred thousand, although the fronts have far more extensive memberships. The PBGMS, the women's front, had a membership of two million in West Bengal in 1990.[10]

While the party is stronger in the countryside than in the cities, it has had little competition from other political parties or other nonparty political formations. In every show of strength, the CPI(M) has won overwhelmingly. When, for example, the CPI(M) wants to protest some policy initiative from the central government in New Delhi, it calls for a general strike, or *bandh*. When it does so, all of Calcutta stays at home. When any other party attempts to do so, life in Calcutta carries on almost as normal. As even its detractors point out, the hold over the state and the city by the CPI(M) is such that it was the only major city to be spared the ravages of the communal riots in the wake of Indira Gandhi's assassination in 1984. Eyewitnesses report that CPI(M) cadres were deployed at street corners to make sure that there was no fighting between Hindus and Sikhs and to prevent the massacre of Sikhs that swept through the rest of the nation at that time. In its twenty years of rule, the CPI(M) has had its moments of increased and diminished popularity, especially in the city of Calcutta. Yet as the election results show, the people of West Bengal are not ready for the Congress to return to power. In fact, the Congress in West Bengal has become increasingly factionalized as it finds itself time and time again unable to regain electoral popularity.[11] The newer, right-wing Hindu Bharatiya Janata Party is still a minor player, although it has won a few seats in recent elections. Organizations unaffiliated to political parties have little legitimacy, while all intermediate organizations of interest representation are almost always affiliated to political parties. Over time, the CPI(M) has increasingly become more and more the entrenched and omnipotent power in all aspects of Calcutta's life. Like the Congress nationally, it has now created a substantial patronage machinery in the state, particularly among the white-collar bureaucracy.

It is within this field that the PBGMS, the women's wing of the CPI(M), has emerged as the dominant force of the Calcutta women's movement. And it has done so largely by piggybacking on the strength of the CPI(M). The CPI(M) may not be resource rich in terms of finances, but it has great strength in numbers and in political power. It is, after all, part of the state, and as part of the state, it has deployed its political resources to facilitate the capacity of favored groups to mobilize. The CPI(M) has given the PBGMS a formal recognition that endows it with certain rights and privileges over other similar organizations. Thus, along with the three other women's organizations affiliated to the parties of the Left Front, the PBGMS is empowered to investigate and bring to court cases of dowry murders. This naturally results in women turning to the PBGMS in large numbers, because they believe that the state will hear them if they take their troubles to the PBGMS.

Second, the CPI(M) favors the PBGMS when distributing funds. Even though the PBGMS is not allowed to apply for a wide range of funds because it is affiliated to a political party, groups of PBGMS members often form non-profit organizations and apply for funds under their new names. In this way, PBGMS members have been able to create many producer cooperatives for women, and it was the PBGMS that was given the opportunity of launching the literacy campaign.

Third, the CPI(M) enables the PBGMS to have access to publicity—publicity that is necessary in the wars over political culture. The CPI(M) does not control the mainstream English-language press, which tends to be more centrist, but it has made its own newspapers and other publications widely and freely available to the public. Therefore, every protest, action, and campaign undertaken by the PBGMS is widely advertised in the pages of *Ganashakti* (People's Democracy). And *Ganashakti* is found daily, free of charge, on walls and boards throughout the city.

In the late 1970s, at a time when political rivals were weak or delegitimized, the CPI(M) emerged as dominant in Calcutta's political field. And along with the CPI(M), the PBGMS emerged as dominant in the women's movement. That the CPI(M) became powerful at precisely the time that the second wave of the women's movement was being born throughout the country has resulted in a women's movement strongly shaped by the power of that party. Indeed, the entire field of politics in post-Emergency Calcutta, both parliamentary and oppositional, can be seen to be overwhelmingly dominated by the CPI(M).

Political Culture

Calcutta is, above all, a city with a long-standing oppositional and anti-establishment culture, largely because of the Bengali *bhadralok* who participated early on in the administration of the colonial state, only to find their paths blocked as they tried to move up the ranks of the British bureaucracy. Armed with the weapons of liberal Western education and administrative experience, it was these *bhadralok* who formed the core of a strongly anti-British movement in the late nineteenth century. During the struggle for independence, Calcutta was at the center of a range of agitational politics, from boycotts to assassinations.[12] The Bengali intelligentsia were particularly active in creating nationalistic fervor and immortalizing, in music, poetry, and prose, the heroism of the people and the repression of the British state.[13] They simultaneously created the image of Bengali women as "the true jewels" of India.

In post-Independence India, oppositional culture continued to flourish in Calcutta in poetry, theater, and music. In moments of particular political tension, such as the late 1960s, Calcutta's coffeehouses, tea shops, street corners, offices, and walls became the sites for struggles over political discourses and strategies. Universities were marked by clashes between students belonging to rival left political parties. Even before the CPI(M) came to power, left culture had established itself firmly in Calcutta. The universe of what was and should be political for women in Calcutta thus came to be shaped not only by the socioeconomic conditions of extreme poverty and inequality and the legacy of political activism, but by a Marxist-Leninist ideology tempered by nationalism. For a gendered issue to be considered legitimate in Calcutta, it had to be framed to resonate with this particular political culture (Snow and Benford, 1988). As we can recall, table 2.4 in chapter 2 showed that autonomous groups in Calcutta claimed as crucial for women exactly the same issues, in exactly the same order, as those put forward by the activists of the CPI(M)-affiliated PBGMS. That is but one illustration of the power of Calcutta's political culture.

What might this mean for women's issues? In terms of Marxist-Leninist ideology it means that in the political-cultural ethos of Calcutta, class conflict is seen as the primary motor of history. It means perhaps that there are traces of the ambivalence found toward the "woman question" in Marxism, in which the family is both attacked and cherished (Landes, 1989). It means that there is an ambivalence between treating "women's problems" as separate phenomena or as a subset of human problems caused by capitalism. It means that there is a proclivity toward maintaining a separation between public and private and toward seeing work as a solution to many problems. It means that while temporary measures must be taken to make life easier for women, the real agenda is the struggle for socialism. It ultimately means that, while women's political participation is encouraged in both women-specific and general struggles, both men and women are supposed to be, first and foremost, foot soldiers in the "larger democratic movement" toward socialism.

In terms of Bengali nationalist ideology, Bengali women are seen, as are women in many nationalist struggles, as the carriers of culture, who have resisted in the past, and must continue to resist in the future, the seductive forces of the West. Indeed, as Chatterjee (1989) has argued, for nineteenth-century Bengali social reformers, if colonialism meant the defeat of "the East" in the material realm (the world), the spiritual realm (home, the sphere of women) was the place where they could assert their superiority. Thus it was women who carried the burden of ensuring that this inner sanctum not be encroached upon by the colonizer.

Bengali women are seen as potentially and actually politically active, but not necessarily on behalf of themselves. Among those women who have been celebrated in Bengali culture are martyrs such as Matangini Hazra, a seventy-three-year-old peasant who was killed while leading a procession in Midnapore in 1942, and Shanti and Suniti Ghosh, who assassinated the district collector of Comilla. They have been immortalized in images that resonate strongly with selfless, protective, self-sacrificing motherhood. The view of mother-woman as symbolic of the motherland has led many to accuse the CPI(M) of doing little to change cultural notions of Bengali womanhood and of "recasting left activity as a familial one" by addressing women repeatedly as "mothers and sisters" (*mayera o bonera*).[14] However, the critics' monolithic image of Bengali womanhood is not congruent with the diverse and varied representations of women in Bengal's political culture. To be sure, *mayera o bonera* should be "respected" and protected, but they are also portrayed as articulate, independent, and spirited fighters.[15] Both these images find resonance in Calcutta's political culture.

It is not just in ideological content and representational spheres that the left has made its mark on Calcutta's political culture. Two organizational innovations in particular militate against nonparty organizing. As the Communists first began to gain popularity in the late 1950s, they gained visibility by means of two specific instruments of mass agitation—massive demonstrations and the general strike (Chatterjee, 1990:30). The new locus of agitational politics became the brigade parade grounds and the massive Calcutta *maidan* (field). Marching on the *maidan,* filling it up with hundreds of thousands of bodies, became—and has remained—the ultimate show of political strength. Similarly, a total response to a *bandh,* or strike call, is also a sign of political strength. Both of these instruments of agitation take the form of highly public spectacles, one by its presence and one by absence. These widely accepted forms of doing politics require an organizational capacity not easily compatible with decentralized autonomous groups.

Because of the city's long-standing left tradition, political parties are the legitimate carriers of people's interests in Calcutta, rather than nongovernmental organizations (NGOs), which have critical roles in civil society in

other parts of India and the third world. Foreign and multinational foundations, whether commercial or nonprofit, are looked at with suspicion. The
CPI(M), like other communist parties before it, is hostile to the possibility of
organizational autonomy of social movements, including the women's movement. Calcutta's history of involvement with the left effectively means that
political initiatives are considered more legitimate when taken in the name
of the working class or peasants—or the party. In a situation that is similar
to the "operaismo" or workerist tradition in Turin, political women can be
most effective on workerist issues, or issues that do not smack of the essential conflicts of interest between men and women (Hellman, 1987).

Radicals and proponents of social change, including feminists, have basically two choices in Calcutta. They can either attempt to work from within the party because of its vast resources and reach or they can attempt to
affect the government from without. Given Calcutta's history with the
Congress Party, there is an added complication for those who would distance themselves from the CPI(M). For most radicals, the CPI(M) is, warts and
all, the preferred government. It is not, after all, the tarnished and corrupt
Congress.

The Women's Movement in Calcutta

We have, then, in Calcutta a hegemonic field that is powerful and concentrated. Dominated by one party, it also has a homogeneous political culture
that stems from its leftist and nationalist traditions. It is within this field that
the women's movement has had to establish itself. And it is both because of
the shape of the field and because of the dominant position of the PBGMS
within it that a campaign such as the literacy campaign can be successfully
undertaken.

Within this field, various women's organizations exist, some old, some
new, some that are born and swiftly die, depending upon their adaptability.
There are three sorts of organizations in Calcutta. The old established nonpolitical organizations, such as the All India Women's Conference, the All
Bengal Women's Union, and the Saroj Nalini Memorial Association, which
started in the 1920s with the first wave of woman-centered organizing, still
exist. They provide training for women in traditional skills such as arts and
crafts, catering to women who have for one reason or another no home to
turn to. They also help create and run hospital wards and schools. They are
what might be called "social work" agencies and are headed by highly respected elite women who publicly eschew "politics."

The second sort of organization is the politically affiliated organization.
These are wings of political parties and include the National Federation of

Women, affiliated with the CPI; the Mahila Congress, with connections to the Congress Party; the PBGMS, a wing of the CPI(M); and the women's wings of the Forward Bloc, the Revolutionary Socialist Party, and the Socialist Unity Centre of India (SUCI). These are the sorts of organizations that most easily find a home in Calcutta. The third sort of organization is the newly formed autonomous women's organization, born during the second wave of the women's movement in India. These include Sachetana (which means self-awareness), the Women's Research Centre, and Nari Nirjatan Pratiradh Mancha. These are the sorts of organizations that exist uneasily in Calcutta but more comfortably in Bombay. It is the relationship between the affiliated and autonomous women's organizations that forms the focus of this book. In particular, I analyze the relationships between the Paschim Banga Ganatantrik Mahila Samiti and Sachetana, on the one hand, and between those two organizations and Calcutta's political field, on the other. I treat the PBGMS as an example of a dominant organization, the only possible choice in Calcutta. Of the possible subordinate (in Calcutta, these are autonomous) groups, I have chosen to study Sachetana, since it was founded as a deliberate alternative to political parties. I end this chapter with an introduction to the two groups and turn, in the next, to a closer look at their membership, ideologies, and strategies, placed as they are in Calcutta's political field.

The Dominant Group: Paschim Banga Ganatantrik Mahila Samiti

Paschim Banga Ganatantrik Mahila Samiti, or the West Bengal Democratic Women's Association, is the women's front of the CPI(M). Although officially formed in 1981, the PBGMS counts its existence from the formation of the Mahila Atmaraksha Samiti in 1943 and thus celebrated its fiftieth anniversary in 1993. In response to the devastating Bengal famine of 1943, several preexisting women's organizations formed the Mahila Atmaraksha Samiti (MARS), or Women's Self-Defense Association, to help bring relief to people who were at risk of starvation and death. Yet MARS was always more than a "relief" organization.[16] Dominated by women from the still underground Communist Party, MARS was declared illegal by the Indian government following independence in 1947, yet it continued to function in secret. At its fifth conference in 1949, held underground, MARS declared that women must fight for peace and against exploitation and poverty and demanded free primary education and maternity leave (Chakravarty, 1980). In 1954, the Communist Party of India formed the National Federation of Indian Women (NFIW), which became, after the older All India Women's Conference, the second all-India women's organization. When, in 1964, the Communist Party split in the wake of the Sino-Indian War into the CPI and the CPI(M), the women's group tried initially to stay unified, but ultimately separated in 1970.

Through the 1970s, the CPI(M) did not have an organized women's wing, since the NFIW remained with the CPI. Finally, the national-level All India Democratic Women's Association (AIDWA) was officially formed in 1981, with the slogan "Equality, Democracy, and Women's Liberation." It had its first convention in Madras, its second in Kerala, its third in Bengal, and its fourth in Coimbatore in 1994. In 1991, the PBGMS, the West Bengal branch of the AIDWA, had 2,012,000 members, with 1,890,000 members in Calcutta itself (P5, P10). However, as Bonani Biswas, the general secretary of the Calcutta district committee warns, there is obviously a large difference between activists and membership: "We can get 50 percent of our members to vote and about 25 to 30 percent to participate in campaigning. Active membership is no more than 3 to 4 percent" (personal communication, October 1990).

The structure of the women's organization closely approximates that of the party. At the grassroots level there are primary units, and the task of these workers is to maintain day-to-day contact with women at the grass roots and also to mobilize them for demonstrations. Above them are the local, district, state, and national committees, in that order. The Calcutta district, which forms the focus of this study, has 310 primary committees and 64 local committees. The organization runs on the principles of democratic centralism, in which the hierarchy is clearly defined and the majority decision, arrived at after debate, must be accepted. The Calcutta district office of the PBGMS is located on one side of the CPI(M) offices in Alimuddin Street, in a narrow lane in a poor, primarily Muslim, area. The office consists of a small room with a couple of benches and tables and a few metal folding chairs. The walls are lined with rickety shelves overflowing with files and membership books and cards. This office is clearly action oriented. The women who visit the office come to report on an accomplished task or to discuss tasks to be undertaken. Women who need legal counsel are directed to the legal aid cell situated on the other side of the building in the PBGMS state offices. Others who come to the office with problems and concerns simply talk to the PBGMS women sitting at one of the two tables. In the meantime, at the other table, membership slips continue to be registered and party politics continue to be discussed over tea.

The PBGMS functions both as an arm of the state and as a women's organization pushing for change. This duality is the source of both its strength and, as we shall see in the subsequent chapters, its weakness.

The Subordinate Group: Sachetana

Sachetana, one of Calcutta's few surviving autonomous groups, was formed by a group of academics and development workers in Calcutta in 1981, the same year as the AIDWA. It was initiated by a Bengali social worker trained in Bombay, who felt the need, while engaged in social work in rural Bengal, for a support group for herself and for a better understanding of women's issues. She wanted to know how to better "articulate and insert women's issues" into the main political debate—away from the dominant "charity" and "victim" discourses (S1) that she felt were the prevalent modes of discussing women. The group, she decided, should be neither social-work oriented nor party affiliated. Through common friends she met academic women who were sympathetic to the left in Calcutta, and together they organized a seminar on gender issues—the first of its kind in the city. Sachetana emerged from this seminar. Some of these women were CPI(M) activists and sympathizers and others were partial to the CPI. They began meeting in the spare room of a friend, and soon decided that since they were, by and large, intellectuals, academics, and journalists, they would be most effective as a consciousness-raising group.

While the group has remained small, they continue to meet once a week in the Sachetana office. Situated in Rashbehari Avenue, a middle- to upper-middle-class area in south Calcutta, this tiny office has a couch and mats on the floor for women to sit on. On the walls are a few feminist posters, and on one side of the room, locked cabinets filled with their files and some books. The room is located on the mezzanine floor of the house of one of the activists. Sachetana meetings take place either here or in the house of another activist who lives around the corner.

Sachetana offers legal aid and counseling services, holds discussions on both academic and political subjects, and publishes a magazine, *Sachetana*, that addresses a wide range of issues. It has a reputation for being populated with upper-class women, yet is fairly well respected. While Sachetana has a formal division of labor—a secretary and a treasurer—it is quite nonhierarchical in its daily operations. According to one member, Sachetana has "basically all leaders and no followers." Sachetana has about 150 members on paper, and about 10 or 12 active members. The activists are not paid for their work with Sachetana.

One of the most intriguing features of Sachetana's membership is the maintenance of a wide variety of party affiliations. There are women in Sachetana who are active members of or affiliated to the CPI(M), the CPI, or the CPI(ML). Indeed some members feel that the diverse composition of

Sachetana in such a politically charged city is Sachetana's biggest achievement. Sachetana's dilemma stems from being an autonomous feminist group in a city with a political culture as strong as Calcutta's and a field so dominated by the CPI(M).

In chapters 4 and 5 I focus on the effects of Calcutta's particular political field on both Sachetana and the PBGMS, and pay special attention to the ways in which activists within these two groups understand their position within the field, their strengths, and their weaknesses and how they accordingly negotiate their strategies.

Chapter 4

Negotiating a Homogeneous Political Culture

We do not go to posh areas. Where we go, women have no idea of separate problems. So their problems are food, money, and so on.

—PBGMS activist

Embedded as they are in particular fields, social movement organizations find themselves constantly negotiating with the state, other organizations, and their potential constituents in struggles to keep issues alive and to resolve them in the best possible manner. Chapter 3 foregrounded the interaction between the political culture and the distribution of power in Calcutta's political field. In this chapter and the next, I draw out the implications of the configuration of that field for two types of groups—the powerful PBGMS and the subordinate Sachetana—and for the activists within them. Here we have two organizations, created within a year of each other, whose positions within the field have resulted in two very different logics of organization. This chapter highlights the effects of the field on the ideology of the two groups, while the next concentrates on the actions and strategies of these two organizations as they strive to make the best use of the political field in which they are embedded. This chapter thus deals primarily with the effects of Calcutta's political culture, and chapter 5 addresses the effects of Calcutta's distribution of power.

Let us remind ourselves about Calcutta's political culture. Leftist ideologies dominate a city that prides itself on its revolutionary history. A combination of Marxist-Leninist and nationalist political discourse is the most palatable and acceptable of all discourses to Calcutta progressives, and it shapes and limits the framing of political issues. It is this discourse with which organizations who want to attract adherents must be familiar. While the bulk of this chapter focuses on a comparison of the ideologies of the PBGMS and Sachetana, I turn first to their memberships. It is, after all, the members who constitute these groups, embrace and contest their ideologies, and carry out the actual work. It is my intent in what follows to give the membership of these groups a human face, to make visible the ordinary members of organizations—those women who do not receive worldwide media coverage, but without whom there would be no movement.

Membership

It seems intuitively obvious that in a field where the CPI(M) is so dominant, people would join the PBGMS for strategic reasons. But the reasons people have for participating in collective action or belonging to a social movement organization are complex (Ferree and Miller, 1985; Klandermans, 1984). As we shall see, both women who belong to Sachetana and women who belong to the PBGMS derive a sense of identity from their membership. However, two things clearly separate members of Sachetana from members of the PBGMS: the degrees of exposure to a world outside Calcutta's political culture and economic status.

Mita

Mita is a member of the PBGMS and a clerical worker at Calcutta University. When I asked her if I could interview her, she told me that she would first have to get permission from her leadership. When she returned, she was expansive and forthright, and when I asked her why she had been so honest, she replied that the leadership had said she could be. As I listened to this woman, a little younger than I was, leaning forward with her sparkling eyes and ready smile, her thoughtfulness and her passion, I wrote in my notebook, "If this is the kind of young worker the party can attract, it is no surprise that it has stayed in power for so long."

Mita comes from a family that has several members close to or in the CPI(M) and has herself been in the party since she was in high school. Her parents lived in another state and the four brothers and sisters lived together, "bringing each other up." Mita, who is married, had the party arrange a marriage for her when she felt she was ready. The party found her a husband who was not himself a party member but was a supporter, and who was "liberal" enough to support his wife's political activities. At the time she spoke to me, Mita had been married for less than a year. Her wedding day marked the end of her formal association with the student wing of the party. Today she is active in both the party's youth and women's wings.

Mita lives with her husband, her mother-in-law, and her brother-in-law and his wife. All four of the younger members work outside the home. Mita's average day begins with her waking up early, cooking lunch and dinner, and "looking after" her mother and brother-in-law before she goes to work. After work she usually attends party meetings or activities, making sure to return by nine o'clock so that she can serve dinner to the family and eat with them. That she does this much housework is a strategic decision on her part to ensure that she can continue her political work. She knows that while her husband is supportive, he is the younger brother in the family, and his older brother and mother do not approve of her political activities.

Does she mind doing all this work? Does she ever discuss her problems with her colleagues in the PBGMS?

> I can, but I don't. . . . these are sentimental matters. It is, you know, part of the *lajja* (shame) associated with the Bengali middle class. . . . we feel that we must adjust. . . . my in-laws are nice but they cannot stand what I do, even though they are a political family. I can speak to you about this in this discussion the two of us are having, but what is the solution? I have decided that you have to accept certain things.

Later on she adds, "This is a fight *I* have to fight."

Mita says no more about her own life, but while she says that the two most important problems faced by women in West Bengal are literacy and employment, she becomes passionate about the third problem: "Women do not get the respect they deserve. As hard as they try to hold their heads up, society does not allow them to do so. This affects me deeply."

Mita also feels passionate about the work the Samiti (her organization, the PBGMS) does and about its little successes. She tells me about the social boycott the Samiti engineered of a man who was suspected of burning his wife to death, the literacy camps they initiated, and the joy she feels when women stand up for themselves. But she will not talk to me either about clashes between the party and the Samiti, or about what the Left Front government has failed to do for women. She says she can't think of anything off the top of her head. She tells me that she will always stay with the PBGMS because she feels that she can serve more people in a mass organization than by just being in the party. As a woman, she feels part of the PBGMS: "There are so many problems women face and so much work to be done."

Mita is one of a new generation of women who form the lifeblood of the PBGMS. Recruited out of high school, she had no prior political experience, no prior political affiliation, but came from a family of party supporters. She is thus a fairly typical representative of the PBGMS. Of the PBGMS women I interviewed, 35 percent had no previous organizational experience, but 40 percent had once belonged to student political groups. While the older members often joined the party against their parents' wishes in the 1930s and 1940s, sometimes running away to Calcutta in order to be political,[1] the younger members are usually from families that support the party. This reflects a change in Calcutta's political culture: belonging to the party is no longer a dangerous and challenging political activity, but rather, it has become a family tradition.[2]

While many younger PBGMS members were recruited while in school or college and then moved through the SFI (the student wing) and the DYFI (the youth wing) and eventually to the PBGMS, there are others, especially from the lower-middle and working classes, who were recruited directly by older PBGMS women in the neighborhood. One PBGMS grassroots activist works as a maid in a hospital and is the sole supporter of her son and her husband, who is in a state mental hospital. Another grassroots activist, a single woman in her thirties who treats the party as though it were her savior, gave me this account of why she joined the party. The death of her parents prevented her from fulfilling her dream of being a dancer, she said. Her father had been a member of the CPI(M), and she had often accompanied him on his trips, participating in the cultural activities of the party:

> I came into the party through dancing and singing. I used to sing in the villages on May Day. I saw what the party did for the poor and whenever I saw the suffering of poor people, my heart would overflow. When my sister got married, I was sent to live with my uncle, who could not afford to send me to college. I did not know what was to become of me. I had so many dreams. Now I have no one but the Samiti.
>
> I joined the Samiti in 1985. I told my father before he died: "I will stay with the party. I will not get married. The party is my only family now." . . . I rely on the party for everything. I have put my life into their hands. (P9)

These stories and others draw on images of the party as family, as protector, as comfort and strength. It is clear that women who come from poor and insecure backgrounds join groups like the PBGMS both to break through their social isolation and to gain protection. But if that were all, there would be little difference between the party and, say, a born-again religious group. These women are socially aware of inequalities and injustices, find themselves in instinctive sympathy with the party's approach, and revel in their newfound abilities to understand the world differently and to explain it to others. They are women to whom Calcutta's political culture speaks. They are also women who can expect the party to somehow look after them and thus put their life into its hands. The party may be resource poor, but they will never starve.

The vast majority of the women I interviewed in the PBGMS were married (75 percent; none were divorced) and almost half lived in joint families, as did Mita. More than 60 percent did paid work outside the home, mainly as schoolteachers or full-time party workers. In terms of household income, the distribution was quite wide. Household incomes of grassroots workers tended to be less than Rs 3,000 ($80) a month and over Rs 5,000 ($140) a month for the leadership.

Shona

Shona is a young Sachetana member who was invited to join the group by one of her professors at graduate school. Unlike Mita, Shona went to a well-known university, and her professors were themselves well-known scholars. She comes from an essentially apolitical upper-middle-class family and, as she tells the story, was jolted into politics when the Emergency was declared in 1975. As a college student at the time, she decided to join the CPI(M)-affiliated student wing, the SFI, in opposition to the harassment and threats made by the Congress within the walls of her college. The SFI seemed the logical counter to the Congress in Calcutta. But unlike Mita, who also joined the SFI initially, Shona did not stay with them:

> They [the SFI] were perhaps practical. But I did not like them. We were told to wear saris at demonstrations, as women. Otherwise we would alienate the lower classes. I found this very annoying. . . . I felt that women were ordered around and were not part of the decision-making process. When we had discussions on this, the party boys told us we were being bourgeois.

Shona speaks of the gender-based issues that often concerned her as a young adult. What did she personally want to do about marriage? Did she want to get married? Did she want an arranged marriage or did she want to choose her own husband? How was she to react to the harassment by men on buses? How was she to come to an understanding of where men got their attitudes toward women? But these were not issues she could address in the SFI, whose student leaders "simply quoted Clara Zetkin" at her,[3] and her frustrations led her to leave the organization. Eventually, as she was mulling these issues over in her mind, one of her male professors introduced her to Doris Lessing's *Golden Notebook,* which she describes as "mind blowing." Perhaps in the context of Calcutta's left-wing political culture and her experience with the SFI, the story of Anna, the novel's main character, resonated strongly with her.[4] Shortly after that she joined Sachetana.

Here is a case of a university student who was part of the CPI(M) student movement, felt marginalized *as a woman,* and then left the organization as she encountered alternative influences. These influences were available to her through English literature and her professors. It should be noted that over two-thirds of Sachetana's activists were initially in CPI- or CPI(M)-affiliated groups before moving to Sachetana. Shona is now herself a college teacher married to a professional and has a daughter. In this she is no different from the other Sachetana activists, who tend also to be married (85.7 percent), to live in nuclear families, to be themselves professionals, and to belong to middle- to high-income groups.

Several of the women in Sachetana are academics who came into activism through the desire to fill an intellectual gap. The founding members were women in their late thirties and early forties, in fields such as literature, history, and economics, who came together at a seminar—the first seminar on women's issues in Calcutta—and felt a sense of "entente" with the other women there (S2). These are women who were exposed to and whose sensibilities were affected by what may be called "the New Left," even though they had grown up in the old left world of Calcutta. In telling me about the consciousness of the desire to belong to a women's group, one activist, a widely respected academic, recalled returning from conferences in England and speaking out about her new ideas: "I came back and said something about being a feminist and he [the director of the research institute at which she was employed] went through the roof. He said, 'But you were doing very good work'! I didn't have the courage to say, 'What's wrong with [being a feminist]?' So I made it into a joke." (S2). Perhaps Sachetana can be seen as a flexible space for those who are not entirely comfortable with the circumscribed gender ideology of Calcutta's political field. In particular, it could be seen as a space in which people who have been exposed to cultures and ideas outside of Calcutta can exist.

Shona voiced her frustrations with Sachetana and with its lack of efficacy on several issues, associating this lack with being located in Calcutta. She was equally clear about her need for Sachetana. "It is only in Sachetana that the 'I within the me' can be raised and recognized"—the only place where her subjective self with all its doubts and concerns can be realized. Sachetana gives her a sisterhood, which she thinks of not as a gift, but as a learned process. She worries about the fact that more young women are not members of Sachetana and attributes some of the blame to Calcutta's political culture. Perhaps, she says, because of the Left Front government, young women feel that there is no need for a separate women's organization. Sachetana exists for those who do feel that need.

Ideology

Social movement organizations put forward an ideology, a way to make sense of issues and the world. Since ideologies involve particular worldviews, they influence a group's perception of important goals, appropriate methods for achieving the goals, and possibilities for their realization. It is the way organizations present the world, the way they frame the issues, that attracts the adherents they need. And it is the political culture of a particular space that renders it more or less hospitable to certain framings. While some ideologies are created indigenously, within a certain political culture, others are borrowed from outside. Whether or not these ideologies are accepted depends on both the permeability of the political culture and on the nature of the ideology.

Calcutta's political culture has for years been more open to the borrowed ideologies of class struggle than to the borrowed ideologies of feminist struggle. Yet no political culture is completely monolithic, even if it does command the most of the public space. While there is a clearly dominant political culture in Calcutta and one prevailing vision of the political, there are also emergent pockets of resistant cultures. Within these pockets, small autonomous groups like Sachetana try to carve out spaces for themselves. Sachetana is both part of Calcutta's dominant culture and outside of it. Within Sachetana there is a constant struggle to keep alive those parts of its ideology that resist the dominant culture. In order to survive, however, Sachetana is selective in its use of oppositional rhetoric. In what follows, I document ideological positions put forward by the PBGMS and by Sachetana, indicating the places where Sachetana resists the dominant culture and where it reflects it.

Sexual and Domestic Violence

If there is one issue that has come to be closely intertwined in the popular imagination with the second wave of the feminist movement in India, then it is the issue of violence against women. This is the issue upon which Bombay's Forum Against Oppression of Women, Delhi's Saheli, and other women's groups throughout the country were founded. The PBGMS women in Calcutta, however, seem to hold two views on rape, neither of which correspond to the newer framings of the issue used by groups such as the Forum and Saheli.

On the one hand, rape is committed for political reasons. According to Manjari Gupta, the Calcutta-based president of the AIDWA, atrocities against women in their "most violent and vindictive form take place for political reasons" (AIDWA, 1990). Malini Bhattacharya, a former CPI(M) member of Parliament, views rape and other forms of sexual assault and harassment as stemming from people who are criminal, lumpenized, and usually associated with the Congress Party. For her it is correlated with other crimes: "In areas where anti-social activities of different kinds flourish, sexual harassment of women, particularly poor women, is also a feature" (*Equality,* July–September 1990, 22).

On the other hand, rape is committed by abnormal men. The leader of the Calcutta district office of the PBGMS declares that "healthy, normal people do not do this. There must be temporary insanity for this to happen" (P5). The reconceptualization of the phenomenon of rape, so crucial (as we shall see in chapter 6) to the development of the women's movement in Bombay, is significant by its absence in the public statements made by the PBGMS.

Recent events in Calcutta brought into the open the problems with certain PBGMS leaders' perceptions of rape. When the CPI(M) was accused of sheltering rapists following the gang rape of three women at Birati, PBGMS general secretary Shyamali Gupta responded by suggesting that the women were prostitutes. Other leaders within the organization were horrified and spoke to her about the unacceptability of her views. A senior member and highly respected editor of the PBGMS journal *Eksathe* was outraged and minced no words in her conversation with me:

> What can I say about that statement? I mean, it shows a lack of brains or something to say that. What she said means that the women were "bad" so it is fine that they were raped. The point is that no one should lay a finger on me against my wishes whether I am a prostitute or a "good" woman. . . . If it is OK to do anything to a "bad" woman, what is our fight all about? (P3)

While this statement reveals a shift in the way violence against women is understood within the PBGMS, this sentiment was not made public. No retractions were made by Shyamali Gupta, and no public criticisms of her were made by party activists. Instead, her statement was taken by women's activists nationally to reflect the appalling lack of consciousness on the part of the PBGMS about violence against women.[5]

Rape is understood by Sachetana activists as an act of violence against women, pure and simple, and they are contemptuous of the PBGMS perception of the phenomenon. What separates Sachetana from both autonomous groups in Bombay and from the PBGMS in Calcutta is its attempt to emphasize connections between larger political violence and violence against women.[6] Sachetana activists also struggle with their own fears of rape and try to challenge the fear and stigma attached to that crime. Speaking at a women's college in Calcutta, for example, one Sachetana activist asked why society should regard rape as a fate worse than death for a woman:

> When we tell a woman to come home early it's because we are trying to protect her from rape. Boys and girls can equally well fall under the wheels of a bus, after all. So a girl can get raped and what is one to do with that? If I am raped and still alive, why should I not think that I have gone through an accident, just as if my hand were cut off? I would not give up living if that were the case, would I? I would try to carry on with the rest of my life. (S4)

There is within Sachetana a recognition of the need to fight both the external circumstances that allow rape and the shame and stigma that victims of rape feel within themselves.

Domestic violence is unequivocally condemned by both groups. The official PBGMS rhetoric, however, maintains that while domestic violence is a tragedy, it can be stopped only through economic measures, and thus, until there are viable economic alternatives, there is no point in focusing on it. According to one state-level leader, the PBGMS often gets cases of domestic abuse, but "you must understand, how much protection can we give them? We tell them they must adjust. If we have a good relationship with the husband, we talk to him" (P5). "To adjust" is a phrase so often used by and about women in Bengal that it has become almost a Bengali word. To adjust means to live with the hand one has been dealt because of a lack of alternatives. When women get married into a household, they learn to adjust, as Mita felt she had to. Telling a woman she must adjust is simply repeating the advice she has been given all her life.

Since poor women are more likely to come forward with complaints against their husbands, domestic violence is often considered by the PBGMS to be a non-middle-class problem. In this view, only unemployed and frustrated men beat their wives and children, a perception that makes the economic solution sound even more promising. The overall attitude of the PBGMS toward domestic abuse seems to be that if an individual woman comes to them for help, they will try to do their best for her, which might mean telling her that "she has to adjust." If, on the other hand, the woman is backed by her particular *community*, then they are willing to organize a social boycott: "The washer man, the barber, the fruit and vegetable sellers—no one should go to a batterer's house" (Calcutta district PBGMS general secretary Bonani Biswas, personal communication). Ultimately, though, because Marxist-Leninist ideology frowns upon the separation of women's issues from broader human or democratic struggles, the PBGMS tends to frame issues accordingly. Whatever the form of violence, PBGMS leaders urge people to see it "not just as a women's issue, but as part of the larger democratic struggle" (P1). This is different from Sachetana's insistence that the connections between various forms of gendered and nongendered violence be recognized.

Sachetana targets the belief system behind domestic violence, because, as one activist argues, "before a woman gets beaten up comes the socialization that says a woman gets beaten up only if she is bad" (S4). So when women come to them for help, they focus on changing her consciousness. But this is not a simple matter. One activist now questions the advice they give to the women who seek assistance from them, recognizing that their advice stems from their own location in the social structure but may not fit the situation of other women: "There has not been much violence in our own lives so we are, in a way, rather smug. This makes us glib in our responses to the women who come to us. We say things like 'You don't have to be accountable [*koiphiyot*] to your husband.' But of course they are. Reasons [for action] have to be given, and this is very real." She went on to talk about battered women who are told by Sachetana that there is no way they should return to their men even though they clearly want to:

> We say [to her] you must learn to stand on your own two feet, learn some skills. She says that she is scared. We say, "Why are you scared, we are here! We have done it." "We" means the ten of us! But the fact is there is no guarantee that she will get a job even if she does acquire skills. There is no infrastructure in place. . . . Often in this society a woman knows no man other than the one she has been married off to, and her entire physical and sexual self is enmeshed in that. Promiscuity is unknown or the costs are too high. So if a woman walks out she is doomed to a life of celibacy, and she may not be ready for that. Why should she be? I think I am going to bring this up at the next meeting. (S4)

This level of thoughtfulness and self-criticism is very apparent among Sachetana's members. Both Sachetana and PBGMS members understand that most women will not come forward and report abuse because of prevailing notions of shame as well as cultural and patriarchal constraints. When a woman does come forward, the PBGMS encourages community action but does not urge her to leave her home. Their activists understand external constraints but do not pay much attention to the inner turmoil the woman is experiencing. Sachetana members are increasingly aware of this inner turmoil of conflicting emotions and loyalties but are, I think, trapped in the clientist structure of the advocacy situation.

On the issues of domestic violence and rape, then, the two groups are officially far apart, but it is the PBGMS analysis that better fits Calcutta's political culture. Sachetana activists are well aware of this, and hope that their analysis will have some impact on public perceptions of violence against women and its consequences, but acknowledge that they have been more successful in rethinking and reworking their own assumptions around these issues.

Work

The Marxist-Leninist ideology of the PBGMS entails theoretical primacy being given to issues concerning the relations of production. This does not in and of itself ensure that work and economic issues will be the only chosen ones, but it does mean that the organization will be more receptive to these issues than to others. The clearest break between the PBGMS and other non-communist groups—be they autonomous or affiliated to other political parties—comes in the Samiti's unshaken belief in Lenin's tenet that with economic self-reliance will come women's emancipation. On this point, there is a united front—and faith—on all levels of the party. Grassroots activists assert that women continually ask for jobs, training, and loans. They are frustrated because, as one woman said, "we hear one thing over and over again. 'We don't have money and we can't make ends meet.' They [other women] want jobs from us but the *didis* say we cannot promise anyone jobs" (P8).[7] What needs to be developed, according to the PBGMS, is an infrastructure that will enable women to get the jobs they need.

Although there is unity of analysis within the ranks of the PBGMS and the CPI(M), there is a schism in who can best represent working-class women's interests. Among the women I interviewed were two union activists who worked in a Phillips factory. They claim primary allegiance to the CITU, the CPI(M) trade union, not to the PBGMS. They do not believe that a women's organization can best represent women like them. They claim that they have already won for themselves, through the union, demands that the PBGMS is still fighting for: "We have won maternity leave, a common room for women, and leave for women to go and breast-feed her child twice a day here at Phillips. She is also given a glass of milk at this crèche to add to her nutrition while she is breast-feeding" (C2). Through the CITU, the CPI(M) has also won temporary women workers and female flight attendants the right not to be fired upon marriage. Thus the PBGMS is seen by these workers to represent "other" women. They themselves are represented by the CITU, an organization more prestigious and powerful than the PBGMS. Thus while the PBGMS sees itself as representing all women, particularly in the poorer classes, working-class women see the trade union as the more effective representative of their interests.

For Sachetana, what needs to change, rather than the economy per se, is the *belief* that women are not to be primary workers (outside the home) and the belief that women are not to think of their own interests. For one activist, herself an economist, the problem starts with social practice:

> If I have raised my daughter with the belief that she will get married and her husband will support her, then she is vulnerable on the labor market. No skills, education, or mental capacity. In East Asian and Western countries everybody assumes that women will work. If all sixteen-year-olds assume they have to work, they will use ingenuity, resources, and contacts to get work, as they do in other countries. (S2)

Elsewhere *Sachetana* magazine notes, "Participating in economic activities does not alter the relative status of a woman in her own eyes or in the eyes of her family."

Sachetana members are unanimous in their rejection of the prioritization of the PBGMS that makes them wave the "magic wand of economic independence" (S2) over everything. They consistently argue that, while the economic dimension of women's oppression is not to be overlooked, cultural beliefs are the main vehicle for women's oppression. Sachetana activists do, however, feel compelled to bring up the issue of women's economic oppression and to justify their differences from the CPI(M) with regard to work. Bombay groups like the Forum do not find it necessary to do so. Yet, as we shall see in chapter 5, Sachetana's actions belie its analysis.

Consciousness Raising

While all of the organizations do some form of consciousness-raising work, women in Calcutta tend to view lack of consciousness as a problem far more than do women in Bombay. Activists in both politically affiliated and autonomous organizations in Calcutta tend to be openly judgmental about the ideological backwardness of the majority of men and women. This can be attributed to the fact that in a politically charged state like West Bengal,

ideologies are weighed and ranked and compared with an ideal to which
all—grassroots activists and leaders alike—should aspire. This ideological
linearity has become part of Calcutta's political culture, to which both autonomous and politically affiliated activists subscribe. Thus an activist of
the autonomous Nari Nirjatan Pratiradh Mancha (an umbrella organization
to which Sachetana once belonged) says:

> As we began doing work we realized how *limited the consciousness of
> women is*. They feel that all the women in the in-laws' house are bad
> but the husband is good. They want us to go to their in-laws and effect
> a reconciliation with their husband. . . . women themselves do not
> know what their rights are and what they are entitled to. (NN1; em-
> phasis added)

And one grassroots PBGMS activist bemoans the fact that middle-class
women in particular are not ideologically progressive:

> In general women are not interested in [politics and the outside world]
> and *they do not have an understanding of themselves as women*. We try to
> raise their awareness. We women are used as instruments. Why should
> I not be like other human beings, just because I am a woman? I once
> spoke to a woman professor who said that I should return the next day
> so that she could ask her husband whether she should join the organi-
> zation. I said, "Well, of course, he is your partner so you should discuss
> this with him. Does he also discuss his decisions with you?" But lower-
> class women are not like that. They earn and feel more equal to their
> men. (P7; emphasis added)

One of the longest-lasting Communist contributions to Calcutta culture is the legacy of the Indian People's Theatre Association, which used to
perform political songs and plays that captured the hearts and imaginations
of rural and urban people. Today, to the dismay of many older members,
such cultural groups are defunct. There is simply too much other work to be
done, one activist told me, and thus consciousness raising among the masses
and within their own organizations has had to take a back seat.

While the task of internal consciousness raising may not be a top priority, many members do believe the main function of the PBGMS is providing
political awareness to the masses. The general secretary of the PBGMS
Calcutta district, Bonani Biswas, considered by many a genius at reaching
"the masses," regularly conducts classes with groups of women:

> I tell them: "Your husband made a cup for the Birlas[8] from the re-
> sources of this land. The Birlas did not bring the resources down from
> the sky. The Birlas spend Rs 8 on the product. They give your husband

Rs 4 and sell it for Rs 20. The Birlas get Rs 12 in profit. Your husband brings this money home and since he is the only breadwinner, you pray to the gods to keep him alive. You disregard your own work in keeping the household together. Your husband kicks you away because he thinks it is his right, because the work you do is not valued. So you are doubly oppressed." And they say, "You are absolutely right, *didi*. On top of that they spend Rs 2 on alcohol."

Notice how she deftly weaves in critiques of capitalism and patriarchy in this effective tale. The story makes clear that the problem is not just that the Birlas are profit-mongering capitalists, but also that the devaluation of women's work by men and women alike allows women to be wretchedly treated.

While many of the critiques of "ideological backwardness" refer to customary patriarchal attitudes and values, many PBGMS members fault capitalist culture for diverting women's attention away from the struggle. Samiti activists also frame explanations about lack of political consciousness on the part of students or women in Marxist language. Thus, "feudal-capitalist" or "capitalist" cultures—through television and magazines such as *Sananda*—are blamed for preventing more women from joining the organization, for keeping people isolated, for "trapping women in a web of desire" (P5). Sometimes, it is not capitalist culture but the Congress Party who is the villain of the piece. Seldom is it men's interests in power or patriarchal culture.

The name "Sachetana" means self-awareness, and through its magazine, Sachetana actively tries to raise the consciousness of its readers. One of the first editorials proclaimed that while there are certainly both economic and social dimensions to women's oppression, there would not be this level of cruelty toward women if it were not for centuries of beliefs about women— beliefs that women are incapable, harmful, and susceptible to sinning and temptation. It is because women are thought to possess these weaknesses that it is considered appropriate for them to be in a position in society subordinate to men (*Sachetana*, 1986). And several years later, the magazine similarly stated:

> The unformed consciousness of men and women lies buried under the murky layers of such prejudices and biases. To weed them out and sow seeds of change should be the task of all right thinking and humanitarian individuals. That is why we have named our organization Sachetana. We believe that if we, with our writings, songs, plays and protests, can awaken the consciousness of even a few persons, its ripples will spread out in ever widening circles of men and women. (*Sachetana*, 1991)

Here are shades of liberal humanism reminiscent of Mrinalini Dasgupta's writing about literacy (quoted in chapter 3). Here Sachetana's language appeals to those "right thinking and humanitarian individuals" in the same way that the PBGMS does, in the way that the intelligentsia of Calcutta would best understand.

Consciousness raising is in many ways the raison d'être of Sachetana. But rather than stress the role of the Birlas or other powerful capitalists, Sachetana activists point out the sexual double standards and the "puritanism" that pervades expectations of women, which they blame the CPI(M) for fostering. One of Sachetana's plays, *Meye dile Shajiye* (The bride bedecked) examines the commodification of the woman in marriage, while *Bandar Khela* (Monkey show) is a critique of the dowry system. Privately and within their group, Sachetana activists criticize the nationalist chauvinism of the CPI(M) and its requirement that party women wear the traditional Bengali red-bordered white saris at large public events. Sachetana believes it is struggling against those aspects of Marxist-Leninism and nationalism that perpetuate the oppressive double standards. But they are the more difficult aspects of Calcutta's political culture to counter.

Feminism and Male Domination

Feminism is often a contentious word in the women's movement in India, and in Calcutta, it is a particularly difficult word. Some highly visible national-level CPI(M) activists treat "feminists" (i.e., activists in politically autonomous groups) as the stooges of imperialism in India; to them "feminism" is the enemy more so than "men." Thus in the 1990 AIDWA conference pamphlet, Kanak Mukherjee, a senior CPI(M) central committee member based in Calcutta, writes that feminism is a "subtle intervention of imperialists and other reactionary forces" that creates "ideological confusion among the people through subtle propaganda" by spreading the idea of "feminism" as against "Marxism."

The West Bengal PBGMS general secretary, Shyamali Gupta, articulates in a somewhat confused way what she believes "feminism" is and why she, as a Marxist, opposes it:

> Feminist or womanist groups believe in gender oppression. We do not. We believe in class oppression. Like us, there are men who are oppressed. But it is true that social oppression is a little higher in the case of women because as a section of society, not as a class, women are backward. It is true that family and society are male dominated. I prefer to call it not oppression but domination. (Personal communication)

While "oppression" and "domination" can have analytically distinct interpretations, Shyamali Gupta appears to be ranking these concepts such that oppression is related to primacy given to class and domination appears as less fundamental. Her differentiation between gender and class mechanisms is both labored and contrived. Yet this is the only way party ideology and women's experiences can be reconciled in Calcutta's political culture.

Since Sachetana activists represent a range of the political spectrum, they do not have a "party line" on definitions of feminism and patriarchy. But running through several women's ideas is the sense that feminism is about creating a new gender ideology. It is about recasting and recreating the relationships between men and women, women and their families, and women and themselves. One Sachetana activist would add to this "an examination of our own sexualities and subjectivities" (S1). Furthermore, Sachetana activists believe that feminists do have distinctive points of view and must hold on to them. This is why, for example, feminists should never merge completely with the state, for who then would be its watchdogs?

Because feminism does have a distinctive point of view, it can lead women away from "the party ideas" that permeate Calcutta's political culture. And it is feminism's ability to do this that makes it "so badly needed" in Calcutta, in the words of one Sachetana member. Thus both the PBGMS and Sachetana are aware of the threat posed by feminism to the CPI(M). Both acknowledge the unacceptability of feminist ideas to Calcutta's political culture. The possibility of this distinct and alternative point of view is the danger of feminism to the CPI(M)—the "keepers" of Calcutta's political culture—and the promise of feminism to Sachetana, the "outsiders."

Political Organizing, Foreign Funding, and the State

Sachetana and the PBGMS do coincide on key questions involving the political sphere and organizing, and this is where Sachetana differs most from other autonomous groups, such as the Forum in Bombay. As would be expected, the women of the PBGMS have a flexible attitude toward the state. Aside from obvious loyalty to their government, PBGMS members reflect a view that many Calcuttans share. The Left Front is seen generally as a safer government, one against which—at least until very recently—one could demonstrate and protest without fear of reprisal. It is seen as a government that actively works to combat ethnic tension and one that has been inactive rather than actively hostile toward women. Women in the PBGMS feel strongly that if the left is in power, then women can only benefit. They frequently point out that women in West Bengal are safer, that democratic norms are maintained, and that the ordinary women of West Bengal know that they have a government that will listen to their concerns. That there are costs associated with being part of the state is something that PBGMS activists will only acknowledge off the record:

> Susheela Gopalan once said to me that women must enter each and every committee and group of the party, because if our voices aren't heard, then the party men won't think about us. . . . If those who are directly affected don't speak out, then others don't think about them. . . .
>
> Autonomous women's organizations have a certain suspicion of political parties. They believe that they swallow up the movement. . . . We believe that if the women's movement is not linked with the larger people's movement, then it will not get very far. (Former CPI(M) member of Parliament and PBGMS member Malini Bhattacharya, personal communication)

The resolution of the dilemma for the PBGMS lies in getting more and more women involved in every level of the party, not in leaving it. Working in isolation, that is, divorced from a political party, is a strategic error. Those who choose this path are at worst distrusted and at best considered irrelevant.

Sachetana activists are in general appreciative of the presence of a left government as well as a left political culture. They believe that Calcutta's political culture has encouraged Sachetana members to think and rethink their actions and to consider the viewpoint of other feminist groups, as well as those of the PBGMS. Left culture is seen as something that makes feminists responsible: "Every time I make a move, I have to think twice about its political implications. I don't think we can afford to be spontaneous. . . . the tendency of the feminist movement, particularly with so much emphasis on personal freedom, is just to be completely voluntaristic, . . . which I think is a mistake" (S5). Several Sachetana activists are quick to point out the benefits to women brought by the Left Front, and all the women in Sachetana, save one, would consider working with the state. This government, regardless of its many shortcomings, is perceived to be a better government than others. It must, in some sense, also be protected. According to one Sachetana member, "Unless . . . it does something where we think our constructive criticism might help, we do not want to be actively antagonistic to this government" (S4).

Whether because of pressure from the CPI(M) or because of their belief in the Left Front government or because Sachetana is part of Calcutta's political culture, which legitimizes state-based political action, there is a willingness on Sachetana's part to accept government funds (state and national) but not funds from foreign aid agencies such as USAID and the Ford

Foundation. This is not simply because they have a right as taxpayers to use government money, as several members maintain. Calcutta's political climate acts as a powerful deterrent to accepting foreign funding, and they are too suspect as feminists as it is.

Nevertheless, their autonomy is important to Sachetana. It gives them the space to articulate alternative theoretical positions without having to toe a party line. By maintaining their autonomy, Sachetana activists feel they can still be left oriented without being tied to the opportunistic requirements of party politics. It is the continual submergence of women's issues to the larger interests of the party that is the main problem with political affiliation. At the same time, they acknowledge the cultural unacceptability of autonomy in Calcutta. As one academic, closely affiliated with the CPI(M) and active in the teachers' union, put it, "If I had been just a member of the Communist Party, that is something they [her colleagues] would not consider odd. Nor if I were just an active member of WBCUTA [the university teachers' union], but belonging to a women's organization is an 'aberration'" (S1).

The Personal and the Political

> *No other immediate work at hand, so we chatted about our own problems, which I think should be an integral feature of Sachetana's sisterhood program, don't you?*
> —Entry in the Sachetana diary, February 9, 1986

The slogan, "the personal is political" is not one that finds a happy home in Calcutta. Activists in both groups know quite well that "personal" and "familial" issues pervade and influence the "political" sphere. As activists and women they constantly negotiate the tensions between being a party worker and a wife and mother, as the conversation with Mita revealed, and these tensions are not restricted to PBGMS women. While the PBGMS women I interviewed were not reticent about their ideas about marriage and the domestic division of labor, they were equally clear that these were fights that, as Mita said, they "have to fight alone."

Women in the PBGMS know that in order to be a successful woman activist, one must have the support of one's husband. Support may take the form of a husband defending his wife against his parents or helping out with housework. Some are able to negotiate this successfully, while others are often frustrated: "I do get angry with my husband sometimes when I come back exhausted and he is sitting around and I have to cook. I do tell him. I say I have worked harder than he has so why can't he get himself a cup of tea! My husband, though, is very liberal and has never objected to my working outside the house the way I do" (P14). On the other hand, there are women like this seventy-year-old activist, who has created a household in which her husband made and served me tea and snacks during the interview:

> In my house we have not behaved as if only women do the housework. You wash your own dishes, and so on. We must have the same rights within the house. We who work in the party have started to do this. *We cannot say one thing outside the house and face a dictatorship inside it.* My husband has often cooked when I have been at meetings. (P7; emphasis added)

Nevertheless, PBGMS activists do not pressure women, whether within their organization or outside of it, to challenge the structure of relationships within the family. When asked about this issue, they shrug, smile deprecatingly, or shake their heads sorrowfully. They do not deny the importance of the issue but they will not politicize it. They do, however, encourage women to earn money and assure them that they will be able to make joint decisions with their husbands if they do.

On one level, therefore, there is a line between the personal and political that is not breached—"These are personal matters." On another, however, several of the PBGMS women I spoke with had been married through the party or with the party's permission, thus ceding to the party control over the most personal decisions of their lives, decisions that had hitherto been made only by their parents or by themselves. One woman I spoke with even gave the party control over whether she should leave her husband. When her husband gave her an ultimatum because he felt she was spending too much time in party activities, she opted to leave him, and the party initially supported her decision. However, the local committee in the area in which she worked maintained that if divorced, she would cease to be an effective party worker. The community would not be able to accept it. Thus she was asked to stay with her husband, and, while the party did "speak to him" about their relationship, she knows that she has had to "give in a lot" (C2).

Sachetana plays a complex role in the lives of its members. On the one hand, activists like Shona are attracted to Sachetana because it is the one place they feel free, where they feel a camaraderie, a place of their own. Sachetana is a place where they have seen themselves and others grow. On the other hand, some of its members criticize Sachetana for not being open enough to the personal. According to one activist, the avoidance of personal discussions has resulted in Sachetana's failure to become a truly feminist organization. She herself found it impossible to discuss the painful issues around her divorce with the group (S4).

Sachetana activists are nevertheless more open about conflicts within the household and see the concessions they make to their husbands (and their husbands' families) as political compromises. These compromises are sometimes the topic of discussion in the presence or absence of the woman concerned. Because these issues are seen as political, Sachetana activists are more judgmental about the ability of particular individuals to make these compromises than are PBGMS activists: "Our members have in many ways accepted the values of their in-laws. Therefore there are constraints on their action. . . . I do understand the problem. I have found my way by making myself work harder. Even though my husband often helps me, I find I still work very hard to be the perfect wife, mother, and scholar" (S2).

The effects of Calcutta's particular political culture are clearly felt in the uncomfortable articulations of the personal and political. In attempts to raise their own awareness, Sachetana members sometimes hold discussions about culture and sexuality, as they did at an annual general meeting I attended in 1991. However, there is a level of discomfort that becomes apparent in the group when such "personal" discussions are attempted. Few of the activists actually reveal their own experiences (as familiarity with consciousness-raising groups elsewhere may lead us to expect), and conversations are almost always held in neutral terms ("one feels . . ."). There is a sense of awkwardness about these discussions and relief when they end. Participation in such "baring of the soul" discussions are, undoubtedly, culture specific and must be socially learned. Because many in Sachetana were initially politicized through the CPI and the CPI(M), they are more hesitant and less open to this process than are, for example, the activists of the Forum.

Conclusion

Despite some similarities in ideology, the PBGMS and Sachetana approach issues such as work and domestic violence in fundamentally different ways. It is also evident that Sachetana finds it necessary to react to and refer to issues as framed by the PBGMS, both because the PBGMS is so powerful and because it reflects and epitomizes Calcutta's political culture. Common to most groups in Calcutta is the idea that women are in general "backward" in their beliefs and that consciousness raising will help these women "progress." Common also is a certain nationalism and trust of the state. Because politically affiliated forms of organization are so legitimated in Calcutta, Sachetana is not ideologically opposed to them (unlike autonomous groups in many other cities). Sachetana members condemn what they see as the double standards held by the PBGMS with regard to an array of women's issues discussed in this chapter, double standards internalized by men and women alike. Yet they do so in circumscribed spaces—only within their group. They are more self-reflective about their social status and the impact that might have upon the very women they want to politicize, and they struggle with politicizing the personal.

Ultimately, then, because they are situated in Calcutta's political field, Sachetana is ideologically constrained in three particular areas: (1) The field limits their ability to deal with the intimate and the personal (both organizationally and personally); (2) being suspect as autonomous feminists, they dare not accept foreign funding and so remain dependent on individual and state funds; and (3) their subordinate position within the field, combined with their challenging theorization of issues such as work, sexual double standards, and violence, leads them to choose a multilayered strategy in which these issues are dealt with in ways that do not directly threaten the status quo.

There are signs, however, of subtle changes in Calcutta's political culture. During my visit to Calcutta in 1994, one activist who is a member of both Sachetana and the NFIW commented, "I've seen a new phenomenon in the past five years or so. Now women are less silent about domestic violence and rape. They are less humiliated and shamed by it. I think this is partly the result of the national women's movement and television." What remains to be seen is how these changes translate at the level of the political.

Chapter 5

Domination and Subordination in Calcutta

> To many observers it remains surprising: the Communist dominated
> Left Front government in West Bengal has remained in power for al-
> most two decades now. It has stood the test of numerous national,
> provincial and local elections. It has seemingly remained largely unaf-
> fected by the ever increasing churning in Indian politics.

So begins an article in *Economic and Political Weekly,* arguably India's best
progressive academic journal.[1] It goes on to document the "reasonable" success of the *panchayat* (local government) system in West Bengal, highlighting
the extent to which women and the poor have been brought in from the margins. The article also points to a phenomenon particularly noticeable in eval-
uations of the CPI(M)—that opinions of the government in West Bengal tend
to fall into two distinct camps, "contemptuous dismissal" or "unqualified ac-
claim." The CPI(M) is seen as a failure by analysts such as Ross Mallick and
Ashok Rudra, who view it as a party that has consolidated itself by oppor-
tunistically refusing to challenge the status quo. It is seen as a success by analysts such as T. J. Nossiter and Atul Kohli, who believe that the CPI(M) functions as a social democratic party and has indeed represented the poor. In
terms of what the party has done for women, some say that it has raised the
wages that women earn, that women may have a real shot at leadership
through the *panchayats,* and that, despite lapses, it has kept Calcutta relatively safe for women. Others say that the party has done very little, too little, or
nothing at all. All agree, however, that the CPI(M) is *the* political force to reck-
on with in West Bengal, and many agree that the CPI(M) has too much power.

West Bengal's political field is dominated by political parties, the CPI(M) being the superordinate force in this field. This party operates in Bengal with the help of its massive front organizations and has little competition from rivals from the center (the Congress) or the right (the BJP). Its front organizations are strongest in those sectors of society where traditional support for Communists may usually be found—the peasantry and the unions. The CPI(M) has also built up a substantial patronage machine in the state. Nonparty political formations and institutions as yet have little legitimacy and power. Organizations linked to the CPI(M) can depend on it for both its resources (some finances but mainly people) and for its reach. This enables them to create alliances via the party—a resource denied to those unaffiliated to the CPI(M). As this chapter will show, while Sachetana and the PBGMS share some elements of ideology (that distinguish both of them from women's organizations in Bombay), their respective positions within the field result in two very different sets of trajectories and strategies. The PBGMS trajectory is marked by outward strength, on the one hand, and deference to the CPI(M), on the other, while Sachetana's trajectory is marked by fluctuating attempts to distinguish itself from and accommodate itself to the CPI(M).

Strategies

Just as political cultures are not seamless, neither is power. While the PBGMS dominates the women's movement because of its affiliation to the CPI(M), it does not own it. And while Sachetana is subordinate, it still has an impact in Calcutta. In this section, I turn to an examination of the organizational and personal strategies of Sachetana and PBGMS activists. Individual activists within each organization must constantly negotiate between their ideologies, their knowledge of their groups' capacities, and the possibilities of their groups' effectiveness. The spirit that motivates this section is the desire to understand a rather complicated question: How do activists make decisions about issues and strategies, given the constraints of their organization and the field, as well as their own ideologies and experiences? This analysis will point to some areas of conflict and contradiction, since the mechanisms of decision making are often most starkly revealed to us there and thus help to illuminate the ways in which activists negotiate these complicated relationships.

Paschim Banga Ganatantrik Mahila Samiti

As the women's wing of the CPI(M), the PBGMS is in the peculiar position of being dominant in the women's movement in Calcutta but ultimately subordinate to the CPI(M). It thus operates on two levels: On the one hand, it must be responsive to women's needs, and on the other, it must carry out the party's agenda, since it is, after all, dependent on the party for resources and is accountable to it. As we saw in chapter 3, the party legitimizes the PBGMS by giving it a privileged status among women's organizations and also provides the PBGMS with funds and publicity.

The PBGMS activists I met are passionate, devoted, principled, compassionate, and extremely hardworking. They work for women's "emancipation" but are also active participants in the nationalist gender culture of the CPI(M). Members of the PBGMS always wear saris as opposed to the *salwar kameez,* a more convenient garment favored by women in North India and increasingly worn by young women in Bengal. The first time I met one of the key activists of the PBGMS, she asked me why I wasn't wearing a sari and a *bindi* (on my forehead), adding that she just thought they looked better than did anything else on Bengali women. My short hair (despite my elaborate ruse of pulling it back into a fake bun) caused much amusement and head shaking, but was tolerated because I do, after all, live in the United States. Women of the PBGMS see themselves as women certainly, but primarily as Bengali Communist women.

But the PBGMS is not the party; it is a mass organization connected to the party. It was difficult to understand the exact mechanisms of the party's relationship with the PBGMS, but something of their relationship can be understood through statements such as "all we have to do is not go against the main program of the party" and "we are the auxiliary, not the party." What is crystal clear is that the PBGMS is not an autonomous organization and is accountable to the CPI(M). This means that it must often accept issues handed down from the party leadership. The CPI(M), in turn, can only be in power as long as the electorate keeps it there; it will not be reelected if people do not feel that the CPI(M) is working on issues that most concern them. Thus PBGMS activists find themselves negotiating between the party and their organization, on the one hand, and between the people and the party, on the other, attempting all the while to help women and to fight for their rights.

Mediating between the Government and the Masses in a Time of Change

At the time that I did my initial fieldwork in 1990–91, communist parties around the world were reeling from the shock of changes in the Soviet Union and Eastern Europe, followed by the Tiananmen Square confrontation. The women of the PBGMS were suddenly faced with a more skeptical public, a first-time questioning of the sacred cow that is Calcutta's political culture. This skepticism creates considerable tension within activists because they feel accountable to "the masses"—they owe the people explanations. These activists see their job as politicizing women and leading them to a better life. Yet, as representatives of the state, PBGMS activists find themselves making bold promises to women, promises they know they cannot fulfill. Aware of the people's expectations of them, they are frustrated with their inability to meet them:

> Women come to us, you know. They have been deserted. They have no skills, yet they need jobs. It's a real problem. What does one do? *This is our government so we should have been able to do something about this with state-level resources in the past thirteen to fourteen years.* But we haven't. We always think, how many jobs can we give people, after all; it is more important to explain the basic political concepts to them. But now we see that because our party is in power, women are not remaining satisfied with our answers. Communist countries are crashing all over the world. No longer are merely words convincing. (P6; emphasis added)

Promises of a better day, without any concrete help in the present, can no longer work in the face of changes in the communist world. Calcutta's political culture cannot single-handedly withstand the effect of the crumbling of the Soviet Union. There is, in this activist's mind, a recognition that the state, a state run by *her* party, has not sufficiently prioritized women's needs, and that this fact, together with a new skepticism about socialism, would turn women away. Moreover, there is a second problem along this vein: the longer the party remains in power, the less revolutionary it becomes. One state-level leader confided to me in a moment of unusual candor: "I think it is time for our government to leave office. How long can we keep telling the people that we have limitations imposed on us by the central government? The fact is, a revolution cannot come through parliamentary democracy." (P1)

For women in the mass organizations associated with the party, making promises that are broken and finding themselves in patron-client relationships do not make for rewarding political work. In some sense PBGMS activists see the political culture around them changing as the CPI(M) continues to consolidate its power in the old way. More and more people flock to the party and to its mass organizations because of what the government can give them, not because they believe in socialism. The longer the left stays in power, the longer politics becomes imbued with opportunism. Women of the PBGMS look around them and find their beliefs and their work increasingly difficult to sustain.

The party has often campaigned on a platform of promoting the "digni-ty and respect" of women. Thus when rapes are perpetrated by CPI(M) cadres, the residents of Calcutta hold them accountable. They demand an explanation, and grassroots activists sometimes find themselves scrambling for an explanation in the absence of party guidance. At a district-level meet-ing I attended, several grassroots activists asked the leadership for advice re-garding the complaint that the party couldn't really be concerned with women, given that they were not doing anything about the assault and mur-der of women social workers at Bantala. Both the party and the PBGMS are held accountable to the political culture they have constructed, and the grassroots activists of the PBGMS are the first to know when they are failing the test.

Mediating between the Party and the Organization: The Problem of Male Leadership

The presence and importance of men in the CPI(M) affects the way the PBGMS deals with several critical issues. That the problem of the domestic division of labor is not raised at all is largely due to the dominance of men. The PBGMS activists are well aware of conflicts in the division of labor, since women are frequently late to meetings or skip meetings entirely when they have no domestic help. Some hold the division of labor responsible for the fact that women activists do not have more time to devote to reading or to participating in party activities and hence are underrepresented in the lead-ership (P5).

The presence of men in the organization also affects the way the PBGMS confronts domestic conflicts between party members. If a man refuses his wife maintenance (equivalent to the concept of alimony and child support) in the case of divorce, the PBGMS can start legal proceedings immediately. But when the perpetrator is a member of the CPI(M) or its affiliated groups, the PBGMS does not directly intervene. The matter goes through the union (or other party organizations) and through protracted negotiations, with the PBGMS turning to legal action as a last resort. This dynamic is largely due to the relative position of the PBGMS vis-à-vis the CPI(M) in Calcutta and is not, for example, seen with the CPI(M) and its women's wing in Bombay.

Whether or not individual male leaders agree with each other, the male leadership as a whole is well aware of the embedded nature of patriarchal in-terests. They are also aware that not serving women's needs would turn women away from the organization. Many of the decisions to adopt or to ig-nore issues are a product of this tension.

Mechanisms of Resolution: Service without Politicization

The CPI(M) often co-opts seemingly explosive issues by resolving them in such a way as to eliminate the political edge. And it does so because it can. Domestic violence is one such issue. I was repeatedly told that when domestic violence occurs in couples belonging to the party, the "party takes care of it." Sometimes they expel the husband; sometimes they separate husband and wife and help the wife become independent. In one instance, the wife was given a party office job (P9).

What the party does not do is politicize the issue. While it does not blame women for bringing the violence upon themselves—and in fact appears to have dealt fairly in many cases—it also ensures that domestic violence does not appear in the public arena as an "issue." Therefore party men are not fundamentally threatened, yet individual women feel that justice has been done and the party has stood by them in their hour of need. Consequently, women feel little need to push the issue into the realm of the political. The issue of domestic violence has thus been classically co-opted by the CPI(M) to fit both Calcutta's political culture and the paternalistic culture of the CPI(M).

What do PBGMS women do about domestic violence? Within the PBGMS, one can discern three levels of response. There is, of course, the official position from the national- and state-level leaders: domestic violence is a tragedy, but can only be solved through economic measures. Thus, until viable economic measures exist, there is no point in focusing on it. At the level of the local leadership, there is far more sympathy for victims of domestic violence, even though the women I interviewed did not mention the issue until I broached it. While the political belief that economic conditions matter more than any other factor is held by national and local leaders alike, local leaders who actually work with battered women are deeply unhappy about their inability to provide even temporary protection measures for women (P6). They recognize that domestic violence must be taken seriously.

The grassroots workers in the PBGMS contradict their leaders' views on domestic violence. In their view, it is mistaken to consider it a working-class issue; it is just that middle-class women do not readily report the domestic violence in their lives:

> I see the women as they come to the Samiti—women who are being forced into marriage, women whose married lives are terrible, women who feel they have no choice but to try to bear the tortures inflicted on them—poor women and rich women both! . . . women tell me that they work hard all day and then their husbands beat them. I have seen husbands even in the professional classes beat their wives. (P9)

Two grassroots activists debated this point during one of my conversations with them:

> Poor women talk about the fact that their husbands beat them—but not middle-class women. If women come to us, then we go en masse to their house, we try to talk to the husband or to his elders and we try to find out what is causing this behavior. (P8)

> Middle-class women don't talk about it even though it occurs more in the middle class. After all, if you do not wish to embroil us in your family matters, there is nothing we can do. (P12)

While some PBGMS activists have developed analyses of domestic violence that are very different from the official discourse, that discourse is still maintained. It is publicly maintained both because the PBGMS is working within the bounds of Calcutta's political culture and because it cannot afford to alienate the party men.

Mechanisms of Resolution: Democratic Centralism

Democratic centralism, the political form followed by both the CPI(M) and the PBGMS, should ideally hold the leadership accountable to the people. Issues should filter up from the base, decisions should be arrived at after open argument and debate, and people should be free to dissent. However, once the decision is made, even dissenters must accept it.

In my discussions with PBGMS workers at various levels, it became clear that they take this process very seriously. At the grassroots level, the workers feel that it is their responsibility to report a policy's success or failure to the leadership at their level and that the report should be carried on up through the hierarchy (P15). If there are criticisms of a particular party policy faced by grassroots activists, they carry the information to their local PBGMS meetings and ask for help in answering the criticism.

There are elaborate formalized procedures for decision making in PBGMS. Each level (local, district, and state) has its powers, and only matters on which there is no agreement at a particular level are to be referred to the higher level. In cases of disagreement between the party and the PBGMS that the PBGMS secretariat cannot resolve, the matter is referred to the liaison between the party and the PBGMS. If there is no resolution at that level, it is taken to the party secretariat, whose decision must be accepted by both parties.

This is a clearly demarcated process. Yet, when I asked a leader of the Calcutta district office what was done in the case of disagreements between the mass organization (PBGMS) and the party CPI(M), she replied:

There should not be any. I am in this organization because I agree with it. I have a space to say what I believe within the organization. We go by majority decision. We debate and argue but ultimately must accept the decision of the majority. But then I cannot go back to my district and talk about my disagreements.

When pushed further about hypothetical dissenters, she elaborated:

They cannot [refuse to implement a decision]. We will explain to them why it is necessary to implement it. We do not say it is a party decision. It has to be first passed at the Samiti, and then carried downward. If there is a problem we will bring it back to the party, resolve it, and then repeat the process. If people still disagree, we discuss it. But if, in spite of this, someone is not satisfied, then she must have an ill motive and we realize that she must have moved away from the values of the organization. (P5)

Dissent is not easy in an organization with such strong norms against "deviationism" as this. Indeed, there are harsh penalties involved in being labeled a dissenter or deviant.[2] The distance between conception and execution in the political process does not bode well for true democracy. This mode of decision making also means that while issues may arise from the base, they may, in the normal course of events, be weeded out by the leadership.

Many grassroots workers in the PBGMS revealed that they simply work from an agenda sent to them by the regional leadership. If they are asked to sell five hundred copies of *Eksathe,* they ensure that they make their quota. The leadership has used and does use its power to discipline its cadres by publicly chastising, suspending, or expelling them. The ideological and resource powers of the CPI(M) keep individual activists of the PBGMS in line.

Mechanisms of Resolution: Individual Self-Censorship

Knowledge of PBGMS ideology and capacity and fear of party discipline cause PBGMS activists to censor themselves. An incident related to me by a Sachetana member makes this evident. At a public meeting on women in *panchayats,* the state finance minister commented on the importance of thinking about women's issues without being "feminists." In response, the Sachetana member warned that the problems of women in development would not be resolved if the government continued to ignore the problems faced by women in their homes. A CPI(M) and PBGMS member responded by saying, "We are not like Bombay feminists. Relationships between men and women are not the important problem here," but then went on to outline women's problems within the family and with other men in the *panchayat.*

Once outside, she thanked the Sachetana member for bringing up the issue of gender relations within the home, and assured her that if Sachetana kept raising such issues, she would keep working on them within the party (S2). She felt that she simply could not publicly raise the issue to the party, which has not hesitated, in the past, to brand particular individuals as "feminists"—a word infused with anti-Communist, pro-Western, pro–United States meaning. This incident is important not only because it shows that a fairly powerful member of the PBGMS and the CPI(M) felt uncomfortable in directly challenging the party-mandated way of looking at problems, but also because of the disjuncture between action and speech it revealed, a disjuncture that I suspect has become fairly commonplace within the PBGMS.

A second organizationally linked self-censorship mechanism involves the awareness that the PBGMS lacks the capacity to take certain actions. This is made particularly clear in one grassroots leader's response to the issue of domestic violence. She no longer raises the issue at party meetings, both because she has understood that these issues are not dealt with politically and because of her assessment of the constraints:

> If we could give the women who come to us economic independence and protection, things would be a lot easier. As things stand, how do we tell them to leave their husbands? Where will they go? In situations where reconciliation is impossible, what should women do? The homes we have for women to go to are hopelessly inadequate. (P6)

This grassroots leader knows quite well that domestic violence is a problem that plagues many women. She is constantly frustrated with her inability to help women whose husbands abuse them, as she was initially unhappy and disappointed with her government's inability to solve the problem of domestic violence. Today, she deals with cases of violence on an individual basis but does not treat it as a major political issue. In her perception, given structural constraints, the party can do little to help abused women in the immediate future, thus there is no point in bringing the issue up at meetings.

The PBGMS: Strength and Deference

> *That which we desire we desire in our foolishness. And that which we have we fail to desire.*[3]
>
> —Bengali saying

There is no organization for women as powerful as the PBGMS in Calcutta. With its roots in the anticolonial struggles in pre-Independence India, the PBGMS has faced obstacles in its path to constantly recreate itself—until recently. It has shown that it can survive and that it is capable of success. Its ideologies fit Calcutta's political culture with ease, and its affiliation to the CPI(M) endows it with great strength. The price of that strength is deference to the party.

Once a source of profound politicization and mobilization of women, the role of the PBGMS has undergone a change since the CPI(M) ascendancy to power in West Bengal. Now it finds itself protecting and defending the state and even offering protection and patronage to others. Its members are increasingly mass recruited rather than trained as cadres, and free-riderism is emerging as an increasing problem. Indeed, it is the very protection and patronage possibilities of the post-1977 PBGMS that draw new members to it. Many activists are aware that people join the PBGMS because "they know we can do something. They know that with political power comes economic" (P14). Further, "women always want something in exchange for their membership—a job, a loan, etc." (P12). While activists try to convince potential recruits that the party cannot guarantee jobs or loans, but only their possibility through joint struggle, they are aware that women want membership in the PBGMS for instrumental reasons.

The CPI(M) may pay a price for its power. It first took the reins of government at a very favorable moment in Calcutta's political field—when it was marked by a weak and delegitimized Congress in the absence of any other political force, a left-friendly oppositional and Bengali-nationalist political culture, and a loyal and devoted cadre. And over the past two decades, the CPI(M) has grown steadily in power. In her book *Two Faces of Protest,* Amrita Basu argues that while the CPI(M) blames structural constraints for its declining radicalism on gender issues, the party has had greater latitude than it claims, deliberately choosing the less revolutionary options every step of the way. As others, both reformers and detractors, have pointed out, it is indeed the party's determined reformism that has allowed it to establish and extend its hold over the state. Part of its increasing power has come at the expense of mobilization and at the expense of its front organizations. In other words, the party has grown in power not only in the political field, but also in relation to its front organizations. This shift in power may ultimately be debilitating for the CPI(M), if the disillusionment and dissatisfaction of PBGMS activists is an indicator of the reaction of the front organizations in general.

PBGMS activists are communist women in a communist state. They are ideologically, emotionally, and materially tied to the CPI(M). Given the size, age, and power of the PBGMS and its position in Calcutta's political field, there are powerful reasons for the willingness of members to allow issues of concern to be filtered out and yet not abandon the organization. There are, I suspect, different logics that explain why older members and younger members stay in the organization. For older members, there is a sense of loyalty, a common belief in an ideology (a belief that sustained them through many years of repression), and a recognition of having made history. Their entire lives have revolved around the party and its struggles, and they are unlikely to leave even if they are frustrated with the party.

Perhaps the younger members would like the PBGMS to focus more on relations of gender within families, but even if it does not, they know that it will look after their particular family problems. The PBGMS provides members with protection, possible job opportunities, and power. As long as the PBGMS delivers on at least some of its promises and as long as it continues to be the only game in town, the newer members will remain. But as soon as it begins to falter, it will lose the trust and loyalty of many of its members. When that time comes, the PBGMS will have to recreate itself once again if it is to survive. Until then, the PBGMS will continue to promote some issues and silence others. And PBGMS members will continue to make necessary trade-offs, given the significant advantages of being affiliated with the dominant organization in a political field.

Sachetana

In every conversation I had with members of Calcutta's autonomous groups, I would hear phrases such as the following:

- "You can't remain outside established political groups and hope to get a big crowd in Calcutta."
- "The political climate is geared toward large groups."
- "There cannot be a large-scale Sachetana in West Bengal, but it does not need to be as limited as it is."
- "Autonomous women's organizations don't mean a thing in Calcutta."

What is an autonomous group to do if it wishes to mean something in Calcutta? Given that Sachetana is small and autonomous, what must it do to survive in Calcutta's political field? Even though it was formed in 1980, when the PBGMS did not formally exist, Sachetana has struggled in the shadow of CPI(M) dominance ever since its inception. In the past decade, Sachetana has fluctuated between sharply distinguishing itself from and accommodating itself to the all-powerful CPI(M). It has also found itself struggling with the inflexible, impermeable political culture of Calcutta. The combination of Calcutta's monolithic culture and the strength of the CPI(M) has created in Sachetana a trajectory marked by oscillation. A brief description of this trajectory will make clear the ways in which Sachetana has been deeply affected by Calcutta's political field and the CPI(M) position of dominance within it.

Sachetana announced itself to Calcutta through the production of a play, *Meye Dile Shajiye,* written by Malini Bhattacharya, one of their members. The play highlights the marketing and selling of women as brides and the use of dowry in marital exchanges. For the first few years of Sachetana's existence, these cultural performances formed the main thrust of its endeavors.

The antidowry campaign met with no opposition from the CPI(M). The PBGMS was created within the year (1981) and soon adopted the campaign as one of its issues. Shortly after that Sachetana initiated—and quickly abandoned—a literacy drive that involved holding classes for slum-dwelling children, with the objective of getting closer to their mothers. They found that they had neither the training nor energy nor resources to attract women to this program. As the mammoth PBGMS began to make its presence felt, Sachetana activists, realizing that they could not compete with the PBGMS, tried to differentiate themselves from the Samiti, returning to their original goal of political and self awareness—*sachetana.*

In an attempt to increase their strength in the face of CPI(M) power, several of the new, non-CPI(M)-affiliated, women's organizations came together in an umbrella organization called Nari Nirjatan Pratiradh Mancha (Forum against Oppression of Women) in 1981. While initially part of this group, Sachetana soon left, uncomfortable with what it considered to be sensationalist and politically irresponsible actions of the Mancha, particularly because of its constant criticisms of the CPI(M). While Nari Nirjatan Pratiradh Mancha (NNPM) still exists, it is no longer an umbrella organization. It is now a smaller organization with unofficial links to Maoist parties.

The organizational power of the CPI(M) affects Sachetana in multiple ways. As the governing party, the CPI(M) makes available funds for select projects, thus forcing Sachetana to choose between adopting CPI(M)-sanctioned projects or ignoring the money. Once the funding has been obtained, Sachetana activists still have to negotiate with the party for spaces in which they can do their work, as the more recent experience of the adolescent girl project shows.

In the wake of the declaration of the Decade of the Girl Child by the South Asian Association for Regional Co-operation (SAARC) in 1992, Sachetana applied to the Urban Development Centre of the West Bengal government for funds to launch a project to educate adolescent girls. They chose a slum near their office, in the neighborhood in which several of the activists lived, as the targeted site for this project. It then took over a month to get permission from the CPI(M) party activists who controlled the slum to use their facilities for classes for the girls. This permission was at first given and then withdrawn. The task of negotiating the maze of party politics was left to a Sachetana member who has been active in party politics for many years. When I last spoke with Sachetana members in 1994, a year into their project, Sachetana had found itself providing elementary education, help with homework, and some art and craft classes. Gender awareness, the real aim of the project, had somehow remained out of reach.

Sachetana has neither the legal recognition nor the numbers to be effective in the ways that the PBGMS can be. Feeling that it is not allowed to be effective because of the enormous popularity and power of the CPI(M), it has evolved several adaptive strategies in order to ensure its survival in Calcutta's political field. All of these are what Bourdieu (1975) has called strategies of succession rather than strategies of subversion. That is, they are strategies of adaptation, not of separation, strategies that stem from positions of weakness rather than strength.

Strategy 1: Compatibility with the CPI(M) Agenda

Despite their analysis that "participating in economic activities does not alter the relative status of a woman in her own eyes or in the eyes of her family," Sachetana decided in 1990 to get funds from the government to initiate a nontraditional employment program. In conjunction with several other autonomous groups in the city, Sachetana launched Naba-Swadhikar. The objective was to promote "greater participation of women in self-employment and entrepreneurial ventures" (letter circulated on August 23, 1989). A year later, the project began to fall apart for a number of reasons. In order to facilitate this program, Sachetana activists had to learn how to work with the government, how to procure funds and how to distinguish good proposals from bad. Sachetana simply felt ill equipped to do this work and came to rely heavily on an activist-entrepreneur from another group, a person who had a great deal of experience negotiating with the government—a person whom they eventually found they could not trust. Moreover, they discovered that against their best intentions, the goal of the program began to shift. Success began to be defined as the act of getting a job, not the creation of durable skills. In working with government bureaucracies, they felt pressured to create leaders and hierarchies within their organization. Participating in this program meant turning Sachetana into something it never wanted to be, a government-sponsored distributor of funds. In 1992, they made the decision to pull out of the program.

Both the political culture of Calcutta and the fact that the CPI(M) controls funding for these projects periodically pull Sachetana in the direction of programs such as literacy and self-employment, but their efforts are invariably short-lived because of their limited capacity and lack of recognition by the powerful forces in the city. At the same time, fear of being condemned by the CPI(M) inhibits them from acting on issues that would mark them as distinctly outside of that culture.

Sachetana has molded its issues within boundaries acceptable to the CPI(M). In order to be subversive and to sharply differentiate itself from the PBGMS, Sachetana would need to have a more powerful alternative resource or cultural base or both. The absence of an alternative cultural base from which Sachetana can mobilize against women's oppression is a direct consequence of the power of the CPI(M) universe of political discourse in Calcutta, a power that extends to at least some members of Sachetana.

Given that Sachetana members consider themselves to be feminist and given that feminism has been successfully labeled as Western (read: decadent and bourgeois), Sachetana members do indeed face an ideological and cultural quandary. They are undoubtedly more westernized. For example, some of the younger Sachetana members smoke and do so in the meetings. And this, according to an older member who is more rooted in Calcutta's political culture, has cost them dearly: "Why did she insist on smoking in the office? People aren't used to this. They are not comfortable." Calcutta's women, this activist feels, have stopped coming to Sachetana partly because the sight of women smoking is such a striking marker of cultural and ideological difference. The CPI(M) has also used such deviations from social norms to discredit Sachetana.

The combination of its lack of effective power in the political field with its distinctive ideology often puts Sachetana on the defensive. If it wants to engage with an issue that is not yet accepted in the culture of Calcutta and the CPI(M), it is obliged to defend its position. When Sachetana decided it was time to politicize the institution of marriage, for example, there was a strong concern that the campaign would be denigrated as an excuse for airing middle-class women's problems. An editorial introducing the newsletter's focus on marriage, therefore, stated defensively: "It is possible that Sachetana's detractors will use it [the issue of marriage] in evidence against the organization. 'Aha,' they would say, 'Sachetana is now showing its true colours! Like any middle class women's organization, it is turning into a marriage counseling service'" (*Sachetana,* October 1987). The editorial then went on to explain why the analysis of marriage as a powerful institution of domination was so important for all women, and why women should understand the legal and customary codes that govern their lives.

Sachetana is engaged in an ongoing struggle with Calcutta's political culture and the CPI(M) agenda—a struggle that not only defines the group's relationship with other actors and organizations in the field, but also causes conflict within the group itself. In order for Sachetana to survive, its members must carefully weigh their insider/outsider status. To accept the CPI(M) agenda would lead to Sachetana's eventual demise or absorption into the PBGMS, but remaining at the margins of the culture could render it irrelevant.

Strategy 2: Alternative Spaces

One strategy that helps Sachetana productively maintain its insider/outsider status is that of carving out alternative spaces. While Sachetana does still periodically launch large, more visible employment or education projects with the help of funding from the state government, its members organize seminars, film shows, and discussions on various topics of interest on a regular basis. Their raison d'être is, after all, to raise consciousness in themselves and in other women. The report of activities presented to the membership at the annual general meeting in 1986, for example, included discussions on topics as varied as women labor leaders of the nineteenth century, women in China, the women's movement in Hyderabad, the character Bimala in Rabindranath Tagore's novel *Ghare Baire,* and a report on the international film festival. These discussions were held primarily for the regular members. Sachetana has also periodically held workshops on dowry for college students, as well as seminars on women and work and women in media.

A second strategy, then, is to create spaces and issues in which the CPI(M) is not interested. The film festivals and the workshops fall into this category, as do the various internal group discussions. Through seminars in which women on the left are invited to talk about their experiences, Sachetana hopes to have an impact on women within left parties. The expectation is that listening to each others' stories will give participants the courage to push the "woman question" further in their respective parties. It is in these spaces that Sachetana members are at their most subversive, in these corners where formulations that challenge the CPI(M) are put forward. "We survive," says one activist, "by cheating. We have selected a level that political organizations aren't interested in" (S1).

Strategy 3: Working with the CPI(M), or Playing Watchdog

The third strategy appears to be a selective silence about controversial issues, on the one hand, and an overt willingness to work with the PBGMS-CPI(M) on the other. Sachetana frequently invites PBGMS representatives to their seminars and participates in joint forums with the PBGMS when possible.

The PBGMS, on the other hand, does not commonly invite Sachetana to its conferences. It tends to restrict its call for joint actions to the women's organizations of the four left political parties of the Left Front. In the city of political parties, Sachetana's autonomy immediately puts it outside the circle of power. It is not consulted, referred to, or feared. It cannot make powerful alliances with other autonomous groups, although it did make some ill-fated attempts in the past. The only effective alliances it can make are with other political parties—with the CPI(M) or the CPI.

Sachetana is rarely openly critical of the CPI(M) as a party or as guardian of the state. Many Sachetana members as individuals are deeply critical of certain government actions, but their criticisms as an organization are both belated and tempered. This unwillingness to confront the state, which is precisely one of the missions of a social movement, is what often causes a paralysis in Sachetana. Its paralysis extends so far that even when the majority of the members agree on a particular criticism of the CPI(M), they do not take a public stand about it, as evidenced by Sachetana's response to the Bantala and Birati crimes in 1990. These two cases, the first the murders of health and social workers and the second a gang rape, occurred within a few months of each other, and CPI(M) cadres were implicated in both. Additionally, the government was slow, sometimes offensive, and fumbling in its handling of both events—the chief minister was reported to have said, "These things happen." These cases, therefore, came to represent in the public mind a clear indication of the lack of attention by the CPI(M) to women's safety and well-being, as well as its loss of control over its cadre. Sachetana's response was also slow: "The Bantala/Birati case—it's so important. It took so long to even figure out what we wanted to do and when. . . . They were all thinking, shall we do this against the CPI(M)? What will _____ think?" (S2).

This unwillingness to challenge the CPI(M), even in such a clear-cut situation, stems from two distinct sources. First, the political identity of many of the Sachetana activists involves deep ties to feminism and the left, an identity that allows them to deliberately distinguish themselves from other feminist groups outside Calcutta. Second, they fear the power of the CPI(M). They know that as long as they are nonthreatening to the CPI(M), they can survive. Indeed, several activists claim that they can be effective *because* the CPI(M) ignores them most of the time. But if they were to be too critical of CPI(M) policies, the CPI(M) could use all the cultural tools at its disposal (such as its widely read newspaper) to discredit them completely. They wonder whether their quiescence stems from their desire to survive as a group (S3, S5).

Ironically, Sachetana does indeed want to act as a watchdog of the

CPI(M). But it has decided that it can best do so by influencing women within political parties. Some in Sachetana believe that their very existence gives women within the CPI(M) the space they might need to articulate alternative visions of women's issues—the very space denied by the party. These activists conclude that the party line must be changed from within and that Sachetana's role should be to change and draw out women in the party: "There are of course certain issues where when the ten of us shout, it is not going to change the world. We know that. Policy changes, legal changes, interstate changes, we cannot bring about. But we can raise the issue and ask the politically affiliated groups to take it up if they can manipulate within the party" (S3).

As the incident I described in the section on PBGMS self-censorship among the state finance minister, the PBGMS member, and the Sachetana member shows, Sachetana can indeed be effective in this way, but not always successfully. As one activist, a strong supporter of the CPI(M), said ruefully, "I thought that if autonomous women's organizations brought up these issues, then the PBGMS would realize its mistake and start working on those issues. But it has not happened, probably because the PBGMS is too smug" (S7). In Calcutta, the CPI(M) does not need to listen to Sachetana.

Sachetana: Autonomy and Subordination

> *We survive by cheating.*
> —Sachetana activist

As a small, autonomous women's organization, Sachetana has never really become a "contender" in Calcutta's political field (Fligstein and McAdam, 1993). Its members are some of Calcutta's most respected academics, yet its trajectory is scattered and fragmented and not totally within their control. It does not possess the material resources to challenge the CPI(M), which, while lacking in money, can promise patronage and protection. In terms of external support, Sachetana cannot rely on the state, which is governed by the CPI(M), unless it conforms to its ideology. Sachetana does possess cultural capital but has been unable to reach the people with its progressive vision, especially since the decline of its cultural group, which performed street theater. In contrast, the freely distributed CPI(M) newspaper *Ganashakti* (which is posted on boards throughout the city) is widely read, and *Eksathe,* the PBGMS magazine, also enjoys a wide distribution. The journal *Sachetana* is simply unable to compete culturally because of lack of resources. Even though the essays in the journal are scholarly and politically sharp, it is not glossy and commercial enough to be successfully marketed, and Sachetana does not possess the wherewithal to widely distribute it.

The issue of Sachetana's lack of cultural legitimacy is a complicated one. Few feminist movements around the world have achieved cultural legitimacy, because feminism so often means breaking with dominant cultural mores, including the ways of doing politics. So feminists try to gain acceptability through allies in different sectors of society. It is precisely the possibility of making these alliances that is severely circumscribed in Sachetana's case. There are few "free" allies in Calcutta. Further, because there is a more easily accessible women's movement in place, Sachetana seems all the more like an outsider, with even less legitimacy. The NNPM, the group that Sachetana was once part of but subsequently moved away from, is seen as even more outside the realm of acceptability than Sachetana. However, because of the willingness on the part of the NNPM to defy the CPI(M), it has won some grudging admiration from sectors of society less friendly to the party. As one elderly Calcutta man said to me, comparing the NNPM with Sachetana, "At least those girls have spunk. They yell and shout about things. What does Sachetana do?" It is Sachetana's sense of responsibility toward the CPI(M) and its support of a left government that, ironically, delegitimize it further.

Ultimately, Sachetana finds itself answerable to Calcutta's dominant political party and so remains trapped, with neither the capacity of the CPI(M) nor the freedom of such autonomous Bombay groups as the Forum. Sachetana is no longer seen, and no longer sees itself, as a strongly activist group. For its members, Sachetana provides the one place where they can openly discuss their dissatisfaction with the Left Front government's policies toward women and where they can develop critiques of patriarchy that other groups would not encourage. They have created alternative cultural forms, safe spaces or havens, in which they can express their oppositional beliefs, but they cannot do so openly (Fantasia and Hirsch, 1995; Morris, 1984; Taylor and Whittier, 1992). Within these "liberated zones," Sachetana activists question themselves and each other and struggle with redefining problems and seeking new kinds of solutions. While the PBGMS thoroughly dominates the political field, Sachetana has found a space for itself that allows it to survive, if not to grow.

Chapter 6

Bombay: A Fragmented Political Field

A *National Geographic* article on Bombay is filled with photographs of extremes—beggars at the window of a luxury car, squatters near mansions, and poor people cooking their meager fare on the street underneath huge billboards of glamorous women from "Bollywood," Bombay's Hollywood (McCarry, 1995). Photography that revels in such lurid contrasts is standard fare in Western imagery of the third world. What is interesting about this article is the range of people interviewed—actors and actresses, slum dwellers, fashion designers, scavengers, newspaper editors, Roman Catholic priests, and the editor of India's only publication for gays and lesbians. As I skimmed through the article, I thought to myself, there is something about Bombay that makes people think of diversity, makes people seek it out. There is something about Bombay that radiates the word "cosmopolitan." Yet Bombay is also home to the ever powerful Shiv Sena, a nativist group that has grown fat on the resentment of native Maharashtrians against "foreigners"—Muslims and other non-Hindus, as well as people from other states. All these forces—the cinematic world, the advertising world, the Hindu right wing, the poor, and the progressive, secular forces of the left—coexist in an uneasy and scattered way in Bombay.

Unlike Calcutta, the political field in Bombay is dispersed and contested, especially in the social movement sector. I begin the analysis of Bombay's political field with the story of the amniocentesis campaign undertaken by the Forum Against Oppression of Women in conjunction with the Forum Against Sex Determination and Sex Preselection, a coalition of groups that came together to work on this issue. This campaign is representative of

Bombay's women's movement, just as the literacy campaign is representative of Calcutta's.

The Forum's Amniocentesis Campaign

Morchas for Women
The Forum Against Sex-Determination and Sex-Preselection, an umbrella organization comprising various groups in the city, organized a morcha from Azad Maidan to Kala Ghoda today to protest against the misuse of modern medical technologies like amniocentesis, chorionic villi biopsy and super sonography to abort female foetuses and which have become an overt form of discrimination against women.
    Participating in the nearly 100 strong morcha were representatives from different organizations in the city such as the Women's Centre, the Forum Against Oppression of Women, Maitrini, Stree Mukti Sanghatana, Stree Uvach, YWCA, CPDR and also members of the Humanist Party, which actively supports the Forum Against Sex-Determination and Sex-Preselection.[1]

The campaign against sex determination and sex preselection reached its height with the passage of the 1988 Maharashtra Regulation on the Use of Pre-natal Diagnostic Techniques Act. This legislation monitors the use of particular technologies (such as analysis of amniotic fluid, chorionic villi, or tissue) that are used to ascertain the sex of a fetus. It is a strange issue in many ways—one that has, nevertheless, captured the attention of feminists worldwide. How did amniocentesis come to be an issue in Bombay?

The answer, of course, is not a simple one. For years, female infants in India have been killed in a variety of ways—by poison, suffocation, or simply neglect—because of the strong socially and economically created preference for male children. Once amniocentesis tests, whose original purpose was to detect genetic abnormalities, were introduced to India at the All-India Institute for Medical Sciences in 1974, it was found that the main motivation for couples to have the test performed was to determine the sex of the child. A follow-up survey showed that 90 percent of the couples wanted to abort the fetus after learning that its sex was female (Gandhi and Shah, 1991:128). While a few women's groups protested on seeing the results of the survey, little attention was paid to them. This was still the mid-1970s, when the voice of the women's movement was not yet heeded.

In 1982, when a *male* fetus was mistakenly aborted at the Bhandari antenatal sex determination clinic in Amritsar, Punjab, the existence of these commercially run clinics was first brought to public attention by popular national weekly magazines such as *Sunday*. Women's groups, including the newly formed Forum in Bombay, and some progressive medical groups came together to ask for a ban on sex-determination tests; again the protests received little attention (F8). As the test grew in popularity, advertisements for them could be found on billboards proclaiming, "Better Rs 500 now than Rs 5 lakh later," in which Rs 500 referred to the cost of the procedure and Rs 5 lakh (or Rs 500,000) to the dowry one would have to pay in order to marry off one's adult daughter.

In 1985–86, the issue was revitalized, and this time it received far more publicity. The Forum Against Sex Determination and Sex Preselection (FASDSP) was founded by members from health groups, people's science groups, and human rights and women's groups. The FASDSP (1989) maintained that this issue had to be seen as "(a) an integral part of women's oppression and discrimination, (b) misuse of science and technology against people in general and women in particular, (c) a concern of human rights."

Accordingly, the group resolved to demand a ban on techniques for sex determination and to persuade the government to permit amniocentesis only for the testing of genetic abnormalities. Since regulation is easier in government-run hospitals, FASDSP argued that the test should not be allowed in for-profit private hospitals.

The main active opposition to the FASDSP campaign came from the medical establishment, who argued that it was perfectly reasonable, given their economic value, for a couple to prefer sons. They argued further that strong son preference meant that couples would not stop having children until a son had been born. Amniocentesis would thus be a boon, given India's "population explosion," in that unwanted female children could be aborted and family size thus contained. Latent opposition to the campaign came from those who wanted the tests available to them for sex-determination purposes.

FASDSP used a two-pronged approach to achieve its goals. On the one hand, it encouraged already "awakened" public opinion to bring pressure to bear on the government to ban the use of techniques for sex determination. This included nationwide signature campaigns, saturating the media with articles and debates about the issue, and drafting legislation to ban the tests.

On the other hand, the FASDSP also embarked upon a consciousness-raising campaign to change the deep-seated prejudices against female children. This involved a demonstration in which parents marched along with their daughters and hundreds of schoolgirls marched, waving flags that bore the slogan "Ladki na ladke se kum" (Girls are not inferior to boys). Songs highlighting discrimination and urging equality between boys and girls were written and sung, three video films were made, and on Children's Day in 1987, skits and songs emphasizing the need to value girls and boys equally were performed at children's fairs.[2] During the months of April and May of the following year, the Forum held a *Nari Jeevan Sangharsh Yatra,* or a "campaign for women's lives," which linked the issues of female infanticide, feticide, wife murder, and other forms of violence against women. Debates, skits, slide shows, and videos were organized in twelve different sites in Bombay (FASDSP, 1989).

In order to ensure the passage of legislation banning tests for sex determination, the FASDSP worked closely with friendly bureaucrats and sympathetic politicians, such as the socialist member of the Maharashtrian legislative assembly, Mrinal Gore (F8). Herself a long-standing member of the women's movement, Gore strongly supported the legislation. When, at the winter session of the assembly in 1987–88, she made an impassioned plea for the introduction of the bill, the state government assured her that the state would introduce a bill, but would not accept the one drafted by the FASDSP.

When introduced in April 1988, the state-sponsored bill had several major problems—it made these tests available, if regulated, in private hospitals; it made *women* punishable by law if they violated these regulations. It also built a time lag into the process of complaint that would give a doctor enough time to cover his or her tracks (F8). Further, when the state-level committee to regulate the amniocentesis tests was formed, it included a doctor who had herself repeatedly performed the test for purposes of sex determination. The FASDSP held a press conference and forced her to resign. While the state mandated the creation of local vigilance commissions to ensure that hospitals were not performing the tests illegally, no such committee was formed in Bombay until 1991.

The bill and its provisions were far from satisfactory to the women's groups or to the FASDSP, but predictably, enthusiasm dwindled after its passage. On one level the campaign was only partially successful because the legislation was essentially toothless. On another, it was a phenomenal success because it irrevocably changed the way people thought about amniocentesis. How did amniocentesis become an issue in Bombay? How, in the words of one Forum member, was the Forum able to "literally make an issue out of no issue at all" (F8)?

The narratives about the origins of the amniocentesis campaign vary. Some say the issue was in the air and inevitably became central, while others give more personal accounts of its origins. One activist's response made it appear to be a matter of chance. Her mother, who did not live in Bombay, had apparently asked her to make inquiries about amniocentesis tests for a friend in Bombay. In obliging her mother, she realized what these tests were really about. While participating in a demonstration a few days later, she mentioned her findings about amniocentesis to another activist. Soon it became a topic of discussion, and several of the activists went to private clinics around the city to find out what they could about the performance of amniocentesis tests and the abortions that followed. The results of this informal survey were published and the first meeting about it was held in someone's home. With their university connections, Forum and Women's Centre activists organized a seminar at SNDT Women's University. This then was the beginning of the campaign in Bombay.[3]

Clearly this is not the whole story. There were already in Bombay a variety of groups that could be mobilized around the issue. Two of the core members of the Forum were doctors and were particularly interested in the issue. Another member's husband was a doctor and another's was part of the people's science movement, and they, too, began to question the use of amniocentesis to determine the sex of the unborn child. The willingness of two or three key members to invest time and energy to research the issue, to report to the Forum, and to write up their findings resulted in the issue becoming a core focus for the Forum.

The FASDSP, which was formed in November 1985, had three or four members from the Forum and their friends from the people's science movement and Medico Friends Circle, an organization of progressive medical personnel. Thus the reach of the movement was considerably widened, and it became possible for the issue to be raised in several forums simultaneously. The activists went to schools, spoke to individual doctors, and initiated public debates. Few outside those immediately involved knew anything about the use to which these tests were put. Statistics that shocked many sections of the public were reported in the media. A report in the *Statesman* (December 7, 1984) claiming that 7,999 out of 8,000 abortions conducted after sex determinations involved female fetuses was widely cited, even though it is unclear where this particular statistic actually came from. Other more verifiable statistics included the finding that there were 10 Bombay clinics performing amniocentesis in 1982 and 248 by 1986–87, and that a majority of forty-two gynecologists surveyed performed amniocentesis tests for the purpose of sex determination an average of 270 times per month (Gandhi and Shah, 1991:130; FASDSP, 1989).

The issue was created by the Forum. There was no initial interest in it or public backing for it. Rather, in the words of one Forum member, "the amniocentesis campaign was really against the will of the masses but one has to take a stand." Their 1989 publication, "Campaign against Sex Determination and Pre-selection—Our Experiences," says:

While it is true large numbers of women are [themselves going to the clinics for these tests] . . . does this behavior of women show exercising of free choice? Denied an independent existence and identity through cultural values of submission and being subjected to enormous family pressure, their choices can never be termed free choices.

Elsewhere, they acknowledge the irony of their position:

So, here we have the unpleasant option of going against what the majority of people seems to believe in and collaborating with the state which most of the time is anti-people.

Today, those involved in the campaign have raised many questions about it. To some, the outcome of the bill reiterates the problems of relying on the legislative process. They have discovered that "any legislation merely drives the practice underground," and some now feel even more strongly that unless legislation can actually be monitored by women, it merely gives the state more power. And others have come to the conclusion that telling women that they should want daughters, when they don't wish to bring daughters destined to suffer into the world, is a genuine problem, as is the realization that one cannot make choices for other women.

What does this campaign tell us about Bombay's political field? It tells us, as does the excerpt from the *Sunday Observer*, that major campaigns can get initiated in Bombay by small organizations unaffiliated to political parties. These organizations, which usually work independently of each other, are able to cooperate and sustain a movement. Not only do the autonomous groups form coalitions, but they have enough of a relationship with members of the legislative assembly to use those contacts to write and push through legislation. At the same time, the organizations are not powerful enough to maintain pressure on the government or to insist on participating in the process of ensuring the implementation of the new laws.

Much of this campaign was played out in the media—in newspapers and magazines and on television. These were to a great extent cultural wars. Both those in favor of sex preselection and those against it battled for the hearts and minds of Maharashtrians on this issue. Given its links with media and the networks of progressive groups of which it was a part, this was a perfect issue for the FASDSP. The success of the campaign can be gauged in two ways—by whether they won the cultural war (that is, whether their articulation of the issue would become hegemonic within Bombay's universe of political discourse) and by the quality of legislation. If the FASDSP was not able to win the legal battles, it has partially succeeded in winning the cultural one.

Ensuring the application of the new legislation proved to be out of its reach. For a presentation before the Joint Parliamentary Committee on Prenatal Diagnostic Techniques (Regulation and Prevention of Misuse) Bill in 1991, the FASDSP wrote:

> According to us the law against Sex-Determination failed in Maharashtra not because such laws are destined to fail. It failed because the Government had no political will and commitment to implement it.
>
> It appears today on seeing the state of the implementation that the law was passed by the government only because it was under pressure from the campaign which had received support from all quarters. The issue had received international attention and the progressive image of the government was being tarnished. Hence the law probably came in as a saving gesture. (FASDSP, 1991)

The second paragraph in the quotation points to another striking characteristic of Bombay's political field: the international community is a major player in it, serving both as a reference point and an arbiter. Pressure can be brought to bear on the state government not only from forces within the state, but from without.

In the political culture of Bombay, the ideological implications of amniocentesis were clear to the activists—men and women alike—even if it was not clear to the women involved in these tests. This was not a reproductive rights issue. As far as the activists were concerned, the abortions following the tests were an extension of the continuum of violence against women and so had to be fought. While many women who had the procedures performed on them were forced to do so by their families, some genuinely believed it was a good decision, given the position of women in the world. In other words, there were many women who felt that under these conditions it was in their interest not to have a girl child. Thus, unlike the PBGMS, the Forum did not select the issue of amniocentesis because women wanted them to. Rather, rejecting a "liberal" notion of reproductive choice, it claimed that "women's choices in exercising their reproductive rights too have to be compatible with the principles of gender justice and equality" (Gandhi and Shah, 1991:137).

In Bombay, the regulation of amniocentesis became a women's issue not because most women wanted it, but because feminist and other progressive groups believed it to be in women's objective interests. In Bombay, then, it is possible to have legislation initiated by a social movement that is actually against the will of the majority of the people. Such a thing (for better or for worse) would be unlikely in Calcutta.

At the same time that the FASDSP was working with the state, it distrusted its power. It did not seek to ally itself permanently with the state, and worried constantly about inadvertently endowing it with too much legitimacy and authority. The campaign against amniocentesis reveals that despite its influence, a group such as the Forum remains outside the political establishment, firmly in the protest field, a challenger.

Bombay: A Field with Dispersed Power and a Heterogeneous Political Culture

Maharashtra was formed after considerable cultural struggle in 1960 as a state for Marathi-speaking peoples. Bombay, its capital, remains somewhat in conflict with the rest of Maharashtra, since over 50 percent of its residents are non-Marathi speakers. In this discussion, then, I will move back and forth between Maharashtra and Bombay, as I elucidate the important determinants of Bombay's political field.

The major players in Maharashtrian politics have traditionally been the Congress, rich farmers and their sugar lobby, and, increasingly, the Hindu right-wing Shiv Sena. The Congress has ruled Maharashtra virtually single-handedly since the creation of the state in 1960 until recently. As this book goes to press, a coalition of the Shiv Sena and the Bharatiya Janata Party governs the state.

Until the death in 1920 of Lokmanya Tilak, a major force in the Indian struggle for freedom, Maharashtra had been at the forefront of the nationalist movement. It was the site of the first conference of the Indian National Congress. In the early post-Independence years, the Congress under Nehru had tremendous prestige and strength. Left-wing groups like the Lal Nishan Party, Shetkari Sanghatana, the Peasant and Workers Party (which was formed in 1948), the CPI(M), and the CPI did not ever form a serious threat to Congress power (Kamat, 1980). Right-wing groups like the Rashtriya Swayamsevak Sangh (RSS) were based in towns in the interior of the state rather than in the city of Bombay.

Congress dominance over Maharashtra has, through a variety of patronage mechanisms, traditionally been tied to the textile lobby and increasingly to the sugar lobby. Many Congress cabinet ministers have their own sugar fiefdoms (Kamat, 1980), involving control over factories as well as over all the sugarcane workers who belong to the factories (in the form of memberships in sugar cooperatives). It is largely this system of political control that has prevented other parties from making significant headway in the rural areas (Mutatkar, 1990).

The first chief minister of Maharashtra, Y. B. Chavan, was a loyal Congress party member, a supreme pragmatist, and a member of the dominant

Maratha caste. Understanding the need to keep non-Maharashtrian business in Bombay after the creation of the state of Maharashtra, he assured non-Marathi speakers that he would safeguard their interests. It was during his tenure that agroindustrial policy was formulated and the extremely powerful sugar cooperatives were actively encouraged (Talwalkar, 1990). He was also responsible for co-opting and placating the leaders of the scheduled caste (or *dalit*) movement after the death of their leader Dr. B. R. Ambedkar.

The power structure of Bombay is sometimes described in terms of its ethnic groups; thus the most powerful in Bombay are a handful of Marwari, Parsee, Gujarati, and North Indian businessmen, as well as a handful of Maharashtrian politicians. The middle and working classes are primarily Maharashtrian, but also include a sizable Gujarati population and migrants from North and South India.

As economic control remained in the hands of non-Maharashtrians, however, the working people of Maharashtra began to express their resentment by turning to the organized left. In an attempt to crush support for the left, the Congress and big business together nurtured the Shiv Sena (which translates as soldiers of Shivaji, after the seventeenth-century warrior king), a militant Hindu and Marathi chauvinist organization that was created in 1965 (Abraham, 1979). The Shiv Sena's program was dangerously simple: "the reservation of jobs and new economic opportunities for Maharashtrians, mainly in the lower echelons of white collar employment" (Lele, 1995:186).[4] Bombay was the obvious focus for the Shiv Sena, both because it was the industrial heart of the state and because it was home to a large proportion of non-Marathi-speaking peoples.

Among those who felt the initial hostility of the Shiv Sena were immigrants from the south. Many of the local Communist leaders happened to be from Kerala (a state in South India), and they became the first targets of the Shiv Sena "sons of the soil" movement. The unions split along Maharashtrian versus South Indian lines. Bombay's strong industrial base has meant that its political field has always been heavily influenced by trade unions, and thus the creation of the Shiv Sena went a long way toward hastening the demise of the organized left (Kamat, 1980; V. Patel, personal communication, December 27, 1990).[5] By the early 1970s, the Sena had two sources of power—the support of sections of lower-middle-class Marathi speakers and the influence it had as an arm of the Congress. One journalist aptly called the Shiv Sena the "gendarme of the Bourgeoisie," but perhaps no one then could have estimated the extent of its danger (Abraham, 1979).

In the meantime, however, student, farmer, youth, and new left groups such as Magowa and the Revolutionary Bolshevik Group began to burgeon in Maharashtra. Initially, some of them worked in labor unions in conjunction with the communist parties, particularly with the CPI. With the Emergency, however, most of these groups went underground and union activity ground to a halt. The one group that openly continued its activities during this period was the Shiv Sena, which was not on the list of banned groups during the Emergency (Abraham, 1979).

For the Congress, the Emergency resulted in a series of Congress splinter factions, which then joined together to form a coalition government after the 1977 elections. Thus, despite Congress defeats everywhere else, it was returned to power in Maharashtra. Political power in the state remained in the hands of various Congress factions, all of whom were trying to outmaneuver each other and Indira Gandhi up to her death in 1984. The sugar lobby maintained its dominance, and the Congress patronage machine, although wavering, remained at the heart of Maharashtra politics. Until very recently, when the Congress was in power, it spent considerable energy attempting simultaneously to control the Shiv Sena (now grown enormously in strength and brutality) on its right and to undercut the rural mass-based peasant organization, Shetkari Sanghatana, led by Sharad Joshi, on its left. It did so by trying to pacify unemployed youth (the backbone of the Shiv Sena) and to strike deals with farmers (the backbone of the Shetkari Sanghatana) (*EPW*, 1988). But the Congress itself remained in power because of its machine and the manipulative ability of its politicians, and because of the weak and dispersed nature of its opposition, not because it had the trust of the people of Maharashtra.

As I pointed out in chapter 2, because of its close association with Indira Gandhi, the CPI lost much of its credibility after the Emergency, and the vacuum thus created was filled by an explosion of activity from new groups.[6] Peasant groups, ecological groups, women's groups, and civil liberties groups soon dotted the political landscape in Maharashtra, at the expense of established political parties. While attempts to create alliances unconnected with the Congress and the Shiv Sena–BJP are periodically made and have to date failed, these failures do not preclude possibilities for progressive change in Bombay.[7]

Distribution of Power

My argument, then, is that Bombay has a dispersed political field. There is no single dominant force in Bombay, as there is in Calcutta. No one force controls its possibilities and destiny. But rather, there appear to be three main players in the political field of the city of Bombay—the Congress, the

Shiv Sena, and various coalitions on the left. These coalitions include various nonparty political formations and other progressive forces, including peasant, ecological, civil liberties, and women's organizations. However, they are not nearly as consolidated and strong as the erstwhile (Congress) and the present (Shiv Sena in conjunction with the Bharatiya Janata Party) state rulers.[8]

The Congress was voted out of power in Maharashtra in 1994 in an election with a record voter turnout (*EPW,* 1995a). Sharad Pawar, the Congress chief minister of Maharashtra, had allegations of corruption and criminal wrongdoing leveled against him in every sphere, from enormous real-estate scams to ties with the underworld. The Congress government had come to typify unclean government.

Even before the Emergency, Maharashtra had a history of organizing that was not connected to the traditional left parties. Oppositional parties such as the CPI and the CPI(M) coexisted alongside Marxist-Leninist, Trotskyist, and radical Gandhian groups. A strong movement of the lowest castes, the *dalits,* flourished in Maharashtra; the most radical branch, the Dalit Panthers, was influenced by the U.S. Black Panthers. There were also grassroots movements among rural women and tribal women in other parts of Maharashtra. Particularly well known are the struggles against land alienation and agitation for famine relief in the Shahada region led by Shramik Sanghatana, a powerful tribal organization, in 1972–73, in which tribal women were apparently some of the most militant activists (Basu, 1992).

Today, as with other movements in Maharashtra, the "driving force of the Bombay labor movement are union leaders who disclaim allegiance to political parties and their trade union federations" (Ramaswamy, 1988:17). However, observers of Bombay's political scene consider the era of trade union dominance in politics to have declined by the end of the 1970s. The famous Bombay textile strike, involving 240,000 workers, that began in January 1982 and that finally lost more than eighteen months later, is considered the last gasp of unionism in Bombay. This strike was initially led by established unions and then by Datta Samant, a freelance union organizer (who was killed by as yet unknown assassins in 1996). The other major strikes of the 1980s were led by trade union entrepreneurs like Datta Samant and R. J. Mehta, who moved from one strike to the next. It is inconceivable that such individuals would find a niche in Calcutta.[9]

Given a deeply factionalized yet persistently present Congress, a weak parliamentary left (including the socialist and social democratic parties), and an increasingly powerful right-wing party, the choice made by Bombay's feminists to remain outside of parliamentary politics is not surprising. Feminists in Bombay have little to gain by allying with the Congress or the communist parties. They do not trust the Congress, and the communist parties, which are unlikely ever to become "parties of government," are considered ineffectual. When coalition work is required, they are far more likely to forge coalitions with other autonomous grassroots movements around the state. There is a statewide forum to press for changes in women's rights and to defend existing rights, the Stree Mukti Andolan Sampark Samiti, which was formed in 1979 and comprises both autonomous and affiliated groups. Issue-based campaigns and temporary, politically autonomous coalitions such as the Forum Against Sex Determination and Sex Preselection and Ektaa (against ethnic and religious conflict) are common in the city. Acting together, they have the power to make demands on the state, with the knowledge that they cannot be easily ignored. Feminists have power in Bombay largely because of this ability to build alliances with other actors in the field. There are times when alliances with political parties are important, for example, when the movement wishes to push for legislative change. The women's movement has made alliances with important women legislators from centrist and left parties when trying to introduce a new piece of legislation to modify an existing one. The socialist member of the Legislative Assembly, Mrinal Gore, who was an important actor in the amniocentesis campaign, is one such individual.

The state has often responded favorably to demands from women's groups. Under pressure from women's organizations, for example, Maharashtra was the first state in India to introduce the Regulations for the Use of Pre-natal Diagnostic Techniques Act in 1988. It was also the first to establish a state commission for women and the first to create a state policy for women. While criticizing many aspects of this policy, several members of the Forum Against Oppression of Women recognize that to the extent that the policy challenges patriarchy, it does so in order to appease women, whose aspirations have been growing rapidly in response to changes in the economy and the women's movement (Gothoskar, Shah, and Gandhi, 1994:3022).

In the past few years, however, with the increasing strength of Hindu right-wing parties, the balance of power in the field seems to be shifting again. While it is difficult to predict the outcome of these changes in party alignments and ideological tendencies, it seems probable that small groups and issue-based coalitions will be unable to effectively combat rising Hindu fundamentalism. However, Bombay's political field can still be characterized as fragmented—with a relatively porous political culture, weak party structures, and dispersed power. It is within this field that the Forum, an autonomous feminist group, has emerged as culturally dominant in the women's movement.

Political Culture

The very essence of the city's cultural life, as indeed of its economy, is consti-tuted by its openness to winds blowing from all directions, from across the seas and from the mainland of India; its availability as a meeting ground for diverse communities; its prime function as a place of exchange.

—Alice Thorner

If Calcutta's political field is marked by a monolithic and homogeneous po-litical culture, then Bombay's field is noteworthy for the diversity and fluidi-ty of its political culture. Bombay's politics are remarkably receptive to influ-ence from sources external to its field (including international feminisms, economic liberalism, and MTV), and a wider range of issues and groups is considered politically acceptable by its major political players. From its very creation as a city, Bombay served as the gateway to India and as India's win-dow on the Western world. Bombayites are largely immigrants and descen-dants of immigrants.[10] Gujaratis, Maharashtrians, Parsees, South Indians, and others coexist in Bombay, each group with its own culture, mutually in-fluenced but growing independently. And the same holds true for Bombay's various political groups. The ideas of Maharashtra-based thinkers such as Dr. Ambedkar, Jyotirao Phule, and Ram Manohar Lohia, who linked caste and gender oppression, are widely circulated, as are the ideas of Gandhi, Trotsky, Mao, and Lenin. Bombay's political culture has the quality of a large sponge that constantly changes shape.

Progressive politics in Bombay, especially following the Emergency, has been marked by a questioning of the tactics and goals of the traditional left and the evolution of a politically autonomous, grassroots, issue-based coali-tional style. Bombay's political culture is receptive to autonomous groups and non-party-affiliated leaders of every kind. Feminists in Bombay do not need to be legitimated by the established left and have not allowed its agen-das to influence theirs. Issue-based politics are more common, as is the valid-ity of the autonomous demands of marginalized groups such as the *dalits* and women. There is more of a recognition in Bombay than in Calcutta of the need for women to have separate spaces, and indeed to have organiza-tions without men in them.

The women's movement has taken pains to celebrate the histories of un-usual and active Maharashtrian women. Bombay's feminist activists, many of whom work in women's studies departments, have been instrumental in

bringing to the fore women such as the medieval saint and poetess, Bahina-
bai; courageous women from royal families in the seventeenth through nineteenth centuries, such as Jijabai and Ahilyabai Holkar; and late-nineteenth-
and early-twentieth-century reformers such as Pandita Ramabai and Tarabai
Shinde. They also recognize and publicly laud the fierceness of spirit of communists like Godavari Parulkar and Ahalya Rangnekar and socialists like
Mrinal Gore and Medha Patkar, one of the most prominent leaders of the
agitation against the Narmada Dam.

The Stree Mukti Andolan Sampark Samiti epitomizes the political culture of the early days of Bombay's women's movement. This was the umbrella group, formed in 1979, with representatives of both autonomous and
affiliated women's organizations from Bombay, Pune, and other Maharashtrian cities. Archivists of the Samiti trace its origins to the rich tradition of
social reform in Maharashtra, as well as to the left—both the national CPI
and other smaller left parties such as the Lal Nishan. They highlight the existence and creation of various joint forums for women between 1969 and
1975 and the work done by women's activists with trade unions and tribal
women. Sampark Samiti archivists trace the awareness of a shifting consciousness about the nature and content of women' oppression to a conference paper in 1975 that marked the beginning of the "New Women's
Movement"—different from the old because "for the first time, women's issues were being identified as women's issues per se, that is specific to them
alone. It was a recognition that there exists a certain autonomy to the problem" (Lele, Sathe, et al., n.d.). From the very beginning, the Sampark Samiti
called for the struggle for *stree mukti,* or women's liberation, to take place at
three levels—the personal, the workplace, and the social (Stree Mukti
Andolan, 1979). It also recognized the presence of various strands of the
women's movement in Maharashtra and the necessity of not forcing a unified structure on these strands. Its members acknowledged, however, that
the continuing tensions between the party-affiliated and nonaffiliated groups
sometimes threatened the very existence of the coalition. In the analysis of
key members of the Sampark Samiti, the blame for this is to be laid at the
feet of the parties of the left, who persist in their "sectarianism."[11]

In this culture, the state, as the embodiment of power, violence, and
corruption, is not to be trusted—and thus, ultimately, neither are the parties
of the left. If feminists do not trust the parliamentary communist parties,
they have before them a range of alternative radical ideologies within which
their ideas can be framed. The oppositional left in Bombay is composed of a
diverse range of individuals and groups. Bombay is home to *Economic and
Political Weekly,* India's best progressive academic journal; to *Bombay Dost,*

India's first magazine for gays and lesbians; and to the Centre for Education and Documentation, an archive of movement documents. Independent filmmakers such as Anand Patwardhan and Madhushree Datta document civil rights abuses and the struggles of the dispossessed. The Tata Institute for Social Sciences provides politicized social workers who become deeply involved with issues such as the Narmada Dam movement. Cultural opposition is manifested in English, Hindi, Gujarati, and Marathi newspapers.

Within the women's movement in Bombay, diverse political ideologies coexist, sometimes compatibly and sometimes less so. Some of Bombay's groups are more receptive to ideas from other countries, while others try for a stronger grounding in native Maharashtrian culture. As a whole, the women's movement in Bombay is less accountable to "the masses" than to a certain broad vision of feminism. This vision of feminism is one that it tries to relay to the rest of Bombay and to the feminist movement internationally.

The Women's Movement in Bombay

The field within which Bombay's women's movement is embedded is very different from the field in which Calcutta's women's movement finds itself. Given the lack of any unifying political culture—and indeed the virtual impossibility of its creation—and the lack of a dominant political force with which to ally, Bombay's groups have to grapple with the challenge of making their voices heard amid the fragments.

Bombay's women's movement reflects the fragmentation of Bombay's field. It developed rapidly in a dispersed way through the 1980s, and today we have many autonomous groups such as the Forum Against Oppression of Women, the Women's Centre, Stree Uvach, Maitrini, Vacha, Majlis, and Awaaz-e-Niswaan. Several of these groups, it should be pointed out, grew out of the Forum. There are also groups linked to the traditional left, such as Janwadi Mahila Sanghatana (JMS) and the National Federation of Indian Women (NFIW); groups linked to other regional left parties, such as Stree Mukti Sanghatana and Stree Kriti; and social welfare organizations such as the YWCA. In addition, women who are active in other issue-based groups, such as Yuva, and organizations like the Chhatra Yuva Sangharsh Samiti (a radical Gandhian group) or student groups (such as the counseling unit developed out of the social work program at Nirmala Niketan) also count themselves as part of the women's movement. These groups usually work separately, and different subsets of them coalesce around specific issues.

In chapters 7 and 8, I will focus on two of these groups—the Forum and the JMS. I chose these groups with a logic somewhat different from the one that I used to pick the groups in Calcutta. In Calcutta, the dominant group was obvious, and I chose Sachetana because it was the longest-surviving autonomous group. The Forum is, in fact, the dominant group in the women's movement in Bombay, but the nature of its dominance is qualitatively and quantitatively different from that of the PBGMS. This is so both because of the nature of the field and because of the nature of the Forum. I argue that while the Forum is a small, autonomous women's organization, its dominance is cultural, and it has managed to have a powerful effect on the discourse around gender in Bombay. Finally, I have chosen to focus on the JMS both because it is a subordinate group and because it is the sister organization in Bombay of the PBGMS. An analysis of JMS discourse and activities will show the difference regional political fields make to organizations affiliated to the same national political party.

The Dominant Group: Forum Against Oppression of Women

> *In 1979 some 40 or so women felt enraged by a Supreme Court judgement which had acquitted two policemen of raping a 16 year old tribal girl called Mathura. It was not only a rage against the bias and misogyny of the court but against society which treated the victim as an offender and let the offender go scot free. It was also a rage against the fear of sexual violence that every woman carries deep in her heart.*
>
> *We quite spontaneously, formed Forum against Rape in 1980 to demand a revision of the judgment and politically take up the issue of rape.*
>
> —FAOW, *Moving . . . but Not Quite There*

The epigraph presents the Forum's self-description of its beginnings, but as with many social movements and social movement organizations, the beginning was not quite as spontaneous as claimed. Several Marxist-Leninist groups and offshoots of the Fourth International existed in Bombay in the 1970s. In 1977, after one of its members returned from college in the United States, a handful of women from the Fourth International and Revolutionary Bolshevik group formed the Socialist Feminist Group, which subsequently organized a conference the following year, attended by thirty-eight women from New Delhi, Kanpur, Bangalore, and Ahmadabad (significantly, not Calcutta). The now defunct journal *Feminist Networks* and the still popular *Manushi* were outcomes of this conference. At that point, strongly influenced by the left groups from which they had emerged, the members of the Socialist Feminist Group tended to discuss issues such as wages for housework, the double burden of women, the nature of women's work, women in the Telengana struggle,[12] and the nature of patriarchy in India.

Women from the Fourth International and Revolutionary Bolshevik groups continued to work on both feminist and trade union issues, with several of them being involved in the railway union and in community organizations such as the Bombay Slum Dwellers United Front. Issues about political autonomy and struggle eventually began to emerge in an as yet inarticulate form within these groups, as writings of feminists in England and the United States began to be circulated.

In September 1979, when some progressive Delhi lawyers heard about the Mathura judgment,[13] they wrote a letter to the chief justice of the Supreme Court and circulated the letter to progressive individuals and civil liberties organizations all over India. By January 12, the letter had made the rounds in Bombay, and all forty women who received the letter attended a meeting to organize a protest against the judgment. This was the beginning of the Forum Against Oppression of Women, then called the Forum Against Rape (FAR). The FAR held its first public meeting on February 23 and mobilized support for a huge rally against rape on International Women's Day. The Forum women drew on all their resources and contacts in schools, unions, and slums, with the result that over three thousand men and women participated in the March 8 rally. While the same letter was sent to Calcutta, it did not create the wave of mobilization that it did in Bombay.

After the Mathura rape issue subsided, the group had to decide on how to sustain and consolidate the movement. The activists decided then to create the Forum Against Oppression of Women, to serve as an umbrella organization for a cultural group, a group working with trade unions, and a space for interactions with women on a daily basis—the Women's Centre. The Forum would retain an agitational purpose, while the Women's Centre was intended to be a "more open place where we could relate on a long-term basis to women and their individual problems" (W1). Thus, if individual women approached the Forum for help, they would be referred to the Centre.

The Forum has decided not to do grassroots work and to remain an agitational and educational group, a decision that reflects the fact that most Forum members work full time and are only able to devote weekend and evenings to Forum activities (FAOW, 1990:53). Today, the Forum is the most important agitational organization on women's issues in Bombay. It is the group that is expected to respond to issues as they arise—whether it be the sexist remarks of a chief justice or the creation of better rape legislation. Forum members meet weekly at a room in Lower Parel, a primarily working-class and lower-middle-class area, and here they bring up concerns to be addressed, petitions to be circulated, and problems to be analyzed.

Together, the Forum and the Women's Centre are at the heart of

Bombay's new women's movement. They are the innovators, the bearers of new ways of thinking about women. While, like other women's groups nationally, they are still to some extent marginal in the media, their ideas and presence have made them a force to be reckoned with.

The Subordinate Group: Janwadi Mahila Sanghatana

The Janwadi Mahila Sanghatana, the women's wing of the CPI(M), got its start in Bombay in 1989, almost ten years after autonomous groups had begun to make their presence felt. It did not have to build an organization from scratch, since it did exist in Pune, another major Maharashtrian city, under the name Shramik Mahila Sangh (SMS). The Shramik Mahila Sangh, which translates as "organization for toiling women," evolved into the JMS, which translates as "democratic organization of women," in 1985. This change was made because the SMS appeared too "political." In other words, the SMS clearly represented a particular section of women—the workers—while the JMS was to represent all women. The change in name signaled a changing politics.

Today the JMS has many members, but only eight core activists in Bombay. While the JMS is not strong, it does have influence in those pockets of Bombay with a history of CPI(M) strength. It is organized in a fashion similar to the PBGMS in Calcutta, with state committees at the highest level, joint secretaries (thirty-six women who meet once every two or three months), district committees, and area committees. The city of Bombay is divided into four areas.

In its short period of existence, JMS activists have worked on campaigns of tenants' rights (insisting that the landlord make more water available, monitoring and prosecuting cheating landlords) and campaigns for the right to employment and equal wages for equal work. At present the JMS is focusing its energies on the availability of affordable essential commodities such as rice, flour, sugar, and oil, the kind of campaign that CPI(M) groups typically adopt—unless they run the state! On the other hand, since JMS activists are based in neighborhoods, they also find themselves dealing with all sorts of "domestic" problems such as incest, rape, and domestic violence.

The JMS is very much the new kid on the block as far as the women's movement in Bombay is concerned. Its task is not easy, for it must carve out a space for itself in a city in which the CPI(M) does not have much of a reputation and in a women's movement in which legitimacy is accorded to autonomous groups. But as table 2.4 showed, in contrast to the case of the autonomous groups in Calcutta, which mirrored the issues cited by the politically affiliated groups, the affiliated groups in Bombay do not mirror Bombay's autonomous groups. That is, the JMS is not dependent on or as much influenced by the more dominant women's organization. This is only to be expected in a fragmented field where no one group or type of group can easily set the agenda for the entire movement.

Chapter 7

Coexistence in a Heterogeneous Political Culture

To a great extent, Calcutta's political establishment and protest field share a common political culture. That is, they share, to a great extent, beliefs about who and what is legitimately political. Given Bombay's political culture—its heterogeneity, its fluidity, its openness to a variety of influences—dominant and subordinate groups relate to each other in ways that would be inconceivable in Calcutta. There are viable movement subcultures in Bombay that can create and define themselves in contradistinction to the dominant political culture, and thus there is more contestation and conflict about the boundaries of the political. In this chapter, I examine the ways in which the autonomous Forum and the CPI(M)-affiliated JMS coexist in Bombay's political culture. I begin once again with the membership of both organizations, a membership that itself reveals the differences between the political cultures of Bombay and Calcutta.

Membership

Dulari

Dulari was raised in a working-class family in Uttarkhand (a hilly area in the state of Uttar Pradesh) in what she describes as a very democratic household. She met her first husband, a CITU activist and a Christian, when she was only in the ninth grade (about fourteen or fifteen years old) and married him despite great opposition from her Hindu family. However, Dulari soon found herself, a very young woman with little secondary education, married to a man who "never wanted to see me independent." Despite her lack of formal education, she did not hesitate to participate in political discussions in her house and with her husband's friends, but was never able to participate in active politics until her husband's death in 1987. This was both because her husband drank, leading to a long illness, which meant that she was rarely free from household responsibilities, and because of his proscriptions on her behavior and activities. But after his death, she was free. And with that freedom she wanted to "help other women like [her] or worse." She joined the JMS in 1988, remarrying shortly thereafter in 1990. This time her marriage was no less controversial. She, a working-class, tribal woman who had never finished school, married an upper-class, Christian man, younger than she is, who is considered a leading party intellectual. Of this marriage, Dulari says to me with some pride: "We are both full-timers now. And both of us do the housework."

Dulari is a relatively new but vital member of Bombay's Janwadi Mahila Sanghatana. I visited her in her home, a two-room structure in a large slum in the Bhandup area of Bombay. Here she lives with her three children from her first marriage and her new husband, a Ph.D. in physics from the United States, who has returned to work with the CPI(M) trade union, the CITU. Powerful activist though she is, Dulari would not, because of her life history, be a good fit with the JMS sister organization in Calcutta. She is too nonconformist by far.

Dulari and her husband, John, are well known in their neighborhood. When I entered their house, I saw John sitting on the floor, surrounded by drinking straws and bits of wire. With these he was trying to fashion an affordable toy for the children of the slum. While I visited with them, several children came by to see the toy John was devising for them, while women dropped by to consult Dulari. Women come to Dulari with problems ranging from violence and divorce to problems getting their ration cards and dealing with their landlords. "Trouble with jobs and their husbands," says Dulari when I ask her about the worries women have. "Always the same two problems. Jobs and their husbands." As I walked around the area with her, it was clear that she had her finger on the pulse of the neighborhood, as she would point out the various sorts of people who lived in the slum, their problems, their poverty, their hopes, and their fears. From her I learned about the women of a nomadic tribe who have turned to pickpocketing for survival (because of their smaller fingers, children and women are more successful than adult men) and why they drink so heavily. "They drink for two reasons," she said, "it dulls the pain when they get beaten up by the police, and it gives them the courage to do it." Dulari takes great pride in the work she does for the JMS. No one else, she says, looks out for poor women the way the JMS does. While women have always sought her out with their troubles, her affiliation with the JMS gives her the ability to actually do something for them.

But Dulari is not really a typical JMS worker. Unlike Dulari, officeholders of the JMS tend to be urban and highly educated. Shaheen is perhaps more representative. Like Mita of the PBGMS, she joined the student wing of the CPI(M), the SFI, when she was in the eleventh grade. She was introduced to the SFI by her math teacher, a man who encouraged independent thinking: "He would challenge us to question the existence of God." Through the SFI, Shaheen fought in student elections against Shiv Sena students, campaigned against "Eve teasing,"[1] confronted teachers who were not living up to their responsibilities, and held screenings of political documentary films for her fellow students. She soon rose through the ranks of the SFI to become the state secretary. Today, Shaheen is one of the key members of the JMS, in charge of one of the four Bombay districts.

JMS activists tend to be journalists or full-time party workers, as do their husbands. In their marriages, she and Dulari follow what appears to be a pattern in the JMS—the prominent activists within JMS are often married to prominent activists in the party. For example, Shaheen is married to the president of the party's youth federation. But unlike PBGMS activists whose marriages were often arranged for them by the party, JMS women tend to have chosen their own partners from the party, and have more often than not made unconventional and controversial choices—perhaps in and of itself an influence of Bombay's political culture. Dulari is certainly unconventional, but so is Shaheen, who is Muslim but married to a Hindu. Shaheen told me that for her, changing her last name to that of her husband, rather than retaining her name, was a political act.

Because the Communist Party once had an important presence in Maharashtra in decades past, there are still some Bombay-based activists of national renown, such as Ahalya Rangnekar (whom everybody calls Ahalyatai; *tai* is the Marathi equivalent of the Bengali *didi,* elder sister), who have been organizing women for more than fifty years. There is a vast age gap between her and the new crop of activists, without a middle generation to act as a buffer. As a result, the newer activists are sometimes confronted with deeply rooted ideas from their highly respected senior comrades that do not match their own. The younger activists recognize this difference and struggle with attempts to influence the worldviews of older colleagues within their own organization. "It is not easy," said one younger activist, "for people who were politically sensitized in 1942 suddenly to think in a very broad fashion about women's issues. I think that we have to bring these issues into the party. We have to sensitize them to these issues."

Parul

I have chosen to discuss Parul not only because she is a founding member of the Forum but also because her trajectory is representative of those who have gravitated toward the organization. She is an activist well known in the circles of the international women's movement and has written widely about various struggles undertaken by the Bombay women's movement. Like her sister members, Parul came to the Forum after a period of involvement with left-wing parties. Growing up in the neighboring state of Gujarat, Parul was initiated into the politics of Trotskyism by a teacher when she was in the tenth grade. Very quickly she became a key member of the Fourth International and was involved in campaigns to release political prisoners and to create health clinics for the poor, and she worked as well with radical unions. While she translated Kate Millett, Evelyn Reed, and Friedrich Engels into Gujarati, she was not herself interested in the women's movement. It was her marriage that pushed her in that direction. Shortly after she married a comrade, a Muslim, despite the disapproval of her Hindu family and community, she realized that she was being pressured, by the very party that had so praised her political skills, to be a good wife to her comrade husband, quit politics, get a job, and support him in his political work. This switch in the party's attitude toward her came like a bolt from the blue, at the same time that she found herself struggling with her husband's expectations of her as a wife. She decided to move to Bombay, alone, leaving behind, at least for a while, the complications of her newly married life. In Bombay she met women sympathetic to her perspective: "I found that people appreciated me more and were very helpful. There was lots of sharing, support and sisterhood. I was introduced to a completely different set of human relationships among people involved in social issues. There was not the compartmentalization so prevalent in the left." Parul was one of the women from related left parties who formed the Socialist Women's Group in 1978, resulting in the Feminist Network and *Manushi,* India's first feminist magazine. These women were already part of the women's movement, absorbed in the debates around feminist issues, when the Mathura rape case hit Bombay and the Forum was born.

Parul speaks eloquently about the anger of her party and trade union toward her and the other women who became increasingly involved with the Forum: "They said we were shameless, for how could we discuss rape in public?" She finally broke with them in 1983. Although she is still a member of the Fourth International, she refuses to participate wholeheartedly in organizations that "won't take women and feminists into their decision-making process."

Parul's story is repeated time and time again by Forum activists. A woman who left her Gandhian Socialist organization to join the Forum told me how she came to criticize the patriarchal nature of her group:

> I got married in 1980 and at that point began to struggle with ideas about a real partnership between men and women and men's roles at home. My friends and I began to discuss issues relating to women. We were angry young women and developed a reputation within the camp of being argumentative. There were two incidents in particular that shocked me. One was that a woman in the organization who had had relationships with a couple of men in the organization got pregnant. The man ran off. Everyone was shocked and many of the women went on hunger strike and forced him to marry her. Second, one of our leaders molested a woman and nobody was willing to stand by the woman. I became extremely agitated and began to think of autonomous groups. (W2)

These incidents are unlikely to have been restricted to a Gandhian Socialist organization like the Chhatra Yuva Sangharsh Vahini or to India. Many accounts of women in political parties or in New Left movements in the United States who decided to organize autonomously confirm that the trivialization and marginalization of sexual harassment and assault—and women's issues in general—is a common feature in many left organizations. Yet these kinds of problems were never brought up by women in Calcutta.

One of the Forum's few working-class members, who is also from an oppressed caste, reports similar reasons for joining the organization: "I used to be with the Dalit Panthers, along with my husband, but they didn't treat me well. I would have to cook for people during election meetings. . . . the male workers in the Dalit Panthers do not appreciate women's work and they mock and ruin men who help their wives" (F4).

Over and over again, we hear the refrain: these were women already politically aware and active before joining the Forum, but once they felt that they were not being taken seriously and that their priorities were not being valued, they made the conscious decision to leave (or become inactive in) their organizations and invest their energies into a more responsive women's organization. None of the PBGMS women volunteered information about such problems, and clearly none of them had separated from organizations because of them. Indeed, although the women in Sachetana did speak of these problems, none had felt compelled to leave their party as a result.

There is one other element of the Forum's membership that must be mentioned, for it is one that was instrumental in its creation. One of its founding members had just returned to Bombay after college in the United States, where she had been influenced and moved by both the Black Panthers and the feminist movement. She, together with Parul, who belonged to the same political group, began to feel "the need to do something." There was no group in Bombay that they could identify with, so when they started their feminist discussion group, they did so with the help of literature from the West and used its insights in their struggle for autonomy within their party.

For some Forum activists, then, it was married life that pushed them to become radicalized as women, because it was then that the contradictions between being a comrade and being a wife became stark. For some who returned from college in the United States, exposure to the Black Panthers and the politics of feminism widened their horizons. For yet others, the Forum provided a shelter from their broken homes. Women came to the Forum from diverse political and social backgrounds, within and outside Bombay, bringing with them ideas about political struggle. They tended to come from both middle-class and upper-middle-class backgrounds, with a tiny minority from the working class, and included Gujaratis and Maharashtrians, Hindus and Christians. Because of this diversity and range of experiences, the Forum emerged as an alternative space for women—a space to which people from various ideologies could come to make sense of their lives as women.

Ideology

Oppositional politics in Bombay has developed a particular culture, characterized by autonomous and grassroots groups unaffiliated to political parties who generally mistrust the state and tend to work in coalitions. One of the striking markers of difference with Calcutta is the separation in Bombay of the political culture of protest and the political culture of parliamentary politics. Thus in Bombay's political field, multiple political cultures exist, clash, and jockey for legitimacy. No single "injustice frame" exists in Bombay, nor any obvious ideological hook that will resonate with multiple sectors of society. Bombay's field is a hotly contested terrain, whose disparate outsiders battle over meanings and definitions with the insiders, conceding nothing. Dominant discourses have a precarious existence and are constantly challenged in Bombay.

In such a terrain, the Forum has carved out for itself a tenuous leadership within the women's movement. It has managed to shift the terms of the discourse on crucial issues, particularly sexual and domestic violence, and has established itself as the voice of the women's movement in Bombay. It has, in Snow and Benford's (1988) terms, transformed the domestic violence frame. The subordinate CPI(M)-affiliated JMS, entering a field already stamped by the Forum, finds itself negotiating constantly between the Forum's definitions of women's issues and their party's. And from this negotiation arises a new worldview about women's interests and politics. But because of the fragmented nature of Bombay's field, domination, even in the sphere of political culture, can only be partial. As I shall show, while the JMS has absorbed, in whole or in part, the Forum's rhetoric on a range of substantive issues, it remains wedded to the politically affiliated way of doing politics.

Sexual and Domestic Violence

The main issue facing women is violence in its many manifestations—not just rape but the entire system. The fear of everything around you and how that curtails your life.

—Forum activist

Rape mobilized the second wave of Bombay feminists. Anger and horror at the Mathura verdict exonerating two policemen of raping a sixteen-year-old tribal girl acted as a catalyst for the formation of women's protest groups around the country. The target of protest was initially rape by the powerful—policemen and landlords—of the powerless. Groups like the Forum soon moved to developing their own analysis of rape, an analysis strongly reminiscent of that of U.S. radical feminists. Rape came to be seen as an instrument of power used by all men to keep all women in their place. All women were potential rape victims, irrespective of age, dress, or conduct. Rape was redefined, not as a spontaneous outburst of lust or passion, but a preplanned, premeditated action of violence and humiliation. It was an extreme manifestation of the unequal relations between men and women (Flavia, 1992).

Forum activists focused their initial energies on publicizing and reinterpreting rape. Entering a field in which the discourse defined rape as a problem of "law and order," it sought to shift the discourse to rape as a problem of "violence against women." From its very inception, the Forum used the media to politicize the issue of violence against women, to define it as a social problem and analyze it accordingly. They had access to ideas about rape being generated in the United States and used them to build analyses more appropriate to India.[2] Forum members had their work cut out for them, for while the rape cases tackled by the Forum did receive considerable amounts of initial publicity, they would quickly disappear from the media. Forum members soon came to understand that the publicity received by rape cases was largely due to their shock value (F5). As rape cases received increased press coverage, gory details titillated readers, and men expressed a sense of outraged honor, while women were increasingly seen as victims.

While the media was slow to respond to the Forum's new perspective, the effort has paid off in terms of the political culture of social movements. None of the women in the JMS have any doubt that violence against women is a fundamental expression of men's power over women—not the stray act of crazed or sick individuals. It is simply not tenable for an activist in the women's movement in Bombay to put forward the kind of analysis voiced by PBGMS leaders in Calcutta. A curious turn of phrase used by one of the leaders of the JMS alerted me to the way in which the CPI(M) has adapted its rhetoric around sexual violence in Bombay. In criticizing activists in autonomous groups (whom she disparagingly referred to as "these feminists"), she said, "These feminists deal only with rape and they don't like the fact that we say that rape is not just a sexual atrocity, but is used as a class weapon" (JMS1). But in fact, this activist's formulation is not exactly the formulation that autonomous feminists would find objectionable. It is *her* articulation of the issue that has changed from "rape is *fundamentally* a class weapon" to "rape is not just a sexual atrocity, it is *also* a class weapon." This change is a testament to the permeability of Bombay's political culture as well as to the Forum's strength within it.

Sachetana activists struggle both with the history of Calcutta's left culture and its present impact. Forum activists, many of whom emerged from the left, often use the left as a foil. Nandita Gandhi and Nandita Shah, Forum activists and authors of *The Issues at Stake: Theory and Practice in the Contemporary Women's Movement in India,* contend that the "economic reductionist" arguments of the left must be rejected in favor of the claim that "all women, regardless of their class and caste, are oppressed and that violence is as political an issue as price rise and peace" (Gandhi and Shah, 1991:88). This claim is reflected, albeit in a modified way, in the words of younger JMS members. When I asked about their stand on prioritizing violence against women, I was referred by a JMS activist to an article in the AIDWA pamphlet produced for their third national conference, in which Brinda Karat, the general secretary of the AIDWA, wrote:

> Issues like domestic violence, wife beating, dowry murders, rapes, sexual harassment etc. which are on the increase throughout the country and reflect in the most dramatic way the deteriorating status of women

cannot be ignored as being "politically soft" issues. On the other hand attacks on democracy, issues concerning government . . . are of equal concern to [us] and must be emphasized. (AIDWA, 1990)

This appeal to the party reflects the concerted drive being made in both Bombay and Delhi to get the CPI(M) to recognize domestic violence as a political issue "equal" to democracy. That is, there is an attempt to maintain the "political" nature of domestic violence, which is precisely what the Calcutta-based PBGMS does not wish to do.

Domestic violence is, according to the Forum, a subset of the overall violence against women in society and a testament to the dehumanization of women. Women "are beaten because they did not put the correct amount of salt in the food. . . . they are not really burnt for dowry but because of their lack of value and the level of violence in society" (W2). It was a member of the Forum who first spoke out publicly about being battered, thus introducing into Bombay's political culture the legitimacy of speaking out about one's own experiences and allowing women to step out from behind the veil of shame that inevitably accompanied domestic violence. Through her book, Flavia (1990) documented her life as a battered wife and her decision to leave her husband, thus "breaking the silence" on the issue for the first time. It was she who pushed for the creation of the Women's Centre, so that abused women would have a place to go for advice and to be safe. Soon after Flavia had made the issue public, the battered wife of a famous "progressive" film director came forward to seek the Centre's help, bringing considerable publicity to the Women's Centre. The Forum and the Centre together organized protest marches and demonstrations around particularly egregious cases of domestic violence. They used street demonstrations, marches in the victim's neighborhood, slogans against husband and in-laws, and appeals for a social boycott in order to win attention for this issue. On several instances, the JMS marched with them.

In India, domestic violence often culminates in the killing of the wife in what are popularly called "dowry deaths." This phenomenon has put the spotlight on the dowry system and the appalling pressures borne by women and their parents in their attempts to satisfy the demands made by the groom's family. While Forum and Centre women were among the most visible protesters of domestic violence and wife murders, they have begun to rethink their position:

It took us quite a while to realize that these demonstrations (after a woman had been burnt, say) . . . were equally futile as they did not

help change the attitudes of the family. The natal family's aim was "private revenge" and the concern of the family after the demonstration
was to get the next daughter married into a "decent family" with an adequate amount of dowry and keep her married at all costs. The role
women's organizations were expected to play was that of "unhired
goondas" for whose values and way of life, the family would have total
contempt, but would, nevertheless use them only for the sake of caus-
ing public humiliation to the in-laws and for recovering their dowry.
(FAOW, 1990:17)

These feminist activists are seen as destroyers of the "family," a label that is
true to the extent that they advocate the creation of alternatives to it. Much
of what the Forum stands for is a critique of the most private and personal
parts of family life, and it is therefore particularly threatening.

The Forum's analysis of the existence of a culture of violence has led it
to reject the popular language of street demonstrations because of the violence inherent in them. The chant, "Jo humse takrayega, mitti me mil-
jayega" (we will crush into the ground anyone who challenges us), popularly
used and sanctioned by the left parties, is no longer considered acceptable by
the Forum. "The slogans used, the method used . . . are we repeating the
might is right attitude? How then are we different from the Shiv Sena" (F1)?
In this arena, autonomous groups in Bombay, belonging to a variety of social movements, are at odds with party activists whose demonstrations and
marches against domestic violence are liberally sprinkled with threats to the
opposition. Yet in some ways, I noticed that the rejection of violent language
was slowly beginning to shift the political culture of Bombay, particularly in
the movement to combat communal strife between Hindus and Muslims. In
response to the right-wing Hindu slogan, "Garv se kaho hum hindu hai"
(say with pride that we are Hindus), which has encouraged violence against
Muslims as an assertion of that pride, Ektaa (Unity), an anticommunal front
formed by political and autonomous groups, offers instead the slogan, "Pyar
se kaho hum insaan hai" (say with love that we are human beings).

The Forum has introduced to Bombay a new way of thinking about
violence against women and violence in general. They have altered the "cultural coding" of this issue, which, in Ann Swidler's words, "is one of the
most powerful ways social movements actually bring about change" (Swidler, 1995:33). Other autonomous groups and eventually some politically affiliated groups have absorbed parts of their analysis, and the political culture
of Bombay has been at least partially transformed. This has been the Forum's
most profound achievement.

Consciousness Raising

How does one resist the temptation of being saviours of women, maintain
the sisterly support and not mother them or create dependency?
—FAOW, *Moving . . . but Not Quite There*

While Forum and JMS activists do not claim that "ideological backwardness" is a problem as often as do the Calcutta groups, both engage in ideological work involving women. The linearity present in Calcutta is absent here, and the views toward women's consciousness are both more nuanced and more inconsistent.

On the one hand, Forum activists refuse to use terms such as "ideological backwardness," which are regularly used by women from left parties. They do not believe that they should approach individual women with the conviction that they, as feminist activists, have all the right answers. Rather they search for means through which they can share their experiences with other women in a process of collective learning. At the Women's Centre, individual women who seek help are encouraged to unlearn dependence.[3] At their monthly get-togethers, women share their experiences with other women—experiences about marriage, sex, familial problems, and independence. Yet, in one activist's estimation, what differentiates the Forum from other groups is its ability to introduce a "women's perspective" into all issues. These perspectives are arrived at in dialogue within the Forum, and the task then is to "inject" this perspective into other campaigns and groups (F1). Thus there is in the Forum the belief it has have achieved a perspective that others have not.

Given the contours of political possibilities in Calcutta, it is logical that the PBGMS, with its enormous resources and numbers, should focus on broad political education, while Sachetana focuses on consciousness raising within its own organization. Like Sachetana members, Forum activists believe deeply in raising one's own consciousness. Yet, unlike Sachetana members, they know that they can influence the ways in which other organizations in the city think about gendered issues. To them, changing consciousness is politics, but "mass political education" carries the stigma of elitist party politics. One activist contrasts the politics of consciousness raising to the politics of "activism." Activism, according to her,

reflects the traditional idea that social change is activated by arousing mass movements around some demands made upon the government. This idea basically assumes that governmental power is important and that the Government is going to bring about the changes. But the

> process of change has to be viewed as a process which revolutionizes
> the life of people on a daily basis. This process makes them more confi-
> dent and helps them to organize their lives as they wish. It raises their
> consciousness, but if it is not then consolidated in small groups, if it is
> not internalized in consciousness-raising groups, the lives of the people
> will not be revolutionized. (Datar, 1988)

Consciousness raising is revolutionary politics. Petitioning or protesting the
government is not.

Activists of the JMS are proud to claim that their students' federation
makes conscious attempts to recruit girls and to train them for leadership.
They are themselves involved in such a venture. Rather than raise the consciousness of each individual woman, however, they focus on targeting
women with leadership potential, so that those leaders can then articulate
the needs of their communities. In this targeting of potential leaders they are
no different from other left parties. What marks the JMS as different from
the PBGMS is its insistence on female leadership to articulate women's concerns and its acceptance of the need for separate spaces for women.

The JMS leaders treat the issue of consciousness as a give-and-take between them and other women. In their view, if you want to get women from
the *bustees* (slums) to think about the issues you want them to think about,
you must first tackle the issues of their concern—civic issues: "If you don't,
why should they work with you? They are not naive. They test who will really do it for them" (J2). At the same time, they acknowledge that getting
women to move beyond their immediate problems has proved to be difficult. In Calcutta, there is little importance given to the problems involved in
finding out what women want, how they think, and what their priorities are.
Women's interests, as such, are less interrogated there.

Consciousness is an arena in which the younger generation of activists
differs from the older. Younger JMS activists emphasize the importance of independent thought, of *swatantra vichar,* of a woman's wanting and being able
to stand on her own—those are the goals of consciousness raising. For the
older generation, however, the issue is one of superstition versus science.
When I asked Ahalyatai about consciousness raising, she said immediately,
"Yes, yes, that is very important," and went on to tell me of her anger about a
film in which a child becomes sick and its mother wants to take it to the doctor. The father warns the mother that the way to save the child is to take him
to the temple, not a doctor. The woman is torn, but ultimately chooses the
temple over the doctor—and the child lives. Ahalya Rangnekar is particularly
concerned about the effects of this sort of story; she worries that people will
stray from the scientific path and end up losing their children. She gave me

several examples of her intervention in situations where she had to fight superstition in order to save the lives of women. Women need scientific thought, she says, but the right-wing-controlled media gives them superstition.

The rise of the Hindu right wing and the accompanying religious riots have, however, made both groups in Bombay think seriously about the degree of attraction these parties hold for women. As the right becomes more powerful, dividing Hindu from Muslim and native Maharashtrian from non-Maharashtrian, the issue of consciousness is becoming increasingly troubling in Bombay.

Work

The Forum's definition of itself in opposition to left parties is partly responsible for its lack of attention to work-related issues. It is, therefore, not seen as the kind of group that organizes women workers or works on issues of particular concern, such as maternity leave and day care. While issues concerning the relations of production are of much more enduring concern in the Forum than in many women's groups in advanced capitalist countries, they refuse it primacy over and above issues of reproduction.[4] There are, however, individual members of the Forum who work with unions affiliated to left political parties. While this is not an arena in which the Forum has had a substantive effect, the JMS attitude toward work issues and its recognition of the differing interests of male and female workers reflect the acceptance in Bombay's political culture of women as a group possessing interests separate from men as a group.

One area of concern to working women in which the Forum has actively intervened is sexual harassment. It was recently involved in a suit filed by a flight attendant against her male coworkers and has also intervened in a suit against airlines that routinely fire flight attendants upon their turning thirty-five. Yet in the publication commemorating the Forum's tenth anniversary, no mention is made of any employment-related campaigns.

The JMS sees work as a fundamental right and as a necessary but not sufficient condition for women's emancipation. In this they are unlike the PBGMS but similar to Sachetana. "Work by itself is not enough," said one activist, "but without it there can be no liberation." Sounding even more like Sachetana, she continued, "A girl must be brought up with the idea that she will stand on her own two feet." The older women in the JMS have long been involved in trade union politics, and the two issues—trade unionism and gender—are not as far apart as they are in Calcutta. Indeed, Ahalya Rangnekar is a highly respected leader in the JMS and the CITU.

Feminism and Male Domination

We understand feminism as a consciousness of patriarchal control over women's labour, fertility and sexuality. . . . Socialist feminism acknowledges subjectivity and personal experiences but locates these within existing social relations.

—Nandita Gandhi and Nandita Shah, *The Issues at Stake*

The Forum defines itself as socialist feminist. But it defines itself as an alternative to political parties and to politically affiliated women's groups.[5] This ensures that it is more inclined to adopt issues that those groups do not, but it also means that its naming and defining of "women's issues" is somewhat limited. After the 1984 gas disaster at the Union Carbide plant in Bhopal, for example, when many groups across the country mobilized to fight for compensation for its victims, Forum members wondered whether they, too, should join the struggle. Could this be seen as a legitimate women's issue? They decided against participating in the campaign on the grounds that the effects of the Bhopal gas disaster were not woman-specific and that several other groups were already working on it (F9).

Because the Forum has been defined in the Bombay English media as the ideological yardstick by which to measure feminism, its members are regularly asked to comment on events in the news. But this expectation exerts pressure on some of the women in the Forum not to appear to be less feminist than is acceptable: "These 'ideal feminists' would dominate meetings with their extreme positions on various issues and the rest of us were forced to tag along, not daring to voice our doubts in case we got dubbed anti-feminist" (FAOW, 1990).

Feminism is the prized currency of the Forum, and the more one has of it, the more powerful one is. And it is the Forum that has the cultural legitimacy to name issues and people as appropriately feminist. The Forum has few resources and perhaps only twenty active members; what it does have, according to one member, is the power of its name.

For JMS activists, the Forum remains "those feminists," the ones who get the attention of the media and the ones who remain willfully blind to realities. The JMS activists resent the feminists' characterization of them as being dictated to by the party, and resent even more that while they participate in the Forum's issues, the Forum does not participate in theirs. That is, the JMS considers rape, for example, a valid women's issue, but the Forum does not think the rise in prices of basic consumer goods is.

For the Forum, the family is the key institution of women's oppression (W1) and male domination. That women aren't paid the same as men and that there aren't enough women in unions can all be traced to the family. It is the family that must be transformed. The Forum rejects Engels's argument about the simultaneous emergence of patriarchy, surplus, and private property, arguing instead that "women's oppression and subjugation began much before the generation of surplus, the emergence of private property and class" (Gandhi and Shah, 1991:89). In this, too, the Forum has influenced the JMS.

The JMS may choose to work on civic issues, but in a significant divergence from Calcutta's PBGMS, it is open about the family-based origins of women's oppression. While the PBGMS is well aware of the importance of families in the lives of their daughters, they do not give families analytic importance. The JMS, however, does. In a much advertised conference for destitute women, Ahalya Rangnekar argued that "justice for deserted and destitute women was not only a question of getting a share in government schemes and benefits but, more importantly, it was a struggle to change entrenched family and social values and attitudes towards women, and the institutions that perpetuate women's subordination" (AIDWA, 1991:22).

In the resolution of domestic violence cases, JMS activists distinguish themselves from other political parties, who, they claim, do not really have the interests of the women at heart. In discussing reasons for the abuse of wives by their husbands, one grassroots worker decried what she termed the "machismo and will to dominate" on the part of men. She noted further that in her experience men sometimes falsely accused their wives of having extramarital affairs "just to establish [their] dominance" (J3). The sense of men possessing a will to power, *an interest in domination that is separate from the economic,* pervades the discussions of the JMS. Such a view is markedly absent their counterpart, the PBGMS, in Calcutta.

The JMS may deplore the "feminism" of the Forum and may pride itself on having a more inclusive approach to women, but in a myriad of ways, the Forum has come to be seen as the politically legitimate organization representing women's interests. Thus the JMS will never call itself feminist, but will incorporate elements of the Forum's analysis into its own understandings of male domination, an understanding that sets it apart from its sister organization in Calcutta.

Political Organizing, Foreign Funding, and the State

The autonomous women in the Forum and the Women's Centre are adamantly opposed to working with the state. They believe that their experiences have taught them that they were mistaken in their reliance on the state for the creation of prowoman legislation. Legal success, however minimal, diminishes the intensity of mobilization, as both the antirape and the amniocentesis campaigns testify. To some, the fact that the state has refused to consult with them and put them on important committees is further proof that it is on the other side. Many feel frustrated with the tension between asking for intervention and co-optation, and refer to the shortcomings of the new rape and amniocentesis legislation as proof of the problems inherent in involving the state.

Unlike women in the politically affiliated parties, women in the Forum are uncomfortable with the bill in parliament to reserve 30 percent of seats in village *panchayats* for women. They ask, "Are they trying to co-opt us?" (F1) and are steadfast in their belief that the state is not benevolent and cannot be on the side of women. Thus organized women must forever remain watchdogs outside it. No government, right or left, is seen as genuinely supportive of women's rights. Power is a corruptive force, and observing left governments in other states has not convinced them otherwise.

For many Forum activists there is an ideal division of labor between autonomous and politically affiliated organizations. The autonomous organizations are seen to have a better understanding of women's issues: "We have a gut-level understanding of women's reality, lives, and struggles" (F3); "political organizations have to feed on the autonomous organizations for some kind of ideological understanding. They [the latter] have a far sharper understanding of the issues concerning women" (M1). They believe that autonomous organizations have a more genuine concern for women's issues: "Autonomous women's organizations would never subordinate a women's issue. Rape within the working class will never get us any support from left parties, for example" (F3). Ultimately, they are convinced, the party's interests come first for affiliated women's organizations, and the party's survival means more than a woman's. Forum activists are also suspicious of power. They fear and mistrust the totalizing visions of both the left and the right because all political parties see themselves as above autonomous organizations. And if parties think that their ideas, projects, and goals are superior, they also have the ability and desire to gain the power to broadcast those ideas and to implement them.

Not surprisingly, the JMS does not favor autonomy. And there is little the Forum can do to change that. The JMS activists see autonomous groups as being autonomous not only from political parties but from the political process itself. They are suspicious of those nongovernmental organizations that receive funds from abroad, but are more willing to work with them than the PBGMS is with NGOs operating in Calcutta. Members of the JMS are mistrustful of the present state government but not, therefore, of all states. They cite the ever growing phenomenon of Hindu fundamentalism as an example of why progressives should have a massive, united, ideologically consistent (read: party affiliated) front: "Given the state's targeting of women and [given] the women's wings of the Shiv Sena, BJP, and RSS, we must be able to sustain and expand the role of the progressive women's movement. Fundamentalism requires a huge united political force to fight it" (J2). Given that the forces of fundamentalism are politically affiliated, the forces arrayed against them should be, also.

At the same time, the approach of the JMS to politics differs significantly from the PBGMS. Its activists are far from comfortable with the "normal" functioning of left political parties. Criticizing the PBGMS in Bengal for its conservatism, one activist exclaimed: "This top down business has to stop. We have to be able to integrate the direct experiences and needs of women in a real way, not mechanically. The legacy of vanguardism," she continued, referring to the way the CPI(M) functions in Calcutta, "isolates you from your community."

In Bombay's political field, there is both more overt hostility between autonomous and affiliated groups and a greater willingness to work together. This is in part because of the political culture that encourages coalition work and because of a more equal distribution of power in the field, which enables groups to be vocal about their disagreements with each other. In chapter 8 I will discuss this issue at greater length. Bombay's political culture has also encouraged a rethinking by politically affiliated organizations about more democratic political practices and a rejection of the decision-making procedures usually associated with political parties.

The Personal Is Political

One of the very reasons for the Forum's existence is to legitimize the politicization of the personal. Forum activists one and all speak eloquently of deriving from the Forum strength, courage, and a new understanding of patriarchy and sisterhood. In a monograph published after the first decade of the Forum's existence, several women wrote about their experiences in the group. In her contribution to the issue, Lali, a former member who has recently rejoined, discusses her life, her happiness with the Forum and unhappiness in marriage, and her frustration with the "extreme positions" taken by the "ideal feminists" with no domestic and child-care responsibilities. She felt dominated and stifled in both marriage and the Forum. But when her marriage fell apart, she turned to the Forum: "And respond they did. They responded promptly, unconditionally, spontaneously, totally. . . . Their responses overwhelmed me and yet it seemed, somehow, natural for me to turn to them and for them to reach out" (FAOW, 1990:20–21).

In another article in the same monograph, Sonal Shukla described the worlds that opened up to her through her participation in the group:

> Participating in Forum activities can make you very resourceful. Forum has practically no material resources of its own so you have to use your imagination, use all your abilities which were lying dormant, all your personal contacts and other resources. I realized I could sing. I could even write songs. I had been a potential singer all my life. I belonged to a family of professional musicians and felt handicapped by their standards. With Forum one felt authentic even if one was not perfect. (FAOW, 1990:29–30)

Others value the space the Forum provides them to think and reflect. Whatever the reason members chose to associate themselves with the Forum, few of them would choose to permanently disassociate themselves from it.

The legitimacy of the personal means that in the Forum, as in many groups that started in the 1970s in the United States and Britain (and indeed as in the identity politics of today), personal experience is a valid take-off point for a campaign. Thus the train campaign (which demanded police protection in women-only compartments in the evenings) and the surname campaign (which demanded that the retention of a woman's original last name after marriage be legally recognized) were both initiated because it directly concerned the lives of Forum members. According to one activist, "Whatever makes us most angry is taken up" as an issue (F10). Forum members believe and celebrate the politicization of the personal. Indeed, for its members, that in itself is a reason to belong.

There is little talk about the personal as political in the JMS, although there is not the same unwillingness to bring issues of the self into politics that there seems to be in the PBGMS. Members more unselfconsciously raise issues of the domestic division of labor in the house, and Dulari and Shaheen take pride in their ability to make unpopular life decisions and stick with them. They are proud of defying convention. Yet if one were to ask any of the members why they are with the JMS, they would answer in terms of "women's" needs, not their own.

Conclusion

Heterogeneity, fluidity, and partiality mark Bombay's dominant political culture. To this is added the legitimacy of autonomous, identity-based organizing in Bombay's protest field. Bombay's women's movement is therefore a site of constant conflict and change. Bombay's political culture allows the Forum and the JMS to coexist in Bombay, each with their own strengths. Both organizations share some elements of the oppositional political culture—the acceptance of women's separate interests and spheres, for example. But the JMS does not share other parts of the dominant protest culture, such as autonomous organizing and mistrust of the state. The Forum fears and mistrusts political parties. It is, on the other hand, open to influences from the outside, such as U.S. analyses of domestic violence and British socialist-feminist analyses of class. Through the Forum, the international feminist community has become part of Bombay's political field.

The Forum's partially dominant stature can be seen by the fact that while the JMS is influenced by the Forum, the Forum is emphatically not influenced by the JMS. The JMS needs the Forum to give it legitimacy in the women's movement, while the Forum does not require validation by the JMS. It is not easy to claim that the Forum is dominant, but in the arena of naming and defining issues, it is clearly so. It is not dominant in the resolution of those issues; indeed, it is difficult for an autonomous organization to be. But the Forum, applying its finely honed techniques of persuasive communication (Klandermans, 1992), has introduced into Bombay's political culture the legitimacy of speaking out about one's own experiences and a new way of thinking about violence against women and violence in general. It has forced the JMS to take the role of families seriously. And it has forced younger JMS members to push the JMS to refine and change its analyses of gender issues. As the Forum's discourse on gendered subjects develops, JMS activists eventually pull their organization along. Thus, because it is situated in Bombay, the JMS has found itself open to influences of the national and international feminist community (through the Forum), in a way that the PBGMS, in Calcutta, is not.

Chapter 8

Domination and Subordination in Bombay

Today, We Meet, Join Hands, Raise Our Voices in the Spirit of Sisterhood

> *Our Demands:*
> *Ban amniocentesis for sex determination*
> *Changes in the Rape and Dowry Acts*
> *Introduction of a Domestic Violence Act*
> *Family Courts for divorce, dowry etc. cases*
> *Housing for single women/working women*
> *Basic facilities for rural women*
> *Work for all women with training*
> *—Forum Against Oppression of Women, International Women's Day,*
> *March 8, 1984*

The organizations that form the focus of my study in Bombay differ from those in Calcutta in fundamental ways. These differences are due partly to the nature of the dominant and subordinate organizations, but mostly to the type of field within which they are embedded. The dominant PBGMS in Calcutta is affiliated to a political party that governs the state. Therefore, in the state of West Bengal, at least, the PBGMS is an insider and enjoys the benefits of any organization favored by the state. The PBGMS is, then, a dominant organization in a hegemonic field, and its dominance is almost absolute. But no single force controls Bombay's political field. No single political party or grassroots organization molds the field in its image. The Forum Against Oppression of Women forms part of one of the three main players in Bombay's field. As a representative of Bombay's women's movement, it is associated with the constantly shifting alliance of progressive forces that co-exist with the Congress and the Shiv Sena. Both party-affiliated and autonomous organizations exist within this third, progressive force, and no one element is the most powerful.

The Forum cannot hope to dominate the women's movement in any real sense, although it does exert a certain visible influence over it. The Forum's power comes from two sources—its cultural legitimacy within the protest field and its ability to form coalitions with various nonparty political formations and other progressive forces, including peasant, ecological, civil liberties, and other women's organizations, as well as with the politically affiliated left. The Forum is an outsider, but it is an outsider in a field marked by high levels of challenge and conflict, where the boundaries of the field are fuzzy and more easily permeated and where exit and entry are easier than in Calcutta.

In such a field, the boundaries between dominant and subordinate are less clear and less consistent. If Sachetana's trajectory is marked by oscillation, that of the JMS is marked by a limited yet consistently dual focus, largely because of its existence in Bombay, on the one hand, and its allegiance to the CPI(M), on the other. Only part of its policies and programs are locally generated and thus affected by the Forum. The rest of its energies are devoted to election work for CPI(M) candidates and sometimes to major campaigns, decisions for which are taken at the national level.

As chapter 6 made clear, the fragmentation of Bombay's field makes it difficult for any one organization to wield enough power to be effective. Yet its very openness makes it possible for increased numbers of organizations to become contenders. Bombay has thus become a city of coalitions. Both the JMS and the Forum understand this and are often found in various permutations and combinations with other progressive groups, and sometimes with each other.

If, however, an organization does manage to become powerful, as the Shiv Sena has, then the field can become rapidly transformed. A fragmented field can be more easily reorganized as power balances shift. The progressive forces in Bombay can afford to be more radical and can mobilize more rapidly than can the larger, slower-moving progressive forces in Calcutta. But in the absence of a powerful protector, such as the CPI(M) in Calcutta, they are vulnerable to being swept aside. My recent visits to Bombay indicate that this might be one of the many unfortunate outcomes of the triumph of the Shiv Sena.

While Bombay has always been a city of coalitions, there is a renewed urgency evident in both the JMS and the Forum to continue to build a long-lasting progressive coalition to combat the forces of the right.

A Common Strategy: Coalitions and Alliances

In a protest against the Supreme Court order acquitting Sharad Sarda after he had been convicted for the murder of his wife Manjushree by the Poona Sessions Court and the Bombay High Court, about 200 women belonging to various women's organizations under the banner of "Mahila Sangharsha Manch" (MSM) on Wednesday took out a Morcha to Mantralaya and presented a memorandum to Chief Minister Vasantrao Patil. . . . The women's organizations represented by Samajwadi Mahila Sabha, National Federation of Indian Women, All India Women's Conference, All India Association of Democratic Women, North Bombay Women's Joint Committee and

Forum Against Oppression of Women, intend to meet Governor I. H. Latif and appeal for a review.

—*Indian Express,* September 20, 1984

This year the fight against rape is being taken on afresh with public meetings at Madam Cama Hall at Lions Gate at 4 p.m. tomorrow. The organizations taking part are Forum, Mahila Dakshata Samiti, Stree Uvach, YMCA, YWVA, Women's Centre, Mahila Rakshak Samiti, Jagrut Kashtakari Sanghatana, Stree Mukti Sanghatana, Awaz-e-Niswan, Stree Kruti, NFIW and Women and Media.

—*Times of India,* March 9, 1990

In a period of [an] all-round offensive of reactionary forces it is an indication of the maturity of the Indian women's movement that it stood together on crucial issues such as a common stand against fundamentalism and also a consensus, though it took a long time to build, in opposition to the government's economic policies.

—Report of the AIDWA conference, December 1994

Communist party women's groups, Christian groups, and autonomous groups all came together in 1984 and continued to do so, even though the composition of the coalition had changed, in 1990. One activist estimates that there are about fifteen organizations that share ideas and resources around women's issues in Bombay (F3). "When all is said and done," she says, "Bombay is the only city where this happens." The first two epigraphs in this section, both from Bombay newspapers, show the alliance of groups on issues of domestic violence, while the epigraph from the AIDWA conference document indicates that various portions of the women's movement have also joined forces to fight religious fundamentalism and the government's policies of economic liberalization. The nature of these coalitions are a sign of the nature of Bombay's field. They are partial, temporary, issue-based, and increasingly cover a wide range of problems. These broad-based coalitions are markedly absent in Calcutta, where, if and when they exist, they tend to be coalitions of the affiliated left.

While in Bombay, I quickly learned the extent to which the groups that constitute Bombay's third, progressive, force habitually share their issues with each other. I remember going with members of the Women's Centre to a demonstration on the International Day of Protest against Violence against Women. We squatted in a square downtown, handed out leaflets, sang songs, and talked to those who passed by. We were a diverse group consisting of members of the Forum, the YWCA, Nirmala Niketan (a social work school), and clients of the Women's Centre. As we sat there; some fifty of us, we were approached by a member of Stree Kruti, a women's group associated with a Maoist organization that often works with autonomous feminist groups. She reminded us of another demonstration at the Churchgate railway station to protest the death of several tribals who had been shot in an apparent police effort at crowd control when they had gone to see the state home minister. So after our demonstration was over, most of us walked over to Churchgate. We participated enthusiastically in this protest organized by a Maoist group, adding our voices to the demands for accountable government and punishment for the guilty. And after all the demonstrations were over, many of the activists wandered over to a café, where discussions, both personal and political, continued. Someone passed around the latest human rights report on government actions in Kashmir; someone else reminded everybody present about an upcoming rally.

I point to this incident to show not only the way coalitions are formed within the women's movement in Bombay, but the ease with which various parts of the progressive movement work together. Certainly the women's movement realizes that its issues can win only if they are backed by other progressive forces. Both the Forum and the JMS, therefore, are more willing to support actively the issues of other organizations—a strategy dictated by the distribution of power in Bombay's field, to which both politically affiliated and autonomous groups in Bombay subscribe, and a strategy that gives increasing significance to the making of alliances.

So important is the building of alliances, and so difficult is it for groups to make it on their own in Bombay, that the CPI-affiliated NFIW recently took a step rarely seen in the politics of the affiliated left in India. In an effort to expand its area of control, the NFIW is now actively inviting organizations to be "associated" with it, offering in turn, access to its resources. This is an unexpected innovation because "association" is a far looser connection than "affiliation," thus implying a willingness on the part of the NFIW to work with groups that do not necessarily share its ideology. Recently, an autonomous Muslim women's group, based in the heart of Bombay's poor Muslim neighborhood, decided to attempt such an association. Operating in a fragmented field, where the progressive forces are also fragmented, has forced several changes in both the public rhetoric and the internal structure of the NFIW.

The Forum

I have claimed that the Forum is the dominant voice of the women's movement in Bombay, but I have also said that they are outsiders in terms of Bombay's polity. How, given that the Forum is, after all, a small autonomous organization with a handful of members, does it come to matter? The answer lies in the way the Forum's strengths fit with Bombay's political field, especially with its widely dispersed power and its easy entry and exit. Given its lack of money and numbers, Forum activists rely on their cultural legitimacy and on their culturally skilled activists. In this way, the Forum can build upon each small and partial victory, carving out a niche for itself in Bombay's field.

Utilizing Their Cultural Resources

The Forum sees its strengths as the provision of analysis and the creation of awareness. Many Forum members are talented journalists—some in the English language, others in various regional languages. Through their individual writings in newspapers, popular magazines, and books, they attempt to influence public opinion and consciousness. Forum activists are highly skilled organizers, speakers, and writers. They have access to the most influential English media, either through their own members who are journalists or through their friends, such as Pamela Phillipose and Kalpana Sharma, two of the most respected journalists in the city. This access ensures that the Forum's voice, the voice of Bombay's feminism, is always heard. On my last visit to Bombay, for example, during a social evening with some Forum members, one of them received a call from journalists who wanted the Forum's opinion on whether a female lawyer who had posed in her lawyer's robes for *Debonair,* the rather less risqué Indian version of *Playboy,* should be disbarred. Very quickly the Forum turned this incident around to ask whether the male lawyers who read *Debonair* should be disbarred. The next day, the voice of the Forum was presented, along with the voice of *Debonair* readers and the legal establishment.

In another noteworthy occasion in 1990, when Justice Ranganath Misra of the Supreme Court made several derogatory remarks about women, including advising them not to compete with their husbands but to stay at home and look after their children, the Forum called a meeting to plan a protest. They agreed to meet at the Bombay High Court on Friday afternoon of that week. However, Justice Misra issued an apology for his remarks on Thursday, and so it was that I found about thirty women and men milling about outside the Bombay High Court at 3:30 on Friday afternoon, November 23, uncertain as to their next move. Somebody handed somebody else the bullhorn. Should they speak? Should they just go home? People shouted slogans in a fairly desultory way. The High Court was rapidly emptying as the sessions came to an end. All of a sudden, a journalist, a close ally of the Forum, handed the bullhorn to one of the activists. "Say something," she commanded. "If nobody says anything, I have no story."

That mobilized the activists. One after the other, they stepped forward and spoke about the dangers of right-wing judges and the impossibility of getting justice for women. The next morning, somewhat to my surprise, there appeared a photograph on page 3 of one of the two major English-language newspapers. Under the photograph was an account of the rally, complete with excerpts from speeches.

Because of its close ties to the English-language press, the Forum was able to turn what had seemed to me to be a failed rally into a success. As those who have participated in political protest know only too well, if the media does not report the protest, it might as well not have happened (Gitlin, 1980). No matter that there were only thirty people there—their presence had been recorded and noted. At least Bombay's English-reading public knew that once again the Forum had stood up for women.

For issue after issue, the Forum is able to ensure that their perspective gets representation.[1] It does indeed manage to do what it claims is one of its primary objectives—to inject its perspective into every issue.

Between 1988 and 1990, women's groups around the country vigorously debated the National Perspective Plan on women and its various recommendations. They also discussed the proposal to reserve 30 percent of all electoral seats for women. In Bombay in particular, both political party representatives and autonomous groups held meetings, workshops, and seminars to think through the implications of the reservation of seats for women. To some of the autonomous groups in the city, the focus on electoral quotas was unwelcome, since it detracted from the deeply rooted problems that women faced—violence, lack of shelter for battered women, and rape:

> What we would have liked is to have the political parties or candidates incorporate the perspectives and demands of the women's movement. For nearly ten years now, women's groups have raised the problem of harassment of women in their marital homes varying in form from domestic violence to murder using cooking fuel. . . . Most of the issues we have raised during the decade remain as unresolved and therefore as relevant as ever, but they are in danger of being eclipsed. (Ammu Abraham, Women's Centre)

While the autonomous groups in Bombay did not actually work against the bill, their concerns about it were heard in many of the various meetings, and their opinions were solicited and represented in the press.[2]

Forum activists and their allies have cultural capital and know how to use it. Because of the fragmented nature of the field, they are able to have small effects but make those effects count.

State as Both Friend and Foe

As we learned in chapter 6, the Forum's suspicions of the intentions of those who govern remain high. Certainly, the Forum does not have the option of being part of the state, given the present government—but neither would it wish to had the state been run by the left. However, the dispersed nature of Bombay's field enables the Forum to have an indirect effect on the polity, in a way that Sachetana, in Calcutta, cannot.

Forum activists describe their relationship with the state as a "tight-rope walk between making demands from a state and yet establishing and protesting against its oppressive and patriarchal nature" (FAOW, 1990:33), and their experiences with rape legislation, the train campaign, the amniocentesis campaign, and family courts, to take but four examples, bring sharply into focus the "problem of the state."

During their struggle to make rape an issue, the Forum expended considerable energy on attempts to change rape legislation. When all was said and done, the Forum realized that what they had actually managed to achieve was a series of "token laws and amendments to existing laws." They had a bill that did not include any of their recommendations regarding the regulation of police power and the exclusion of rape victims' past sexual history. One activist, who has written extensively about this, asked, "How could a Bill which created such a furor in August 1980 be passed so stealthily in December 1983?" (Flavia, 1992). At present, a decade after the campaign began, Forum members are reevaluating the rape issue and trying to learn from their mistakes. They now question whether rape should have been the first issue of the new women's movement, and question the tactics used to publicize the issue, as well as the reliance on the state to make necessary legal changes. As Costain and Costain (1987) have pointed out, in the case of the United States, certain sorts of tactics require specialized knowledge—working with the state requires a certain expertise that the women in the Forum did not have at that point.[3]

The Forum has had to learn much since its inception about working with various parts of the state. During the campaign to make trains safe for women by prohibiting men from entering the specially designated women's compartments, they went to the railway police for help, only to be told that the railway police were there to protect railway property, not women (W3). They won their demand for family courts, which would speed up justice for women by bypassing the overloaded regular court system, yet they could not ensure that the courts treated women fairly. Family courts, they now find, protect the family, not the woman. Without effective feminist monitoring, any legislation can succumb to existing social pressures and cultural norms (F5).

Their experience with Project Help, a joint program initiated by the Bombay police, was particularly bitter. When the issue of women being burned to death in their marital homes hit the news, members of six women's organizations in Bombay were invited to be at the bedside of women burn victims to take their dying declarations, so that the perpetrators of these heinous crimes could be caught. Forum members soon found, however, that when they started following through on a particular case or pointing out discrepancies in police records, they were told they were overstepping their bounds. Eventually the police terminated Project Help on the grounds that it was not effective, leaving the Forum feeling used. Its members realized that they had saved the police money by agreeing to be on call twenty-four hours a day, but had not been really treated as independent witnesses (Gandhi and Shah, 1991:100; FAOW, 1990:35).

During the amniocentesis campaign, after months of discussion and agitation, the state agreed to pass a bill to "ban the misuse of pre-natal diagnostic techniques for sex determination" in 1988. Yet the Forum's two major demands, that no private clinics be allowed to perform these tests and that the women who had the tests not be punished, were ignored (FASDSP, 1989, 1991). In 1991, the Forum also noted that it had become clear that the law had remained a law only in the books, and that no one had been prosecuted under it. But even as they accuse the government of lack of political will, Forum activists acknowledge that they did make useful alliances with parts of the state. Without the encouragement and help of the health secretary and his staff, they may not have received a hearing from the state. Yet, when he was transferred (since he was a bureaucrat, not a politician), their links to the state government were broken (F8). So the alliances that they did make with the state were tenuous at best.

There have, of course, been times when the state government has consulted the Forum, but, according to a JMS member, the state may consult the Forum but does not take its advice (J2). The Forum has certainly caused many new laws to be created. The passage of the amniocentesis law and the rape law are themselves no mean feat. But while the Forum has been able to make its presence felt up to the point that the laws are passed, once the matter involves implementation and monitoring the state—that is, once the issue crosses over from the protest field to the main polity—the Forum is then excluded from the process. The lack of sustained and institutionalized access to the state is one of the prices the Forum has to pay for remaining autonomous and outside the formal political arena. At the same time, there are few autonomous groups in the world, of the size of the Forum, that could manage to be as effective as the Forum has been in dealing with the state. Had the political field not been so fragmented and had the state not recognized women as a constituency, this could not have been the case.

Accountability to National and International Feminism

The women of the Forum feel first and foremost accountable to their feminist principles. Germaine Greer, one of the feminist names best known to Indians, once declared, "The world will not change overnight, and liberation will not happen unless individual women agree to be the outcasts, eccentrics, perverts and whatever the powers-that-be choose to call them" (quoted in Phillips, 1991:136). There is in the Forum a similar defiance. Given their loyalty to feminist principles, Forum members are active in national and international feminist networks. Thus their field of influence is not geographically bound to Bombay.

The national and international feminist community plays a key role in the politics of Bombay's autonomous groups. The Forum and the Women's Centre undertake campaigns jointly with groups in Delhi and other Indian cities. They respond to events in other parts of India, such as the dismissal of women workers from the Women's Development Program in Rajasthan for attending the autonomous women's conference in Calicut in 1990. Of the five national women's movement conferences that have been held since 1980, the Forum hosted the first and the second (in 1980 and 1985), and was active in setting the agenda for the next three. Before the last conference, for example, the Forum prepared a statement analyzing the membership and the trajectory of the women's movement in India. This statement then served as a base document from which to build an agenda for the national conference. In sum, the Forum is a major player in the national network of the Indian women's movement. It is a crucial part of the constant exchange of information and ideas within the network of autonomous feminist organizations that it is shaped by and that it helps to shape. Within this network, groups challenge and support each other and come to each other's aid when necessary. The Forum's agenda, then, is set not just by the needs of Bombay's women, but by the ideas circulating in the national feminist community. Its understanding of issues, too, is in part shaped through discussions with other feminist organizations.

Similarly, the Forum is part of the international feminist community. While it is closer to feminist groups in other third world countries, such as Gabriella in the Philippines, it is undoubtedly influenced by the issues (and the theorization) of feminist movements in advanced capitalist countries. An example of such an issue is the Forum's fight against contraceptives such as Net-en, which has been banned in the West, and Norplant, which has not been adequately tested. According to a Forum activist who is critical of this campaign, where women have so little control over their fertility, it is wrong to take away the Norplant option, since no alternatives have been proposed: "You say women's fertility is too much in the control of the medical establishment, but if it's not in their control, it is in the husband's and family's control, so why focus on Norplant?" (F5). Madhu Kishwar, editor of India's foremost feminist magazine, *Manushi,* similarly criticizes the campaigns against the contraceptive Net-en as being shaped by movements against it in the West.[4]

Groups like the Forum, which are part of a larger network and are constantly interacting with activists and researchers from other countries, cannot be fully contained in a geographic space. Certainly, the Forum's success is partially due to its existence in a field where oppositional politics is fragmented and where there is no all-powerful state. But its position in Bombay's field must also be attributed to the fact that it inhabits multiple fields and hence has access to multiple networks of potential allies.

Autonomy versus Mass Base

The Forum's surprising effectiveness, given its size, belies the arguments that politically affiliated organizations make about the pointlessness of autonomous groups. Forum members have always argued that it is to their advantage not to have a mass base, because then they are not held back by the reluctance of people to change.

In the initial stages of its formation, Forum members were sharply aware of their distance from the vast majority of Indian women. In 1982, they wrote, "Bridging the cultural gap between the Forum's activists and the mass of women becomes a very important question if the Forum intends to be a mass organization" (Gothoskar and Patel, 1982). Today, however, it is clear that the Forum is not and will not be a mass organization. While the greater capacity of politically affiliated women's organizations is acknowledged by all, the very strength of these organizations is considered by some autonomous activists to be their weakness:

> The advantage that politically affiliated groups have is an entire set of relationships. . . . We can talk about housing but Mrinal Gore[5] can get housing. Yet they have the problem of not taking a stand against the party and the issue of vote banks.
>
> AWOs [autonomous women's organizations] have the advantage of not being answerable to the masses and therefore can take up certain

issues which mass-based groups can [subsequently] take up. Fundamentally, that should be our goal. . . . Forum's job is to identify and
work on strategic issues since it is not answerable to a mass base. (F1)

It is the very fact that autonomous organizations do *not* have to answer
to the electorate or to the political establishment in Bombay that gives the
Forum its power. One of the great advantages that autonomous organizations have over politically affiliated women's groups is, ironically, their lack
of a mass base. Because the Forum does not need to be accountable to "the
masses," it has been able to launch initially unpopular campaigns such as the
campaign against amniocentesis tests. Sachetana is similarly unencumbered,
but it simply does not exist in a political field that enables it to have an effect
on the CPI(M).

The Forum relies heavily on the efforts of its individual members to vol-
unteer to work on issues. Once the importance of an issue has been agreed
upon, the chances of it becoming a focus of the Forum's politics depend on
the willingness of at least two members to work on it. In one Forum member's words: "Say someone raises an issue. We have a dialogue and wait for
volunteers to do the work. If nobody is interested enough to take up a burning issue then it does not get taken up" (F2). Thus the decision to be involved in an issue sometimes makes the issue itself. Not everyone wants to
work on every issue, and so it often happens that two of the Forum's members focus on fertility, while another two focus on following a particular case
with the police. Once again, this fragmentation of an already small group,
which would result in its annihilation in Calcutta, simply keeps more issues
alive in Bombay.

The Forum: A History of Partial Victories

*Forum is a concept and cannot cease to exist. Forum is a thought
process. . . . Its ideology permeates all our work. The only vested interest in
Forum is the name and the concept.*

—Forum activist

The Forum is part of a new culture of politics that flourishes in post-
Emergency India. Small, decentralized, and consensus-based organizations
do not usually survive, and if they do, they do not usually have the influence
that the Forum does. The Forum, however, has its share of problems, stemming largely from its disavowal of explicit hierarchy. Here the founders
(called "old-timers" by one newer activist) have more power than the newer
members, the articulate have more power than the less articulate, and "in-
groups" of friends who socialize closely together outside of the meetings

exert dominance over the agenda. Members of the in-group tend to listen to each other with particular sympathy during the meetings. Yet, because it does not look like hierarchical power, it is more difficult to check (Rothschild-Whitt, 1979). In the Forum, therefore, a combination of the consensus model of decision making and tacit hierarchies has caused it to be a smaller, more homogeneous group than it may consider itself to be.

Not only is entry and exit easy in Bombay's field, but it is also easy in the Forum. Unlike the PBGMS, the Forum is not the only game in town. When members feel that their interests are not being served or that their needs are unmet, they can leave for a while or start another group. This tendency to break into smaller groups is legitimated, as Maren Carden (1978) has accurately pointed out, by feminist ideology's emphasis on personal growth and autonomy. This tendency coexists in tension with the impulse toward uniting in the ideal of sisterhood, which may explain why members of the Forum who withdraw for several years for personal or political reasons frequently return as regular members. There are yet others who attend Forum meetings only if there is a particular issue they are interested in working on. Dissenters can simply withdraw from the organization for a period of time. Nevertheless, while people drift in and out of the Forum depending on the issue at hand, they rarely leave the Forum permanently. The concept of the Forum and its ideology have been able to make their mark on Bombay. The mark is partial, it fluctuates, but it is there.

Over two decades ago, William Gamson (1975) laid down two criteria of social movement success. The first was the acceptance of a challenger as a legitimate representative of a constituency; the second, the gaining of new advantages. To these, others have added criteria such as getting movement demands on the political agenda, getting new policies implemented, and cultural outcomes such as "changes in social norms, behaviors and ways of thinking" (Staggenborg, 1995:341). The Forum has been accepted in the political field, and it has been instrumental in the passage of new legislation at both the state and federal levels. Its participation has also been critical in creating the family courts, while it may have failed at the level of implementation. But its single largest success has been to establish in Bombay the legitimacy of women as a constituency and the importance of listening to their voices, as well as the promise that the abuse of women will not go unnoticed and the assurance that there is a watchdog outside of the state.

The Janwadi Mahila Sanghatana

The Janwadi Mahila Sangathana is in the unusual position of operating both in the field of parliamentary politics and in the field of protest.[6] As the women's wing of the CPI(M), it is tied to party policies in the same way that the PBGMS is. But its existence in Bombay's political field, together with the comparative weakness of the CPI(M) there, changes the dynamic between the CPI(M) and the JMS. Its existence in Bombay also means that the position of the JMS in the field is not as weak as Sachetana's in Calcutta, and JMS strategies differ accordingly. Unlike Sachetana, the JMS does not have to resort to strategies of succession. At the same time, it cannot afford strategies of subversion, strategies that require a certain amount of power. The JMS thus seems to have chosen a strategy of sometimes peaceful, and sometimes contentious, coexistence with the rest of the women's movement.

The Parallel Trajectories of the JMS

The JMS works on issues initiated by the CPI(M), other left parties, and autonomous organizations. It sees itself as working constantly on two levels: the creation of women's leadership at the base, which is intended to exclusively benefit the party and their own organization, and the orchestration of and participation in campaigns. It is at this second level that the JMS works with other women's organizations, but it does not rely on the initiative of autonomous groups.

Articles in documents from the AIDWA, the national women's wing of the CPI(M), and in Bombay newspapers reveal that in its short period of existence, the JMS has been involved in a wide range of activities and protests. The JMS routinely sponsors anti-price-rise agitations either by itself or in conjunction with other progressive party organizations. On one particular occasion, Ahalya Rangnekar and Mrinal Gore (of the Janata Dal) led six hundred women and their children to the seat of state government in order to protest a hike in milk prices effected by the government and to demand a return to normal prices (*Indian Express,* August 24, 1988).[7] On another occasion, the JMS led over a thousand women brandishing rolling pins through a police barricade in their demand for lower prices (*Indian Express,* October 7, 1987). In these sorts of protests, the JMS is almost always accompanied by the CPI-affiliated NFIW and the Mahila Dakshata Samiti of the Janata Dal, but not by representatives of the autonomous groups.

Equality, the official publication of the AIDWA, reports that in 1991, three hundred women under the AIDWA banner demonstrated at a police station in Bombay against the murder of two nuns and the inaction of the police handling the case, and that the JMS had also successfully revoked the cancellation of leave after abortions that had been the right of bank employees until October 1990. At the same time, the JMS was involved in a campaign with other organizations to demand "proper civic amenities" for the people of low-income localities such as Kranti Nagar, Saradanagar, and Araca Colony in Bombay (AIDWA, *Women's Equality*, April–June 1991). The Forum and other autonomous organizations were also involved in the case of the murder of the two nuns, but not in the other two cases.

Part of the focus of the JMS has always been combatting the Shiv Sena. Thus, during the Bombay riots, their members tried to fight against the appeal of the Shiv Sena in the *bustees* and sometimes physically intervened to prevent houses and shops of Muslims from being torched. Engaging with the Shiv Sena at the level of the neighborhood is something only politically affiliated organizations can do, given that the members of autonomous groups do not actually live in those neighborhoods.

The JMS also uses strategies that the autonomous women's movement in Bombay would never agree to use, but it deploys them with impunity because it has the backing of the party. Ahalya Rangnekar of the JMS gleefully recounted to me tales of confronting violence with violence, of groups of women lying in wait for and beating up known harassers and wife beaters. She explained her "perfected" method for entrapping known molesters and told me of an incident in which a group of women had confronted a Shiv Sena *goonda* (thug), then summoned his leader and had the leader watch him touch the women's feet in apology. This is a method that cannot meet the approval of Bombay's autonomous groups! The conspicuous celebration of rape survivors is another example of a method that would make Bombay's autonomous feminists squirm. Here, in Ahalya Rangnekar's words, is the difference between the JMS and "the feminists":

> In Faridabad, the textile workers were not paid for six months, and when they agitated, the wives of four scheduled caste strike leaders were raped. One of the men committed suicide because his wife was now *apavitra* [impure], and the mother-in-law threw her out. We brought these women out on a platform, we garlanded them and said that they have been sacrificed and used as a class weapon. We gave the wife of the man who died a job in the CITU office. After she got a job, her mother-in-law asked her to come home. We made sure the men [the perpetrators of the crime] got arrested and when they were out on bail we beat them up. . . . The feminists would be too scared to do this. They hold press conferences and meetings but we work in the slums.

The incident is wonderful on the one hand, because of the concern for the survivors of rape and their future and also because, in a very cathartic way, it taps into a profound rage about violence against women. I was surprised to find that I had written in my notes, apparently unconsciously,

"YES!" next to the place where Ahalyatai spoke about beating up the culprits. Yet the incident, and others like it, are problematic on more than one front. It suggests an old-fashioned vigilantism that rarely has progressive implications. The public way in which the survivors are acknowledged is also problematic: One wonders about the extent to which these women were symbols first and survivors second.

The relationship between the JMS and the national body, the AIDWA, also reflects the porous boundaries of Bombay's political field. On several occasions, Bombay activists referred me to an AIDWA position paper on an issue or spoke about AIDWA initiatives that they were carrying out in the city. Not one activist in Calcutta deferred to the AIDWA on any issue. For the PBGMS, their ultimate authority was the Calcutta CPI(M), not the Delhi-based women's wing of the CPI(M). The fluidity of the boundaries of Bombay's field enhances the ability of the JMS to derive strength and sustenance from their parent body. It also means that there are many ways an issue can reach the political agenda of the women's movement in Bombay.

The JMS and the CPI(M)

The weakness of the CPI(M) in Bombay has helped the JMS, whose activists, although not equal to party activists, nonetheless approach the party on a footing of equality not seen in Calcutta. The JMS has more power precisely because the CPI(M) has less. The CPI(M) in Bombay relies heavily on a handful of effective activists, several of whom are women. There has thus evolved a culture of the "systematic promotion" of women through the SFI and the DYFI, the student and youth federations of the party (J5).

Unlike the PBGMS, which has shown a marked unwillingness to intervene in the trade union, to the extent that CITU women do not find the PBGMS of much use to them, the JMS does indeed intervene when the union is unfair to women workers. Speaking of their efforts to equalize the wages of male and female *bidi* (cigarette) workers, Ahalya Rangnekar explained:

> First we pushed the union to give priority to working women's problems. Women were considered inferior workers than men and were accordingly paid less. The *bidis* women made were tied with a red thread and the *bidis* men made were tied with a green thread. We switched the threads and tricked the bosses so they were compelled to pay the women more. The unions had not up to then taken up these issues— the men obviously did not mind the situation very much.

Four thousand women *bidi* workers marched in the streets in Sholapur in 1991. Subsequently, the union agreed to fight for equal wages for women.

This incident, together with the obvious delight with which it was narrated to me, suggests a willingness to be independent from the party union and even to challenge it. It also corroborates the acceptance in Bombay of the notion that men and women have different interests and legitimizes the need for an organization for women to represent their interests. Indeed, that logic is more powerful to the JMS than the logic of not criticizing or hurting the union, which pervades the PBGMS in Calcutta.

The JMS and Other Women's Organizations

The older JMS activists have a different relationship to autonomous feminism than do the younger activists, who feel, in some ways, accountable to the feminists in the Forum. Several of the younger JMS members come from backgrounds similar to the activists in Bombay's autonomous groups, and can thus relate to them in ways that the older Communist women cannot. Their dual sense of obligation traps them in a way that is similar to what happens in Sachetana. JMS activists are indeed answerable to their party. They are, however, also answerable to Bombay's feminist community, and when the two clash, younger JMS members are inevitably torn. In 1991, CPI(M) cadres were implicated in the rape of an activist from Kashtakari Sanghatana, a grassroots group working with tribals and peasants in Dahanu. According to members of autonomous feminist groups, JMS activists were in a terrible bind. Although they had individually expressed their outrage at the event and their sympathy for the survivor to their friends in autonomous groups, they were silenced publicly because of their party loyalties. JMS members claim they chose to be publicly silent in order to work on the investigation and to try to influence opinion within the party.

The JMS has worked with the Forum on many issues. The Jalgaon scandal of the early nineties, which involved politicians in a pornography racket, in which they blackmailed, raped, and videotaped young women, was a case in which women's groups around the state were very active. It was, in fact, the JMS that called a meeting of the Stree Mukti Andolan Sampark Samiti (the umbrella group of women's organizations in Maharashtra) to discuss statewide measures of protest (*Equality*, December 1994). Usually, however, if there is to be a joint action, the JMS first calls upon the NFIW (of the CPI), then Swadhar and Mahila Dakshata (of the Janata Dal), and then women's wings of other left-leaning parties, such as the Samajwadi Mahila Sabha and the Shramjivi Mahila Sabha. Autonomous groups such as the Forum come only after these (J2).

Part of the resentment that the JMS holds toward the Forum stems from the fact that the JMS always participates in joint action initiated by the

Forum while the Forum does not reciprocate, for example, by participating in anti-price-rise demonstrations called by the JMS: "They say it [the anti-price-rise campaign] is a *political* issue. They think that women's problems can be solved only by women. But you have to change the social outlook of society" (J1). However, the Forum does not ignore the JMS in the same way that the PBGMS ignores Sachetana, for there are times when the Forum does need to make alliances with the parliamentary left.

Members of the JMS are openly frustrated with their position vis-à-vis the autonomous women's movement and with the sense of not being fully accepted by them. They are envious also of what they perceive to be the Forum's popularity with the media—with the Forum's unchallenged place as the leader in the field. The JMS activists see their work as less flashy and rewarding and more in tune with the "masses" and resent the attention paid to the highly articulate members of the Forum. However, the ability of the JMS to overtly and publicly criticize the autonomous groups (as opposed to Sachetana's inability to publicly criticize the PBGMS) reflects the absence of concentrated power in Bombay's political field.

The JMS: Affiliated Subalternity

The strategies of social movement organizations, as we have seen, depends on their position relative to the strength of the political field. Under subordinate conditions, groups evolve survival strategies with those material and cultural resources they have at their disposal. Both Sachetana and the JMS are subordinate, but they are not subordinate in the same way. The existence of the JMS in a weaker field, combined with its affiliated status, enables it to marshal more power than Sachetana. Sachetana thus tends more toward conformity than does the JMS. The strategies of subordinate organizations depend also on the nature of the field. Specifically, strategies vary according to the dimensions of the field in which the organization is subordinate. Thus Sachetana, being subordinate in terms of both concentration of power and political culture, must oscillate. The JMS, being subordinate only in terms of political culture, can maintain a parallel trajectory.

I have said that Sachetana has found a space in Calcutta to survive but not to grow. In contrast, there are several factors that indicate the possibility of the JMS growing in terms of both power and legitimacy. The weakness of the CPI(M) vis-à-vis its affiliated organizations in Bombay is one of them. This allows the JMS some flexibility to assert its independence. Even though the autonomous groups in Bombay will always, and with some justification, be suspicious of the independence of the JMS, the voice of JMS activists will be increasingly heard in Bombay's CPI(M). That voice is, of course, a voice influenced by the Forum.

Because the political field in Bombay is so dispersed, the JMS can more comfortably find its way through the various large and small pockets not dominated by the Forum. It can thus try to build an alternative mobilization base in areas, such as the *bustees* (slums), where the Forum does not attempt to reach. Like Sachetana, the JMS shows an overt willingness to work with the dominant groups in the city. Yet the fortunes of the JMS, unlike Sachetana's, do not lie purely in the field of politics in Bombay. Its fortune is linked also to the success of the CPI(M) nationally. When the Delhi branch of the AIDWA makes news, the JMS in Bombay receives attention. Thus connection the JMS has to other political fields gives it additional sources of power, an alternative not open to Sachetana.

Epilogue

During December 1992 and January 1993, the city of Bombay was ravaged by arson, murder, and riots arising from tensions between Hindus and Muslims. The victims were disproportionately Muslim. The Shiv Sena was blatantly and triumphantly open about its involvement in attacks upon Muslim lives and property. In the midst of the mayhem, it became clear that women were some of the most avid participants in the violence, particularly the women of the Shiv Sena. Shiv Sena women burned and looted homes. They lay down on the road to prevent ambulances and army trucks from rescuing Muslims. They urged their men, in the name of masculinity, to fight for their families. How did the Shiv Sena attract the devotion of so many women? The answer that journalists and feminists in Bombay ruefully give is that the Shiv Sena built upon the autonomous feminist movement. Yet, they ask, "Having co-opted the issues that were first successfully raised by the autonomous feminist groups, how did these outfits soon overtake the other women's groups in popularity?" (Setalvad, 1995).[8]

The Shiv Sena was able to attract women to them in a way that feminist organizations could not for several reasons. First, they could take advantage of the fragmented nature of Bombay's field. The state government, with a corrupt and delegitimized Congress at the helm, did not have a strong united opposition. The Shiv Sena had the capacity to provide it. Second, their membership came from the anxious and dissatisfied lower middle classes, who had lost their jobs and had no strong representatives, given the decimation (with the Shiv Sena's help) of the unions in the early eighties. Third, their middle-level leadership lived among their membership in a way that

Bombay's feminists did not (Banerjee, 1995). Fourth, the Shiv Sena was able to build upon the feminist movement in many subtle and subversive ways.

Because of the success of groups like the Forum, political parties in Bombay began to talk about women's rights and domestic violence in the mid-eighties. Some political parties even started their own counseling centers. Women had been placed firmly on the agenda. Capitalizing on this new awareness, the Shiv Sena began to promote income-generation projects and crèches and began to talk about the power of women, using images of motherhood and the goddess Durga, encouraging women to save the nation in the way only feminine strength could. They did what the feminist movement, because of its consciousness of and commitment to diversity, did not and would not do. They built a unified identity of Hindu womanhood.

In this cultural construction, according to Flavia, the Shiv Sena was actually helped by the feminist movement, which had initially relied on Hindu images of Shakti and female power and celebrated the might of Kali, partly in order to stave off accusations of being westernized. This reliance on "Hindu iconography and Sanskrit idioms denoting woman power thus inadvertently strengthen[ed] the communal ideology that Indian, Hindu and Sanskrit are synonymous" (Flavia, 1994). While the women's movement in Bombay was the first to make it acceptable for women to march on the street for their rights, Shiv Sena women now take to the street with ease. Shiv Sena women march down the street, threatening Muslims, selectively shouting the slogans of the feminist movement: not "Hum sab ek hai," or "We are all one," but "Hum Bharat ki nari hai. Phool nahi chingari hai," or "We are the women of India—not flowers but smoldering flames." Ironic, indeed, that the permeability of Bombay's political culture and the strengths of feminism should lend themselves to such a possibility.

Madhushree Datta, a member of the Forum and the Majlis and a remarkably shrewd observer of politics, said in an interview with Sikata Banerjee (1995) that when ordinary women outside of feminist circles come to them, they may or may not get help, but they "definitely do not belong; now our [i.e., feminist] weakness is we did not realize this desire to belong," but the Shiv Sena did. That sense of belonging, that sense of community, is not something that an autonomous organization can create in any but a handful of people. Cadre-based political parties can do that—parties such as the CPI(M) and the Shiv Sena. While the CPI(M) mode of operation has been severely criticized in the new movement culture in Bombay, the Shiv Sena has sneaked by and benefited from the fragmentation of Bombay's political field and the openness and permeability of its political culture.

Chapter 9

Identity, Autonomy, the State, and Women's Movements

Third world women's movements, when not ignored or dismissed outright as derivative phenomena or products of collective hysteria (as they are in Iran and much of the Islamic world), have often suffered from the erratic critique and analysis not only by first world scholars and activists, but in some cases by participant analysts as well. Other times they have been taken less than seriously as the inevitable and homogeneous outcomes of modernization and development, or have been romanticized and idealized by well-meaning sympathizers and supporters (for example, in revolutionary Cuba, Nicaragua, and South Africa). In this book I have tried to address and rectify these problems. Through the experiences of the women's movements in Bombay and Calcutta this book has shown that women's movements are neither homogeneous nor pure products of modernization and development, but rather are embedded in particular histories and geographies. Political fields, which are the dynamic outcomes of local and regional processes, have thus shaped the women's movements in Bombay and Calcutta and elsewhere in India in very different ways. Activists within these movements consciously work to understand and assess the possibilities offered by the field within which their organizations are embedded, negotiating optimal results given existing conditions. At the same time, their identities are shaped by the fields within which they are acting collectively.

My arguments can be extended to consider the environments that shape women's movements around the world. In each case, a focus on fields argues against excessive structuralism (women's movement demands vary with levels of development) and an excessive individualism (women's movements are led and defined by certain exceptional women). It also argues against ahistorical reliance on cultural explanations for the absence or presence of women's movements. Fields, and with them the possibilities of women's movements, may change with new state regimes, such as the transition from a military to democratic government in Brazil (Alvarez, 1990) or the reunification of Germany (Ferree, 1995); new world orders that mandate new economic policies (liberalization); or resurgent ideologies, such as Islam (Moghadam, 1993). Similar phenomenon (such as veiling) may take on one meaning within one field and entirely another within a new field, and similar strategies (such as consciousness raising) may be successful in one field and fail dismally in another.

Political Fields and Organizations

For too long activists in politically autonomous groups and those in politically affiliated groups have disparaged one another, members of each doubting the others' authenticity and ability to represent women's "true" interests. But, as this study has shown, organizations are constrained in their ability to represent women by the nature of political fields. The activists of the four organizations treated in this study experience their activism, and understand their possibilities and environments, in ways that indicate that organizations similar in form (such as political affiliation or autonomy) do not necessarily have the same effects.

The Shifting Nature of Political Affiliation

Paschim Banga Ganatantrik Mahila Samiti activists are communist women in a hegemonic field dominated by the left. Their strength—their ability to make allies and to effect change—is closely tied to the continuing success of the CPI(M) in Calcutta. Because of the dominance of the CPI(M) in Calcutta's political field and its affiliation to the PBGMS, it is difficult for the PBGMS to be defiant in cases of disagreement. In Bombay, on the other hand, as the relationship with the CPI(M) union, the CITU, shows, JMS women in Bombay are more willing to criticize men in the CITU than are women in the PBGMS. Although both are affiliated to the same party, their existence in different fields allows a different range of behaviors and tactics to be available to the two organizations.

There may be internal dissent in the PBGMS around key issues such as work and sexual violence; however, its public position is to insist that food, work, and literacy are the most important issues for women and to fault the twin forces of capitalism and superstition for much that ails women. Even if PBGMS activists recognize the salience of domestic violence, which many clearly do, they do not articulate it as part of the discourse in the public sphere. The leaders of the PBGMS stubbornly refuse to politicize the personal, keeping domestic violence at the level of a private tragedy or vice, even though the grassroots activists may be more willing to speak of it in political terms. At the same time, the meaning that the PBGMS bestows on literacy is profoundly political and moving, reminding us to politicize that which many of us take for granted. In their analysis, literacy is what makes us human in the modern world, and thus to deny a little girl literacy is to deny her a chance at full humanity.

Although PBGMS activists subvert the party in little ways, they are, in the final analysis, subservient to it. They identify with the state—the ruling party, in this case—even if they are troubled by their excessive convergence with it. Because the CPI(M) is in power, the activists of the PBGMS feel that the state is in good hands. However, they feel increasingly constrained and frustrated by the inability of the state to provide for the basic needs and wants of the people. Some may therefore blame the institution of parliamentary democracy and others the party itself, but in the final analysis, PBGMS strengths and weaknesses in Calcutta stem from the same source—the dominance of the CPI(M).

JMS women are communist women in a fragmented field. The CPI(M) in Bombay is strong in neither organizational nor cultural terms. JMS women are open to influence from sources other than their party, which PBGMS women are clearly not. JMS women's understanding of issues such as domestic violence and the need for separate spheres for women is closer to that of the autonomous Forum than of the PBGMS. Thus, JMS women go so far as to claim that domestic violence is, at least in part, caused by a "will to dominate" in men. Indeed, they are nonconformists compared with their comrades in Calcutta. The younger activists understand the issue of consciousness raising, not as the PBGMS (and their own older generation) does, as something needed to rid women of superstition, but as that which enables independent thinking. Yet, unlike the Forum, JMS activists do not trust autonomy, and while they may not like those who govern the state today, they are open to working with the state when it is in friendlier hands. Indeed, they do not believe that autonomous groups can be very effective, especially when faced with a force like the Shiv Sena.

The JMS is certainly affiliated to and loyal to the CPI(M). Yet it is sharply critical of what one activist, at least, terms the "top-down business" of vanguardism that seems prevalent in Calcutta. Through their existence in Bombay's political field, JMS activists have come to appreciate the need to take women's experiences seriously, rather than to rely on leadership for answers and analysis. Although JMS activists are few, which would make them an insignificant political presence in Calcutta, they are able to function independently and effectively in their chosen areas in Bombay. Ultimately, the strength of the JMS comes from its very existence in Bombay's field and, paradoxically, the relative weakness of the CPI(M).

The Shifting Meaning of Autonomy

The Forum is a partially dominant organization in a fragmented field, and this makes it perhaps the most remarkable organization in the study. Although it has only a few members, the fragmented nature of Bombay's field makes possible its effectiveness both in initiating legislation and in influencing public culture. The Forum is also open to ideas from many directions, which means, in this case, both affecting and being affected by national and international feminist communities. The Forum's skilled activists and access to the media have enabled it to represent its views on sexuality, reproductive technologies, and violence against women to the public in ways that may not be hegemonic, but that nonetheless have reached and influenced many people. The process by which the Forum has gained legitimacy has persuaded other women's groups to reflect its views—at least in Bombay. Yet, as the political field shifts with the rise in power of the Shiv Sena, the Forum may well become less effective, since it is not equipped, in its present form, to operate successfully in a field with a higher concentration of power.

Sachetana is an autonomous organization in a hegemonic field dominated by the left. It exists in a field that privileges political affiliation and large organizations. It is also a field whose political culture continues to be shaped by a left and nationalist sentiment. Thus while Sachetana's views on work and on sexual and domestic violence may not be in accordance with the PBGMS, its views on the state and funding are not in accordance with the Forum. The power of the CPI(M) in Calcutta may lead one to assume that it is this power alone that ensures Sachetana's compliance. However, this book has shown that Sachetana members are themselves influenced by Calcutta's political culture, so that older Sachetana members are not comfortable with open discussions of issues of sexuality. Further, Sachetana's views on the nature of the Indian state incline it to work with rather than against the state—a move that the Forum would not make. Sachetana's strategies for existence are complex and serve to differentiate it further from the Forum in Bombay. On the one hand, it is willing to initiate work and literacy projects and to be openly friendly to the PBGMS. On the other hand, it constantly strives to explore precisely those spaces that the PBGMS considers nonpolitical and therefore of little relevance. Sachetana's experience shows that the definition of autonomy must always be a relative one, since hegemonic fields clearly allow a lesser degree of autonomy than do fragmented fields.

Political Fields, Women's Organizations, and the State

While national states share many characteristics in their treatment of women—their economic policies frequently hurt or marginalize women, they attempt to control women's sexuality and reproductive capacities, and they often treat women only as mothers to a new generation of citizens—the effects of states, and indeed their natures, as this study has shown, vary *locally*, and these local differences make an enormous difference to the lives and actions of women living within them.

The organizations in this study cover the range of options vis-à-vis the state, and these options are fundamentally shaped not only by the organization's energies but also by the field in which they operate. Thus the Forum was born out of a mistrust of the Congress-run state, and its members have always feared co-optation, even when they are trying to influence the state. Precisely because they acknowledge the power of the state, they refuse to become part of it, believing that the state rarely has the interests of women at heart and is more likely to use them as pawns. Their experience with the rape and amniocentesis campaigns and with the issue of domestic violence has only heightened their suspicions.

Now that the state is in the hands of the right wing, the Forum is even less likely to work with it on the local level. Yet it must then pay the cost of being marginalized, if indeed the Shiv Sena manages to make the political culture of Bombay a more homogeneous one. While it is not surprising that an organization affiliated to the parliamentary left should be willing to work with the state, the attitude of the JMS toward the effectiveness of autonomous organizations is clearly influenced by what it perceives to be the well-organized and mass-based forces of the right—a force that needs one of equal strength to counter it. Coalitions of autonomous organizations cannot match the Shiv Sena's might, but political parties can. In Bombay, as in Calcutta, the state is the most powerful actor in the political field. But those who govern the state are considered legitimate by the women's groups in Calcutta and not by the women's groups in Bombay.

PBGMS women are now part of the state—a state they consider their own. They benefit from it, and yet are increasingly aware of the price that membership in the polity demands. Their attitude toward the state reflects the attitude of the CPI(M) nationwide. The state can be friend or foe, depending upon who controls it. Indeed, participation in party politics in a parliamentary democracy means that you must be prepared to be part of the state. Thus

PBGMS women rejoice with the others in the CPI(M) with each election win, but the more thoughtful of them worry about losing their militancy.

Sachetana is an autonomous organization that is quite open to working with the state. While it knows well that the state is often an agent of exploitation, Sachetana, far from being an implacable foe of the state, believes that the interests of the state are formed out of struggle and negotiation and is thus willing to continue interaction with the state, even when recognizing its own lack of success in that arena. Sachetana's existence in a field in which an elected left governs gives it a confidence in the state that the Forum does not have.

Political Fields and Collective Identity

Weaving a middle ground between claims that identity springs directly from experience and that identity is fluctuating and discursively constructed, this book has demonstrated that collective interests and identities are shaped within political fields. I have attempted to show that the issue of the politics of personal transformation is not simply one limited to new social movements (Melucci, 1985; Cohen, 1985), but rather an issue, as Taylor and Whittier (1992) suggest, that is important for all movements. While both Calcutta's and Bombay's activists take the politics of personal transformation seriously, such transformations mean different things in the two cities, and their possibilities are contextually constrained. Activists do indeed construct and negotiate their own identities, but they do so within constraints.

It is less possible in Calcutta than in Bombay to claim a "we" that is not class based. Women's interests are thus less easily articulated in terms of individual rights. The definition of the political has been contained effectively by the CPI(M), such that only women's actions for a "larger good" are considered legitimate. In this way the party does perpetuate the perception of women as being especially active on behalf of others and for the larger good of their communities and families, not for themselves. The fight for reform within the family is, however, not considered political, but social. In this way, when a woman is engaged in struggle for democratic rights she is being political, but when she is fighting domestic abuse, she is engaged in social reform.

In Bombay's political field, however, it is possible to maintain an identity that is not class based. Thus groups like the Forum, having created a distinct "women's movement culture," are able to sustain a feminist identity and judge each other and themselves by that standard (Taylor and Whittier, 1992). They do not judge themselves against a larger Bombay-wide political culture, but forge their identities within the feminist community. The Forum defines as political precisely that which the CPI(M) leaves out, attempting to shift the understanding of the term. Thus politics does involve protesting domestic abuse and the misogynist statements of judges, but it also involves the way one protests—the language used and the stance presented.

Activists in both Bombay and Calcutta engage in actions that reinforce their collective sense of self and share common discourses that help bind them together (Snow and Benford, 1992). If Bombay activists have isolated the idea of woman from other identities, those in Calcutta have immersed that identity in so many others as to render her only partially visible. Yet, precisely because of this, Calcutta activists understand, unlike those in Bombay, that women become women not only in opposition to men but also in opposition to other women (Alarcón, 1990). That is, identities are never based purely on gender, but always on class, religion, and other complementary and competing categories as well.

Political Fields and Change

Over the course of this book, I have primarily dealt with the question of the effects of fields on the organizations within them. However, the construction and maintenance of fields is clearly a dynamic process. The contours of fields shift because of the actions of organizations within them, as well as in response to forces from the outside. These shifts, which can occur in either dimension of the field, will take different shape in hegemonic and fragmented fields. The effects organizations can have in Calcutta are obviously not the same as those they can have in Bombay.

Each time the CPI(M) gets reelected in West Bengal, its power becomes more deeply entrenched in all sectors of society. Ironically, every CPI(M) victory comes at the expense of its grassroots organizations. Thus it becomes correspondingly difficult for the PBGMS to influence a party that seems to need it less and less. While the PBGMS is powerful compared with Sachetana, its existence in Calcutta means that it is cut off, to some extent, from alternative sources of change. Its activists may differ ideologically from the party leadership, but have neither the alternative cultural resources nor the power base from which to challenge the CPI(M) to change.

Where might change then come from in a hegemonic field? The answer may lie in sources external to the field. The Indian state at the national level and the CPI(M) government in West Bengal at the regional level have tended to monitor and regulate foreign NGO activity. However, with the quickening pace of economic liberalization and India's increased openness to the world economy, there is a substantial increase in the amount of money available to NGOs from international bilateral and multilateral aid sources and, at the same time, less state regulation and intervention. This means that there now exists the possibility of resource-rich NGOs that can offer resistance to the PBGMS and the CPI(M). The increasing presence of NGOs may also help create an alternative political culture, one that perhaps will offer more space for a diversity of interests and voices.

In Bombay, the Forum has been able to alter the universe of political discourse around gender. However patchy and tortuous the process, there is little doubt that Bombay's political culture has been affected by the Forum's presence. But the alternative discourses offered by the Forum do not necessarily constitute a fully developed, singular ideology, nor does the Forum have the strength as a group to insist that its programmatic discourses be implemented in particular ways. Thus participants in Bombay's political culture face a marketplace of competing ideas, among which they are free to pick and choose, borrow and return. Precisely because change is so fractured and piecemeal in Bombay, the nativist-turned-Hindu nationalist Shiv Sena has actually been able to appropriate slogans generated by the women's movement for their own purposes (Sarkar and Butalia, 1995). In addition, the influx of NGO money into Bombay has resulted in a further splintering of groups in an already fragmented protest field at the very time that the Shiv Sena has moved from the protest field to the wider political field. The shape of Bombay's field is, at this very moment, being remade.

As the delegates made their way home from the Fourth United Nations Conference on Women in Beijing, the question on everybody's lips was, What now? What would the effects of this massive conference be on the lives of women around the world? This book has argued that the effects of the conference will vary from political field to political field, will vary not only between Zaire and Australia, but also between Calcutta and Bombay. This book can thus be read as a call, in an era of globalization, for attention to the local, because it is there that the global has its effects. If we do not closely understand the dynamics of the local, we fall once again into the trap of universalizing and homogenizing, a trap into which feminist analysts, no less than others, have readily tumbled.

Women in the same country, facing similar grievances and problems, articulate different needs and interests. Interests are not created or articulated in a vacuum, and it is through examining the operation of political fields that we will be in a better position to understand their creation and their deployment. Operating, on the one hand, without essentialist notions of women's interests, the appropriate vehicle to represent their interests, or the nature of the state, and, on the other, understanding how movements are shaped, constrained, and enabled by political fields ultimately allow for a more optimistic and open view on the possibilities of effective action for and by women. Such an approach allows us to understand both the Phoolan Devis and the Indira Gandhis, as well as the thousands of unsung, courageous, and committed fighters for a better, safer, and more just world for women.

Methodological Appendixes

Appendix A: The Study

This project was conducted over several years and involved several phases—establishing the differences between the women's movements of Calcutta and Bombay; studying the conditions under which women lived, to see whether the differences could be due to them; understanding and tracing the development of the two political fields; and finally, exploring the effects of the fields on the dominant and subordinated groups within them, as well as the ways in which they were understood and negotiated by activists. Together, these phases involved studying politics at the level of the city, region, nation, organizations, and individuals within them, which meant that an eclectical methodological approach would be most useful. I therefore varied my sources and methodology with the phase of research, using, within the broad frame of the comparative method, archival sources, newspapers, interviews, and participant observation. In this appendix I deal briefly with each.

Interviews

Interviews were my primary source of data, and I used them to establish the differences between the women's movements of Calcutta and Bombay, to understand how activists thought and strategized about the issues, and sometimes for corroboration of my understanding of particular events. Between the months of September 1990 and July 1991, and from May 1992 through July 1992, I conducted sixty-five interviews. In 1994, between August and December, I reinterviewed many of my best informants and

interviewed five activists I had not had a chance to speak to in the earlier
rounds, partly to even out the balance between Calcutta and Bombay. Thus
I had seventy informants, thirty-five from each city. The respondents were
activists from a range of women's organizations. While I ultimately focused
on four organizations, I was led to those four largely on the basis of my interviews. The respondents were from the following organizations.

Calcutta

Autonomous:

All India Women's Conference
Saroj Nalini Dutt Memorial Association
Women's Research Centre
Nari Nirjatan Pratiradh Mancha
Sachetana

Politically Affiliated:

National Federation of
    Indian Women (NFIW or PBMS)
CITU
Paschim Banga Ganatantrik
    Mahila Samiti (PBGMS)

Bombay

Autonomous:

Forum Against Oppression
    of Women
Women's Centre
Stree Uvach
Women and Media
Awaaz-e-Niswan

Politically Affiliated:

Mahila Dakshata Samiti
Janwadi Mahila Samiti
National Federation of
    Indian Women
Stree Kruti
Swadhar
Stree Mukti Sanghatana

Those who were interviewed were selected in a number of ways, but primarily by means of a "snowball" sample. First, through the newspaper accounts and my previous visits, I was able to identify some "stars." I approached them initially and asked them to name five other activists I should
talk to (I did not specify whether they were to be from politically affiliated
groups or autonomous groups, in order to double-check my assumptions
about dominant groups). This generated several overlapping lists and provided me with the second round of interviews. Soon, I narrowed my focus to
the two dominant organizations—the Forum in Bombay and the PBGMS in
Calcutta. When it became clear that to fully understand the effects of fields,
I had to study subordinate groups in each city, I widened the study to include Sachetana and the JMS. I chose Sachetana based on its autonomy and
visibility, and rounded out the study with the JMS, which was affiliated to
the CPI(M), yet subordinate within its field. Once I chose my groups, I interviewed proportionately more people from them.

I interviewed most of the active members in the the Forum, the JMS, and Sachetana. The process of interviewing PBGMS members was more complicated because of its hierarchy. Thus I interviewed the national president of PBGMS, three members of the West Bengal state committee, and then focused on the Calcutta district specifically. Within the Calcutta district committee, I interviewed the general secretary and president and three other committee members. After that I searched for grassroots leaders and activists by asking the Calcutta district committee members whom I should talk to. I also met activists at several events I attended and made appointments with them so that I could get the opinions of activists who were not necessarily the ones favored by the leadership.

How representative was my sample? I am certain of its representativeness with regard to the activists in the two cities as a whole. Since I interviewed most of the active members in Sachetana, the Forum, and the JMS, I can be sure it was representative of them, as it was of the state and district leadership of the PBGMS. I cannot be certain of representativeness with regard to the grassroots activists of the PBGMS. The only check I had for that was a consistency in the answers I received from them.

The length of the interviews varied from between forty-five minutes to all day, and the vast majority were tape-recorded. Those I could not tape—either because it was an all-day interview or because of malfunctioning equipment—I took copious notes on. Women who were used to being interviewed, especially the leaders, were clear and concise in their answers, and my interviews were correspondingly shorter. I approached activists in person or called them by telephone to make initial contact. I often met them in person even after the phone conversation in order to make them comfortable enough to agree to an interview. Interviews were conducted in Bengali, English, and Hindi, depending upon the region and the circumstances. Two interviews were conducted in Marathi with the help of a translator.

I asked each interviewee approximately the same set of questions, varying them according to their group and, in the case of the PBGMS, their position. We began with their initiation into politics, and then moved through their political lives chronologically up to the present. During this discussion, I prompted them by asking them about whether their families and partners supported their work. We then moved to the key issues and problems faced by women and possible solutions before moving to the goals of and work accomplished by their particular group. Here we discussed the details of specific campaigns the group had been involved in and problems faced by them in the course of these campaigns. The next set of questions involved the relationship of the group with other groups in the city, the state, and international funding agencies. We then returned to details about the functioning of the group and the processes by which issues were selected (questions 8 and 9; see appendix B). The logic for having these questions toward the end was that these were the questions that my respondents tended to resist most. However, after they had spoken to me for a while and were comfortable with my style and with the kinds of questions I was asking, they were more open in their responses. The final set of questions asked about the group's successes and failures, as well as about potential and actual threats to the women's movement.

After each interview, I handed each respondent a questionnaire that asked for details about their socioeconomic status, whether they worked outside the home, whether they had children, and so on. A rough schema of the order of questions and the questionnaires are presented in appendices B and C.

People's responses to the interview and indeed to the entire interview situation varied widely. There were some who never ceased to regard me with suspicion for being a researcher from the United States. Fortunately, these were very few. There were some who were curious about me and encouraged me to spend time with them after the interview, during which they asked many questions about my life in the United States. Many, especially in the PBGMS, had never spoken of their politics and their beliefs before and so took this opportunity to share their lives with me over sessions that began at ten o'clock in the morning and continued through lunch and many cups of tea. On more than one occasion, I was moved beyond words to find that the women had cooked fish and other Bengali specialties for me, knowing that I could not get these dishes in the United States.

Interviewers are haunted by questions of their relationship between themselves and their interviewees. There have been a great many essays written about the interview process, not only in terms of how to get the best interview, but also how to best balance the power relationship between oneself and the interviewee. While earlier sociological and anthropological texts advised distance, a limited friendliness and the withholding of information, feminist discussions of interviewing have rejected those standards, opting instead for more personalized, involved interviewing relationships.

I had no problems rejecting many of the old ways of interviewing. I saw no reason to hide my interest and curiosity, nor to deny others the right to expect honest answers from me. During the course of my interviews, however, I found myself playing certain roles. I realized that PBGMS leaders (who tended to be at least ten years older than I was) were more comfortable if they could treat me as a young woman who had come to them for information, to learn from them. It was only when they did not feel challenged that they dropped their guard. This was true of all the older leaders affiliated to political parties in Bombay and Calcutta. Members of the autonomous women's groups, however, enjoyed far more being challenged and respected me more if it was clear that I had done my homework. Since several members of Bombay's autonomous groups routinely write about their activism and their experiences in the women's movement and have been written about by many others, they were, not surprisingly, sometimes less patient with my questions than were members of other groups.

Participant and Nonparticipant Observation

My interviews were supplemented by my participation in and observation of meetings and events organized by the groups in this study. With the PBGMS, these included spending days at the office, helping with routine tasks, simply absorbing the atmosphere and listening to conversations and informal meetings, and attending events like the immunization camp mentioned in chapter 2 (which resulted in my photograph appearing in *Ganashakti* the following day), a memorial service for one of the founding members of the organization, and marches initiated by the samiti. I also observed the proceedings of the legal aid cells and one large formal district-level meeting. With Sachetana, I simply attended the regular Monday evening meetings, as well as their larger annual general meetings and seminars. Because I decided upon the JMS fairly late, most of my information about the JMS comes from a series of long interviews, some of which took place in the activists' homes, and observation of activists at work within their neighborhoods rather than at events.

In the case of the Forum, previous experiences with researchers had led some members to be suspicious of those who attended a few meetings and then went away to write about them. They felt that Forum members had a history with each other and that observers could never understand why people reacted in certain ways to what others said in meetings. Because of this, I did not attend any Forum meetings. I did, however, attend events and talks organized by them. These included discussions on sexuality and "gender and justice" and a protest against Chief Justice Ranganath Mishra. Other Bombay events included a discussion on turning forty by Stree Uvach, meetings of groups such as Stree Kruti and Stree Uvach, a feminist play, study circles sponsored by Vacha, a workshop on the "girl child" organized by Yuva, and rallies for the rights of female domestic workers and against domestic violence. I spent many days at the Women's Centre, talking to the activists and to people who dropped in, attending counseling sessions and their monthly "get-togethers," and reading their impressive collection of feminist periodicals.

In December 1990, there was a large gathering of women's groups in Calicut. While it was attended by members from both autonomous and politically affiliated groups, it was by and large a national meeting of autonomous women's organizations. In order to return to the women's movement at least a little of what I had received, I traveled with some members of the Forum to Calicut several days early to help with the arrangements. In that week, as we arranged sleeping, eating, and sanitation facilities for two thousand women, I met activists from around the country and spent hours deep in conversation with them about numerous aspects of the women's movement. The image of this event, more than any other, with all its exuberance and intensity, sustained me through the many long hours that fieldwork necessarily involves.

Movement Documents

In order to supplement my information about particular events as well as to learn more about the histories of the groups I was studying, I relied initially on the archives kept by the groups. This was rarely done systematically, so I had to depend far more on what individual activists had in their possession. Through members of autonomous groups in Bombay and Calcutta, I collected newsletters, press releases, position papers, minutes of meetings, letters to editors, and notes on the proceedings of previous conferences. Since autonomous groups are more openly self-reflective, these provided me with a wealth of information. Particularly helpful was the Forum publication *Moving . . . but Not Quite There,* published on their ten-year anniversary, and the Sachetana diaries.

Where the PBGMS and the JMS were concerned, however, I had access only to printed material—newsletters circulated among their members (*Sanghatan o Sangbad*) and those for sale (*Eksathe* in Bengali and *Equality* in English) and the party newspaper in Calcutta, *Ganashakti.* I supplemented these with autobiographies written by activists who had either left the party (e.g., Manikuntala Sen) or who were still in the party (Aparna Pal Choudhury and Kanak Mukherjee). I did a close reading of all these materials as much for content as for style and tone. These have been mentioned where appropriate.

Socioeconomic Data

I relied on several sources of data for the information about the socioeconomic conditions in the two cities. These include government documents found in various archives, such as annual labor or crime reports, the census, detailed national surveys based on census samples conducted by the National

Sample Survey Organization, and statistics provided by international agencies. Where such statistics were questionable, as in the case of violence against women, these reports were supplemented by other government-released statistics found in newspapers and by statistics previously compiled by other scholars. These sources are included in the bibliography.

Newspapers

The analysis of newspapers was to accomplish two tasks: to document the differences in the presentation of women's issues in Calcutta and Bombay and to provide me with the names and activities of the women's groups in Calcutta and Bombay.

To that effect, with the help of my research assistants, I closely read several newspapers for every day of the period on which this project focused. The two primary newspapers were the *Statesman* (Calcutta) and the *Times of India* (Bombay). The analysis of these newspapers, however, soon became a less important part of my project, for several reasons. While the second goal was easily accomplished, the first proved to be an impossibility, because the newspapers that actually existed for the entire period were national rather than regional, even though the *Statesman* was more focused on Calcutta and the *Times of India* more focused on Bombay. Yet, because they were national, they did not accurately reflect the fields of Bombay and Calcutta.

I thus abandoned my initial emphasis on these newspapers and have used them primarily as a means of information about certain groups and events and to get a sense of which groups were emerging in power through the decade and which were declining. My new focus on the coverage of events permitted me to expand the number of newspapers to include the *Indian Express,* the *Sunday Observer,* and the *Telegraph.* While I read the *Statesman* and *Ganashakti* in the newspaper offices, I relied on Bombay's Centre for Education and Documentation (CED) for articles from the *Times of India* and the *Indian Express.* The CED clips newspaper articles every day and maintains files on a wide variety of topics. Files on women included women and work, women and law, women and health, crimes against women, and the women's movement. This proved to be an invaluable resource because most Indian newspapers are not indexed. Thus the task of perusing a decade's worth of news for coverage on the activities of women's organization would have been even more onerous without the CED.

Appendix B: Interview Questions for Activists

(translated into Bengali, Hindi, and Marathi where necessary)

1. Tell me a little bit about yourself. When did you join _____?
   Why?
   Were you a member of any organizations before this?
   How did your parents/partner react?

2. What do you think are the key issues facing women in West Bengal/
   Maharashtra today?
   What do you think the causes are for these problems?

3. What would you say is the goal of _____?
   What issues has it mainly concerned itself with these past 3/5/10 years?
   Why that issue?

4. What is the relationship of _____ with other groups in the city? Under what
   circumstances have you acted together?

5. On what issues do you think autonomous/affiliated groups are more
   effective than affiliated/autonomous groups?
   Why?

6. What is your group's relationship to the state?
   How is your group funded? How do you feel about accepting funds from
   Indian government sources or foreign sources?

7. (For Calcutta) Do you think the Left Front government has been good for
   women?
   (For Bombay) Do you think that the condition of women in Maharashtra
   would improve if a left coalition came to power?

8. How is your group structured? Can you describe a typical meeting to me?

9. How do issues get raised at meetings? When was the last time you personally
   raised an issue?
   What makes the group choose one issue over another? For example, why
   did you choose _____ to work on?
   How do you think the membership of your group influences the kind of
   issues that are selected?
   Are there issues that you think need to be raised, but haven't been? Why not?

10. What have you personally gotten out of _____? Would you ever think of
    joining another organization?

11. Where do you think the biggest threat to the women's movement in West
    Bengal/Maharashtra comes from?

Appendix C: Background Questions for Activists

1. Please check your age group from the following categories:
   20–25 _____   30–35 _____   40–45 _____   50+ _____
   25–30 _____   35–40 _____   45–50 _____

2. Are you single/married/divorced/widowed?

3. How many people live in your household?

4. If you have children, how many children do you have?
   How old were you when you had your first child? _____ Last? _____

5. What is your approximate household income?
   Less than Rs 2,000 a month _____   Rs 5,001–7,000 _____
   Rs 2,001–3,000 _____   Rs 7,001+ _____
   Rs 3,000–5,000 _____

6. What is your educational background?

7. Do you get a salary or honorarium for the work you do in the movement?
   If not, do you have another job?

8. Do you contribute to the income of your household?
   About what percent?

9. Who handles the money in your house? That is, who makes decisions about
   expenditures?
   Who made these decisions in your family as you were growing up?

10. If members of your family were ever or are at present politically active,
    please write down what you can about their involvement.

Notes

1. Women's Movements and Political Fields

1. The term "scheduled caste" refers to castes at the lowest rung of Indian caste hierarchy.

2. Phoolan Devi was elected from Mirzapur in the state of Uttar Pradesh in the elections of 1996 from the Samajwadi Party, and lost in the 1998 elections.

3. The first women's organization was the Bharat Stri Mahamandal, formed in 1917, followed by the Women's Indian Association (WIA) and the All India Women's Conference (AIWC) in 1927. Both the AIWC and the WIA began with "women's issues" such as education and social and legal reform, but refused to admit any alliance with Western feminists. Although officially apolitical, there were always strong links between these organizations and the nationalist movement. The AIWC became the best-known recognized organization representing women and grew from an initial membership of 5,000 to over 25,000 in 1945 (Omvedt, 1987). While they were surely influenced by the tradition of male reformers, their demands were eventually far more radical. Particular victories for the AIWC included the Child Marriage Restraint Act of 1929, struggles against purdah, and the campaign for women's suffrage (Forbes, 1981). Alongside the AIWC, however, there grew a Communist-led women's movement. In Bengal, they formed the Mahila Atmaraksha Samiti; in Punjab, the Women's Self-Defense League; in Andhra, the Mahila Sangam (Chakravarty, 1980).

4. For more detailed histories of the Indian women's movement, please see Gandhi and Shah (1991); Kumar (1989, 1993); Calman (1992); N. Desai (1988); Gothoskar and Patel (1982); Jayawardena (1986); and Omvedt (1986b, 1987, 1993).

5. I refer throughout this study to "women's movements" rather than to "feminist movements" to avoid entering into a discussion of which movement is more "feminist." I argue that preconceived notions of "legitimate" women's issues limit our ability to

understand the profound gender implications of, and struggles around, every aspect of women's lives. I do, however use the term "feminist" for those who self-identify as such.

6. See, for example, DiMaggio and Powell (1991). Other definitions are offered by Bourdieu (Bourdieu and Wacquant, 1992:97): "In analytical terms, a field may be defined as a network, or a configuration, of objective relations between positions." In the words of Fligstein and McAdam (1993), a strategic action field is "designed to capture the socially constructed, internally self-referential negotiated nature of the arenas within which strategic action takes place."

7. In a recent volume, Kriesi and Koopmans et al. (1995:33) reject the concept of political culture, finding it too vague and ultimately unhelpful. Rather than consider the role of "political culture" in the emergence of social movements, they prefer what they call "prevailing strategies," or those informal ways in which particular political traditions deal with challengers. This highly instrumental and narrow approach to culture is precisely the problem with the adoption of the Political Opportunity Structure approach.

8. The notion of "political culture," first popularized by conservatives and modernization theorists such as Almond and Verba (1964) and Pye and Verba (1965), carried with it strong biases about possibilities for democracy in developing countries. Here I employ a newer use of the concept, revived by scholars such as Gamson (1988), Inglehart (1988), and Wildavsky (1987). See Tarrow (1992) for a useful review of the application of the concept of political culture to collective action.

9. Jenson (1987a) terms this the "universe of political discourse," which is a consequence of the basic social arrangements in any society.

10. Jenkins (1983) distinguishes between power and mobilizing resources; McCarthy and Zald (1977) list money, facilities, labor, and legitimacy; Tilly (1978) lists land, labor, capital, and technical expertise; Etzioni (1968) lists coercive, utilitarian, and normative assets; and Freeman (1979) writes about tangible and intangible assets.

11. The examples I give here are at the national level, while my analysis is conducted at a subnational level. Political fields exist at both levels, and the relevant field would depend on the nature of the movement. If we take, for example, the women's movement in Italy as described by Hellman (1987), the political field of Milan is fragmented, while Turin is hegemonic.

12. Ryan (1989) offers an account of the U.S. women's movement, in which internal movement dynamics play a crucial role in the way it unfolds, while Whittier (1995) argues that the meaning of feminism is shaped by the interaction of both internal and external (context) processes. I am grateful to Verta Taylor for this insight.

13. See Conell and Voss (1990) for an example of this.

14. For a smattering of the vast literature on this topic, see, for example, MacKinnon (1983); Barrett (1980); Phillips (1991); Eisenstein (1984); Fraser (1989); Laslett, Brenner, and Arat (1995); Afshar (1987); Charlton, Everett, and Staudt (1989); and FAOW (1990).

15. See for example, Laslett, Brenner, and Arat (1995); for Latin America, Molyneux (1981, 1985), Chinchilla (1992), Alvarez (1990), and Barrig (1989); for Iran, Moghadam (1994b); for China, Gilmartin (1989); for the U.S., Costain and Costain

(1987) and Staggenborg (1991); and for Western Europe, Gelb (1989) and Ruggie (1984).

16. See, for example, Ferree and Yancey Martin (1995) and Rothschild-Whitt (1979).

17. See, for example, the lead essay in *Women and Revolution* (Sargent, 1981) by Hartmann and the responses by Young, Joseph, Vogel, and others; Rowbotham, Segal, and Wainwright (1979); Evans (1979); and more recently Segal (1991) and DuBois (1991).

18. Gilmartin (1989) shows that while the Chinese Communist Party (CCP) started out with the position that women's issues had to be addressed in the course of the revolution, rather than after, they began to revise women's programs drastically when threatened by the Guomindang. The Guomindang seized upon Communist women as a way to separate themselves from the Communists and labeled women organizers as promiscuous and immoral. The CCP began to revise its position on women when it was pushed into the hinterland by the Guomindang.

19. Today this debate has come to be called the equality-difference debate. The crux of the debate focuses on the extent to which one emphasizes women's similarities with or differences from men. Clearly the issue carries with it many political repercussions. For a recent anthology on this, see Hirsch and Fox Keller (1990) and Butler and Scott (1992). See also feminist standpoint theorists such as Smith (1987) and Collins (1991) for notions of identity based on experience.

2. From Lived Experiences to Political Action

1. In table 2.1, the issue *employment and poverty* refers to the view that women's problems stem primarily from the fact that they (and their families) are poor and that they have no jobs. Thus they suffer from malnutrition and the health problems that arise out of lack of availability of clean drinking water and adequate sanitation. *Literacy and skill acquisition* is linked to the issue of employment and poverty. In order to get jobs, women must be trained. In order to fight for their rights they must be made literate. *Violence* refers to all aspects of violence toward women—by husbands and other family members, the state, strangers, and so on. *Consciousness* refers to the idea that women are unaware of their rights and are hesitant, because of cultural taboos and superstitions, to act in their own interests. *Family-related issues* refer to the range of controls that families place on women. Families are considered to be the locus of patriarchal control. This category also includes struggles for a more equal division of labor within the family. *Fundamentalism* refers to the idea that the rise of religious fundamentalism affects the way women are viewed and treated. It refers to Hindu and Muslim fundamentalism as well as that of other religions. As religious identities become more prominent, religious differentiation often takes the guise of increasingly circumscribed rules of conduct for women. *Low social status* is a medley category that refers to the overall conditions and lack of respect within which women have to live. This response reflects a belief that it is a mixture of opportunities, socialization, and values that is responsible for women's oppression. *Consumer issues* reflect a variety of concerns—the availability of water and electricity,

paved roads, the price of essential commodities, and so on. *System* refers to the notion that it is the capitalist system or patriarchy that is the main problem. That is, the problem is the way the entire system within which we live has been set up. *Ecology* refers to problems, such as deforestation, that are seen to affect women more than men. *State co-optation* of women and their issues is seen as one of the main problems facing women today, a situation that reflects a deep lack of trust in the state.

2. While I do not discount the possibility of entrepreneur-created movements, as suggested by McCarthy and Zald (1977), such movements are clearly limited to particular moments in affluent nations such as the United States.

3. Gutentag and Secord (1983) hypothesize that a surplus of females (in a situation of male privilege) in the population acts as an impetus to the development of women's movements because under these circumstances, women are more independent from men and tend to participate in the labor force in larger numbers.

4. Nirmala Banerjee reports that in urban areas of India as a whole only 9 percent of women were married by age 19 in 1987–88 (Nirmala Banerjee, 1992:19).

5. Rossi (1988) hypothesizes that unattached women play a key role in women's right's movements because of their relative freedom from men. It is difficult to find "unattached" women in India, because even if they are not married, they are attached to their fathers and families. This kind of argument may have more validity under two sets of conditions—when women earn enough money to be independent or when they control their own assets (such as in many African countries where women own plots of land).

6. As reported by Safa (1990), a study of women's voting patterns in Chile found that two months prior to the plebiscite in 1989 intended to bring an end to military rule, more housewives than working women supported military dictator General Augusto Pinochet.

7. Thus, women doing subcontracted work in isolation in their homes are less likely to organize than are women working in a factory. (See, for example, Beneria and Roldan, 1987.)

8. Of the women she interviewed, Standing found a clear division between natives of West Bengal and those who had come to Calcutta as refugees from East Bengal. (This refers to Hindus who migrated to West Bengal after the partition of India in 1947. Approximately 15 percent of Calcutta households are refugee households.) West Bengal natives were more likely to be conservative in their outlook with regard to women's work, preferring their women to work in teaching and public-sector clerical jobs. Financial pressures in refugee households led to the acceptability of a far wider range of jobs for women from East Bengal.

9. Mutatkar (1990) reports that prior to 1981, Maharashtra led the country in industrial employment proportional to population.

10. While there have always been disproportionately more male workers in industry, partly because of the patterns of migration, this does not account for the historic decrease in numbers of women in manufacturing. In a fascinating study of the Bombay textile industry, Kumar (1983) attributes the decline in women's employment to changes in official colonial discourses about "the male worker," family, housing, and morality be-

tween 1919 and 1939. Kumar demonstrates the ways in which government surveys ignored the numbers of women workers and the complexity of family forms and persisted in defining the family as one that had a male breadwinner, a female homemaker, and children—much as it was being defined in England at that time. Further, in a study of Bombay's textile industry, Savara (1986) concludes that it was protective legislation that had the strongest negative impact on women's work in factories. While there were also enormous decreases in women's employment in manufacturing in Calcutta during this period, the causes for this are less clear-cut. Trade unions in both cities were certainly responsible for some of the decline, since they did press for either protective legislation or the principle of family wage, thus helping to push women out of the labor force.

11. According to an estimate by researcher Bela Bandopadhyay (personal communication, February 1991), 60 percent of unorganized working women in Calcutta are those who work as housemaids, part-time maids, and cooks.

12. Hindu women are governed by the Hindu Marriage Act of 1955 and the Hindu Adoption and Maintenance Act of 1956. Christian women are governed by the Christian Divorce Act of 1869, while Muslim women are governed by the Dissolution of the Muslim Marriages Act of 1939 and the Muslim Shariat Laws Application Act of 1937 (A. R. Desai, 1990).

13. The Muslim Women (Protection of Divorce) Act of 1986 was the site of enormous struggle around issues of religious freedoms and women's rights. This act made invalid a judgment (popularly called the "Shah Bano judgment") in 1985 that awarded to an elderly Muslim woman the right to maintenance following her divorce.

14. The early social reform movement was led by men, many of whom wanted to prove to the British that Hindu traditions contained within them ideals of womanhood superior to those of the British (Chatterjee, 1989; Mani, 1989). As the British launched strong critiques of Hindu civilization, Indian reformers, trying to emphasize the glory of the ancient past, sought to reinterpret the Vedic texts and challenge British interpretations of them (Omvedt, 1987; Jayawardena, 1986).

The earliest issues involved the banning of sati (the burning of a widow on the funeral pyre of her husband), polygamy and child marriages, the encouragement of widow remarriage and widow's property rights (a woman had no claim on her husband's property upon his death), and girls' education. The beginning of the movement is dated to Raja Ram Mohan Roy's inauguration of the campaign against sati in 1818 and its abolition in 1829, often considered the colonial government's first intervention in the sphere of "personal law." This was followed by Ishwar Chandra Vidyasagar's campaign for widow remarriage.

Because the impetus behind many of the male social reformers was ultimately resistance to the British, the social reform movement was soon divided in two. On the one hand there were the liberal democrats and rationalists of the Brahmo Samaj, such as Ram Mohan Roy and Jyoti Rao Phule, founder of the Satyashodhak Samaj (which linked caste and gender oppression). These were men who based their arguments on bourgeois individualism and liberal ideology rather than on the ancient Vedas. In contrast, other organizations, such as the Prarthana Samaj, defined themselves within the Hindu tradition.

Their leaders themselves married child brides and attempted only those bits of progressive legislation that did not interfere with Hinduism. Later organizations within this tradition, such as the Arya Samaj (founded in 1875) and the Ramakrishna Mission (founded in 1897), encouraged women's education and were ready to raise the age of marriage, but all these changes were to take place within the framework of Hinduism.

15. However, while state and local employment accounts for at least 50 percent of public employment, the states have little autonomy with regard to industrial and commercial licensing powers, nomination of the governor, selection of bureaucracies, and shares of central taxes and levies, which are apportioned by the central government (Vanaik, 1990:124).

16. In a CPI publication titled *Emergency and the Communist Party*, the authors declared the Emergency to be a "preemptive strike against the conspiracy of counterrevolution and fascist forces," in which Indira Gandhi represented the progressive forces and J. P. Narayan and others the reactionary forces. Further, addressing the concerns of those who could not accept the curtailed freedoms imposed by the Emergency, it explained: "Unfortunately the demagogic propaganda of reaction has affected some genuine democrats also. Steeped in formal bourgeois democratic ideas, they are taken aback by the press censorship, certain curbs on the functioning of legislatures, curbs on judicial institutions etc. . . . They do not see that the main blow is directed against reaction."

17. While some writers claim that the CPI(M) did not defy the Congress strongly enough at this time and that only Maoist parties did (Vanaik, 1990), this was clearly not the perception in Bengal.

18. Because of the separation of the study of "regular" politics from the study of social movements, we often fail to see the intimate connections between the two. See Aminzade (1995) for the importance of looking at electoral and movement politics in conjunction with each other, and see also Tarrow (1990).

19. These figures come from the analysis of the *Times of India, Indian Express, Loksatta* (all Bombay based), and the *Statesman, Ananda Bazaar Patrika,* and *Ganashakti* (all Calcutta based) between the years 1980 and 1990. The figures do not add up to 100 percent because I have not included references to organizations such as women's organizations in other countries, religious organizations, and social work organizations.

20. "Autonomous" refers to those organizations that are independent of political parties with regard to funding and organization, while "affiliated" refers to those organizations that are linked to political parties.

3. Calcutta

1. *Sanghatan o Sangbad,* the intraorganizational journal of the PBGMS, outlined a three-stage project implementation plan (*Sanghatan o Sangbad,* January 1990). The first stage was to involve a detailed report about the levels of education among their members, to be compiled by each district. The second stage was to involve holding camps for educators that would last for two to three days in each district. This was to yield fifty educators. Each of these educators would then train three other educators and so on. Soon the literacy camps were to be opened and each camp was to last for approximately four

months (between April and July, so that it did not interfere with farmwork in July and August), by which time each educator was to make thirty people literate. The plans were worked out in infinite detail with regard to timing, personnel, and expected outcome. It was also specified that before the opening of any camps, there were to be neighborhood meetings to ensure the backing and enthusiasm of the local people.

Writing in *Eksathe,* the widely distributed publication of the PBGMS, Mrinalini Dasgupta explained the logic by which these camps were to be conducted. Explaining the need to live with and be one with those whom they were trying to educate, she urged patience and humility. She cautioned those who were involved in educating adults not to treat them as if they were children incapable of sophisticated thought, but rather to draw upon their already existing knowledge. The actual plan is a clear modification of the method popularized by Brazilian radical educator Paolo Freire.

Freire suggested starting with words already understood by people—words that had meaning in everyday life, such as "favela," or shantytown, and then breaking up the syllables of the word ("fa", "ve," and "la") to combine them in ways that would create other words (Freire, 1970). Similarly, the PBGMS recommended starting with the words "khhat-bo khhabo," which means "we will work and we will eat."

2. This notation will be followed for my interviews with women activists in Bombay and Calcutta, conducted in 1990–91, 1992, and 1994. F represents the Forum Against Oppression of Women; W, the Women's Centre; J, Janwadi Mahila Sanghatana; P, the PBGMS; S, Sachetana; N, the NNPM; and M, Women in Media. Here P stands for the organization and 11 for the number I assigned the respondent.

3. The Lenin-Roy debates at the Second International centered on the question of supporting national elites in their struggle against colonialism. Lenin supported this idea while M. N. Roy opposed it (Mallick, 1993:11).

4. Literally "gentlemen," *bhadralok* refers to the middle-class intelligentsia that emerged in colonial Bengal. Bengal was the first to experience westernization, and the opportunities of Western education provided Bengali Hindus a foot in the door in the civil service of the British Raj.

5. Partition also marked the end of the predominance of Bengal in Indian politics, since with the division of its land, West Bengal was left with only forty-two members of Parliament (Mallick, 1993:24).

6. Mallick (1993:27) notes that in the early 1970s, only 34.8 percent of managers in the Calcutta Management Association were Bengali.

7. For a sample of writings on the Naxalites, see Sumanta Banerjee (1984), Dasgupta (1975), and Ghosh (1974).

8. Out of a total of 294 seats in the West Bengal Legislative Assembly, the Left Front Coalition won 230 in 1977, with the CPI(M) winning 177 of those. In 1991, the CPI(M) won 188 seats, although it slipped to 150 seats during the last election (1996). Other members of the coalition have included, at various times, the CPI, the Revolutionary Socialist Party, and the Forward Bloc, among others.

9. See, for example, Przeworski (1980), Esping-Anderson (1985), and Basu (1992).

10. Obviously, the profile of the PBGMS, with its two million members, does not fit the profile of a standard women's organization. This is just the number of members on the rolls, not the number of active members.

11. The two most popular leaders of the Bengal Congress, Somen Mitra and Mamata Banerjee (who has now formed her own political party), were often embroiled in public quarrels with one another, each cutting the other down publicly in an attempt to promote him- or herself as the ultimate leader of the Congress in Bengal.

12. With the outbreak of World War II, Calcutta, together with the rest of the country, resented the assumption that Indians would fight on the side of the British. But unlike the rest of India, many Bengalis threw their support behind Netaji Subhas Chandra Bose, who refused to cooperate with the British in any way, choosing to ally with the Germans and the Japanese against the British army and enlisting Japanese help to liberate India.

13. See, for example, the writings of Nazrul Islam, Sukanta, and Tarashankar and the plays of the Indian People's Theatre Association.

14. See, for example, the writings of Tanika Sarkar (1991, 1992) on rape and gender ideology and nationalist images of women, respectively.

15. See, for example, the writings of Mahasveta Devi, particularly the play *Hajar Churashir Ma* and the short story "Draupadi," and the writings of Ashapurna Devi, particularly the novel *Pratham Pratisruti.*

16. According to veteran CPI and National Federation of Women activist Vidya Munshi, while MARS did not consider itself a feminist organization, it was involved with what are now called feminist issues such as the Hindu Code Bill (to fight for better rights for Hindu women): "If we did social work, it was through the lens of joint activity to solve women's problems through mutual help."

4. Negotiating a Homogeneous Political Culture

1. One older woman was thrown out of her hostel for reading "communist propaganda," while another sixty-five-year-old activist joined the student wing of the party secretly and then started teaching private classes in order to be economically independent of her father.

2. As Basu (1992:56) points out, most of the young women who joined the party between 1939 and 1942 were from wealthy, conservative families. Several of these women, who left their families and moved to Calcutta to be politically active, stayed at a communal house run by an older Communist woman, Manikuntala Sen. This house, in which both men and women lived, is the subject of much speculation and is often cited as evidence of the potential the party once had to break down gender barriers. It is, of course, not something either the CPI or the CPI(M) would consider today.

3. Clara Zetkin was a German Marxist feminist who had heated debates with Lenin over the "woman question."

4. "And yet," says Anna, "there were always two personalities in me, 'the communist' and Anna, and Anna judged the communist all the time. And vice versa" (from Lessing, 1962).

5. See Velayudhan (1991) and Karat (1991) for a defense of the relationship of the CPI(M) with women and a condemnation of Shyamali Gupta's statement. Velayudhan and Karat are both high-ranking AIDWA leaders.

6. On the last page of their newsletter, which came out at the time of the Gulf War, is a demand to stop the war. Sachetana activists deem it important never to focus on narrowly defined women's issues. If they are against violence, they are against all of its manifestations.

7. *Didi,* or elder sister in Bengali, is often used as a term of respect for a woman who is older than the speaker. Here it refers to women leaders.

8. The Birlas are one of the largest industrial families in India. They are largely based in Calcutta, but are not Bengali. They belong to an immensely successful entrepreneurial ethnic group from Rajasthan—the Marwaris. It is not surprising that it is easier to rouse anger against the Marwaris, who in popular perception own half of Calcutta, than against Bengali entrepreneurs.

5. Domination and Subordination in Calcutta

1. G. K. Lieten, "For a New Debate on West Bengal," *Economic and Political Weekly* 29 (1994).

2. The question of the possible disagreement between the PBGMS and the CPI(M) was the single most difficult of all the questions I asked during my year of fieldwork. It was this question that made people decide to stop talking to me or to look searchingly at me before they answered to gauge how far I could be trusted. In one case, I was told point blank: "Before I can answer that I must ask whether you completely and fully support the party." When I answered that I supported many things the party had done and stood for, I was told "very well, I will reply accordingly." I never quite figured out what "accordingly" meant under those circumstances.

3. This is similar to the English warning to be careful what you wish for lest you are granted it.

6. Bombay

1. *Sunday Observer,* November 23, 1986. The word "morcha" is best translated as "demonstration."

2. In India Children's Day is celebrated every year on November 14, the birthday of India's first prime minister, Jawaharlal Nehru, who is said to have loved children.

3. It is, of course, likely that amniocentesis might have become an issue even if the activist's mother had not made the request of her daughter, and that it was simply a trigger for the campaign, which was already in the consciousness of Bombay activists. I have reported the account of this part of the campaign exactly as it was told to me.

4. When the Shiv Sena gained enough of a voice in the late 1960s and early 1970s to wage their relentless campaign calling for the reservation of jobs and seats in universities for native Maharashtrians, the Maharashtra state government succumbed to its demands more than once (Weiner and Katzenstein, 1981).

5. The Shiv Sena described capitalists as *annadatas,* or food-givers, on the one hand, while describing the people from the South, or *lungiwalas* (those who wear *lungis,* a style of clothing prevalent in South India), as "criminals, gamblers, illicit liquor distillers, pimps, goondas and communists" (Gangadharan, 1970:19–20).

6. Sujatha Gothoskar, who worked with a CPI-affiliated union during the Emergency, recalls how workers would ask her how she could support an oppressor. When she began telling them that she did not support the actions of the Congress, she and her coworkers were thrown out (Gothoskar, personal communication, December 20, 1990).

7. Most recently, the attempt to create an alliance between the Progressive Democratic Front (composed of the Janata Dal, the Peasant and Workers Party, and elements of the Republican Party of India) and the Bahujan Shramik Samiti (composed of the parties of the left) in order to contest the 1996 election fell apart (*EPW,* 1995b).

8. While the Shiv Sena is now in power in Bombay, this was not so for the period of my study, 1977–92.

9. In trying to explain what came to be called the Datta Samant phenomenon, journalist Sandeep Pendse wrote: "The limitations of the red flag unions created a vacuum of leadership and representation among the Bombay working class. The Datta Samant wave could only be conceivable in such a vacuum" (Pendse, 1981).

10. It is Pune, not Bombay, that is the Maharashtrian cultural capital.

11. In making the case that affiliated groups owe their allegiance to the party, the authors of a comprehensive article on the successes and failures of the Sampark Samiti narrate this story about a women's delegation meeting with the chief minister of Maharashtra. The women's delegation submitted a comprehensive list of demands, mostly related to women's problems. At the end of the long list were added two demands—the first for world peace and the second a call to stop nuclear warfare. In the course of the subsequent face-to-face discussion with the chief minister, these last two were stressed by the party-affiliated women, who were a part of the delegation. The chief minister seized upon the opportunity and expressed "complete agreement" with the agitators on these points. But this only led to sidetracking the main demands relating to women. It is not as if the non-party-affiliated women were not in agreement on such issues as peace and a call to end nuclear warfare, but the disagreement related to the "priority" allotted to each (Lele, Sathe, et al., n.d.).

12. The Telengana struggle, immortalized in the history of popular movements in India, took place in the late 1940s and early 1950s in Telengana, Andhra Pradesh, under the leadership of the Communist Party. Women were at the forefront of this war of landless laborers and peasants against landlords and the state.

13. The policemen accused of rape in the case were at first acquitted and then found guilty at the High Court level. The Supreme Court then overruled the High Court verdict, claiming that Mathura willingly submitted to intercourse with the two policemen.

7. Coexistence in a Heterogeneous Political Culture

1. Eve teasing is a peculiarly Indian term that refers to the male practice of harassing women in public spaces such as roads, buses, and cinema halls. It is also a term that

Bombay's feminists have protested because it is a cute name for what is actually an act of molestation.

2. The consciousness of feminist work in the West and the connections with the international feminist community are often revealed in the writings of Bombay's feminists: "Rape has been quite a sensitive and sensational issue for the women's movement in the west for quite some time. Some of us feminists in Bombay have received posters and books from feminist friends abroad, but we had never thought that an effective campaign could be built up in India" (Chhaya Datar [1988], writing about the beginnings of the Forum's antirape campaign in 1980).

3. The Women's Centre Newsletter of January–April 1989 discusses a case in detail to give readers some sense of the complexities involved in helping individual women. The case involves a woman, Sarla, married to a rich doctor for nine years. She once worked at a bank but her husband insisted she give up her job. At the time she approached the Women's Centre, she was a housewife with a seven-year-old daughter. Her husband, who was having an affair, sued her for divorce on the grounds of mental cruelty: "He says that his is a 'joint Hindu family' and Sarla does not know how to behave in such a family. She was reluctant to give up her job on marriage and the process of persuading her to do so has caused her husband a lot of anguish." Another incident mentioned by her husband was that when he hurt his leg she was not sympathetic. The judge ruled in his favor and granted him a divorce on those grounds. Sarla challenged the verdict: "Sarla is an ordinary, conventional woman, who had an arranged marriage with a man chosen by her parents. She feels that her marriage, its underlying presumptions were a lie. Her husband has betrayed those presumptions. But society has not punished him." The question asked by the Centre is, Should Sarla simply have granted her husband the divorce and accepted some money from him? If she did that, she would have to start life over again, "jobless and houseless, burdened with a child, shattered, feeling humiliated. . . . in their community back in the village, he would appear to be the victor and she the rejected and vanquished. . . . 'Give me back my years', Sarla said to her lawyer, 'bring me back to where I was and what I was when I got married. I will then give you a settlement and will not ask for any money. Can you do that?'" (Women's Centre Newsletter, 1989). The activists in the Women's Centre know that Sarla has an enormous fight ahead of her—a fight to keep a bad marriage. What Sarla sees as in her strategic interest is in fact against her human interest. They also note that only two of the thirty-seven women who have come to the Centre between the months of January and April 1989 mentioned their desire for a divorce.

4. In her discussion of the U.S. women's movement in the 1970s Phillips (1991: 137) writes of women who "gloried in having released themselves from the preoccupations of a purely socialist politics. . . . Class had been too much tainted by Neanderthal socialists who saw in feminism only a Bourgeois concern."

5. As Echols (1989) has demonstrated in her account of radical feminism in the United States, its tendency to speak in universalistic and hyperbolic terms about gender was in large part a reaction to the traditional left's subordination of gender. While the Forum can by no means be called "radical feminist" in orientation, the process of setting itself up in opposition to the traditional left has had a similar effect.

8. Domination and Subordination in Bombay

1. During the amniocentesis campaign several of their male friends, members of the Medico Friends Circle and People Science Movement, wrote feature articles in both Marathi and English-language newspapers. A 1983 article by two activists discusses the case of the abuse of two women in a rich Muslim community as well as the march initiated by the Forum in their support (*Sunday Observer,* February 13, 1983). There are many such examples.

2. See, for example, *Times of India,* June 10, 1989, June 18, 1989, July 23, 1989; *Sunday Observer,* July 30, 1989; and *Indian Express,* May 30, 1990.

3. "When we were at the initial stage of each issue, everyone could talk about everything. But now we must deal with complexities and we need expertise. There should be serious study and analysis" (F5).

4. Author's interview with Madhu Kishwar, WORT-FM, Madison, Wisconsin, April 1993.

5. Mrinal Gore, known affectionately as "Paniwalibai," or "the lady who gets water," is a socialist and member of the Janata Dal who tried to bring water to all areas of Bombay.

6. The JMS is a new organization in Bombay. Since it officially started in 1988 and seems to have expanded only in the last few years (their membership in the state of Maharashtra doubled from 7,000 to 15,000 between 1992 and 1993), an account of its activities cannot be as rich as those of the other organizations in this study. It simply has not existed as long or done as much.

7. Ahalya Rangnekar is one of the best-known political figures in Bombay. She has been an elected member of Parliament and of the Bombay Municipal Corporation. People may not know the JMS but they know Ahalya Rangnekar. Thus the JMS often finds itself dealing with cases ranging from sexual harassment to discrimination at work because people have come to Ahalyatai for help.

8. Since these events took place after the bulk of my fieldwork I rely here on conversations with feminist and filmmaker Madhushree Datta and feminist lawyer Flavia Agnes, as well as the writings of Teesta Setalvad, Sikata Banerjee, Tanika Sarkar, and Flavia.

Bibliography

Secondary Sources

Abdo, Nahla. 1994. "Nationalism and Feminism: Palestinian Women and the Intifada—No Going Back?" In *Gender and National Identity,* edited by Valentine Moghadam. London: Zed Books.

Abraham, Amrita. 1979. "Gendarme of the Bourgeoisie." *Economic and Political Weekly* 14 (15): 685–86.

Afshar, Haleh. 1987. *Women, State, and Ideology: Studies from Africa and Asia.* Albany, N.Y.: State University of New York Press.

Agarwal, Bina. 1988. *Structures of Patriarchy: The State, the Community, and the Household.* London: Zed Books.

Ahooja-Patel, Krishna. 1993. "Gender Distance among Countries." *Economic and Political Weekly* 28 (7): 295–305.

Alarcón, Norma. 1990. "The Theoretical Subjects of *This Bridge Called My Back* and Anglo-American Feminism." In *Making Face, Making Soul,* edited by Gloria Anzaldúa. San Francisco: Aunt Lute.

Alexander, M. Jacqui, and Chandra Talpade Mohanty. 1996. "Introduction: Genealogies, Legacies, Movements." In *Feminist Genealogies, Colonial Legacies, Democratic Futures,* edited by M. Jacqui Alexander and Chandra Talpade Mohanty. New York: Routledge.

Almond, Gabriel, and Sidney Verba. 1964. *The Civic Culture: Political Attitudes and Democracy in Five Nations.* Boston: Little, Brown.

Alvarez, Sonia E. 1990. *Engendering Democracy in Brazil.* Princeton, N.J.: Princeton University Press.

Aminzade, Ronald. 1995. "Between Movement and Party: The Transformation of Mid-Nineteenth-Century French Republicanism." In *The Politics of Social Protest,* edited by J. Craig Jenkins and Bert Klandermans. Minneapolis: University of Minnesota Press.

Andreas, Carol. 1985. *When Women Rebel: The Rise of Popular Feminism in Peru.* Westport, Conn.: Lawrence Hill.

Arunachalam, A. B. 1978. "Bombay: An Expanding Metropolis." In *Million Cities of India,* edited by R. P. Mishra. New Delhi: Vikas.

Bala, Usha, and Anshu Sharma. 1986. *Indian Women Freedom Fighters, 1857–1947.* New Delhi: Manohar, 1986.

Banerjee, Nirmala. 1989. "Trends in Women's Employment, 1971–81: Some Macro-Level Observations." *Economic and Political Weekly* 24 (17): WS10–23.

———. 1991. *Indian Women in a Changing Industrial Scenario.* Indo-Dutch Studies on Development Alternatives 5. New Delhi: Sage.

———. 1992. "Poverty, Work, and Gender in Urban India." Occasional Paper no. 133. Calcutta: Centre for Studies in Social Sciences.

Banerjee, Sikata. 1995. "Hindu Nationalism and the Construction of Woman: The Shiv Sena Organises Women in Bombay." In *Women and Right-Wing Movements: Indian Experiences,* edited by Tanika Sarkar and Urvashi Butalia. London: Zed Books.

Banerjee, Sumanta. 1984. *India's Simmering Revolution: The Naxalite Uprising.* London: Zed Press.

———. 1989. *The Parlour and the Streets: Elite and Popular Culture in Nineteenth Century Calcutta.* Calcutta: Seagull Books.

Bardhan, Pranab. 1984. *The Political Economy of Development in India.* Oxford: Blackwell.

Barrett, Michele. 1980. *Women's Oppression Today: Problems in Marxist Feminist Analysis.* London: Verso.

Barrig, Maruja. 1989. "The Difficult Equilibrium between Bread and Roses: Women's Organizations and the Transition from Dictatorship to Democracy in Peru." In *The Women's Movement in Latin America: Feminism and the Transition to Democracy,* edited by Jane S. Jacquette, 114–48. Boston: Unwin Hyman.

Basu, Amrita. 1987. "Grassroots Movements and the State: Reflections on Radical Change in India." *Theory and Society* 16:647–84.

———. 1990. "Indigenous Feminism, Tribal Radicalism, and Grassroots Mobilization in India." *Dialectical Anthropology* 15 (2–3): 193–209.

———. 1992. *Two Faces of Protest: Contrasting Modes of Women's Activism in India.* Berkeley: University of California Press.

———, ed. 1995. *The Challenge of Local Feminisms: Women's Movements in Global Perspective.* Boulder, Colo.: Westview Press.

Beall, Jo, Shireen Hassim, and Alison Todes. 1989. "'A Bit on the Side'? Gender Struggles in the Politics of Transformation in South Africa." *Feminist Review* 33:30–56.

Beneria, Lourdes, ed. 1982. *Women and Development: The Sexual Division of Labor in Rural Societies.* New York: Praeger/ILO.

Beneria, Lourdes, and Martha Roldan. 1987. *The Crossroads of Class and Gender:*

Industrial Homework, Subcontracting, and Household Dynamics in Mexico City.
Chicago: University of Chicago Press.

Bookman, Ann, and Sandra Morgen. 1988. *Women and the Politics of Empowerment.*
Philadelphia: Temple University Press.

Boserup, Esther. 1970. *Women's Role in Economic Development.* London: Allen and
Unwin.

Bourdieu, Pierre. 1975. "The Specificity of the Scientific Field and the Social
Conditions of the Progress of Reason." Translated by R. Nice, in *Social Science
Information* 14 (6): 19–47.

———. 1991. "A Reply to Some Objections." In *Other Words: Essays Towards a Reflexive
Sociology.* Stanford, Calif.: Stanford University Press.

Bourdieu, Pierre, and Loic J. D. Wacquant. 1992. *An Invitation to Reflexive Sociology.*
Chicago: University of Chicago Press.

Brand, Karl-Werner. 1990. "Cyclical Aspects of New Social Movements: Waves of
Cultural Criticism and Mobilization Cycles of New Middle-Class Radicalism." In
*Challenging the Political Order: New Social and Political Movements in Western
Democracies,* edited by Russell Dalton and Manfred Kuechler. New York: Oxford
University Press.

Briet, Martine, P. Bert Klandermans, and Frederike Kroon. 1987. "How Women
Became Involved in the Women's Movement of the Netherlands." In *The Women's
Movements of the United States and Western Europe: Consciousness, Political
Opportunity, and Public Policy,* edited by Mary Fainsod Katzenstein and Carol
McClurg Mueller. Philadelphia: Temple University Press.

Burawoy, Michael, et al. 1991. *Ethnography Unbound: Power and Resistance in the
Modern Metropolis.* Berkeley: University of California Press.

Butler, Judith. 1992. "Contingent Foundations: Feminism and the Question of
'Postmodernism.'" In *Feminists Theorize the Political,* edited by Judith Butler and
Joan Scott. New York: Routledge.

Butler, Judith, and Joan W. Scott, eds. 1992. *Feminists Theorize the Political.* New York:
Routledge.

Calman, Leslie. 1989. "Women and Movement Politics in India." *Asian Survey* 29 (10):
940–58.

———. 1992. *Toward Empowerment: Women and Movement Politics in India.* Boulder,
Colo.: Westview Press.

Caplan, Patricia. 1985. *Class and Gender in India: Women and Their Organisations in a
South Indian City.* London: Tavistock.

Carden, Maren Lockwood. 1978. "The Proliferation of a Social Movement: Ideology
and Individual Incentives in the Contemporary Feminist Movement." In *Research in
Social Movements, Conflict and Change,* vol. 1, edited by L. Liriesberg. Greenwich,
Conn.: JAI Press.

Centre for Monitoring the Indian Economy (CMIE). 1996. *India's Social Sectors.*
Bombay: CMIE.

Chafetz, Janet Saltzman, and Anthony Gary Dworkin. 1986. *Female Revolt: Women's Movements in World and Historical Perspective.* Totowa, N.J.: Rowman and Allenheld.

Chakravarty, Renu. 1980. *Communists in the Indian Women's Movement.* New Delhi: People's Publishing House.

Charlton, Sue Ellen M., Jana Everett, and Kathleen Staudt. 1989. *Women, the State, and Development.* Albany: State University of New York Press.

Chatterjee, Partha. 1982. "Caste and Politics in West Bengal." In *Land, Caste, and Politics in Indian States,* edited by Gail Omvedt. Delhi: Authors Guild.

———. 1989. "The Nationalist Resolution of the Women's Question." In *Recasting Women: Essays in Colonial History,* edited by Kumkum Sanghari and Sudesh Vaid. New Delhi: Kali for Women.

———. 1990. "The Political Culture of Calcutta." In *Calcutta, The Living City,* vol. 2, edited by Sukanta Chaudhuri. Calcutta: Oxford University Press.

Chaudhuri, Sukanta. 1990. *Calcutta, the Living City.* Calcutta: Oxford University Press.

Chernin, Kim. 1983. *In My Mother's House.* New York: Harper Colophon.

Chinchilla, Norma Stoltz. 1992. "Marxism, Feminism, and the Struggle for Democracy in Latin America." In *The Making of Contemporary Social Movements in Latin America,* edited by Arturo Escobar and Sonia Alvarez. Boulder, Colo.: Westview Press.

Clemens, Elisabeth S. 1993. "Organizational Repertoires and Institutional Change: Women's Groups and the Transformation of U.S. Politics, 1890–1920." *American Journal of Sociology* 98 (4): 755–98.

Cohen, Jean. 1985. "Strategy or Identity: New Theoretical Paradigms and Contemporary Social Movements." *Social Research* 52 (4): 663–716.

Collins, Patricia Hill. 1991. *Black Feminist Thought.* New York: Routledge.

Conell, Carol, and Kim Voss. 1990. "Formal Organization and the Fate of Social Movement: Craft Association and Class Alliance in the Knights of Labor." *American Sociological Review* 55:255–69.

Costain, Ann N., and W. Douglas Costain. 1987. "Strategy and Tactics of the Women's Movement in the United States: The Role of Political Parties." In *The Women's Movements of the United States and Western Europe: Consciousness, Political Opportunity, and Public Policy,* edited by Mary Fainsod Katzenstein and Carol McClurg Mueller. Philadelphia: Temple University Press.

Custers, Peter. 1987. *Women in the Tebhaga Uprising.* Calcutta: Naya Prokash.

Dalton, Russell J., Manfred Kuechler, and Wilhelm Burklin. 1990. "The Challenge of New Movements." In *Challenging the Political Order: New Social and Political Movements in Western Democracies,* edited by Russell J. Dalton and Manfred Kuechler. New York: Oxford University Press.

Dasgupta, Biplab. 1975. *The Naxalite Movement.* Bombay: Allied.

Datar, Chhaya. 1988. "Reflections on the Anti-Rape Campaign in Bombay." In *Women's Struggles and Strategies,* edited by Saskia Wieringa. Aldershot, England: Gower Press.

Davis, Angela. 1983. *Women, Race, and Class.* New York: Vintage Books.

Debi, Bharati. 1988. *Middle-Class Working Women of Calcutta: A Study in Continuity and Change*. Calcutta: Anthropological Survey of India, Ministry of Human Resource Development, Department of Culture.

della Porta, Donatella, and Dieter Rucht. 1995. "Left-Libertarian Movements in Context: A Comparison of Italy and West Gemany, 1965–1990." In *The Politics of Social Protest*, edited by J. Craig Jenkins and Bert Klandermans. Minneapolis: University of Minnesota Press.

Dennis, Peggy. 1977. *The Autobiography of an American Communist: A Personal View of a Political Life, 1925–75*. Berkeley, Calif.: Lawrence Hall.

Desai, A. R., ed. 1990. *Women's Liberation and Politics of Religious Personal Laws in India*. Bombay: C. G. Shah Memorial Trust.

Desai, Manisha. 1990. "Affiliation and Autonomy: The Origins of the Women's Movement in Western India." Ph.D dissertation, Washington University, St. Louis, Mo.

Desai, Neera, ed. 1988. *A Decade of Women's Movement in India*. Bombay: Himalaya.

Desai, Neera, and Maithreyi Krishnaraj. 1987. *Women and Society in India*. Delhi: Ajanta.

Devi, Ashapurna. 1965. *Pratham Pratisruti*. Calcutta: Mitra and Ghosh.

Devi, Mahasveta. 1997a. *Mother of 1084 (Hajar Churashir Ma)*. Calcutta: Seagull Books.

———. 1997b. *Breast Stories: Draupadi, Breast Giver, Choli ke Pichhe*. Calcutta: Seagull Books.

Dietrich, Gabriele. 1986. "A Perspective on the Women's Question." *Marxist Review* 19 (3): 160–78.

DiMaggio, Paul J., and Walter W. Powell. 1991. "The Iron Cage Revisited: Institutional Isomorphism and Collective Rationality." In *The New Institutionalism in Organizational Analysis*, edited by Walter W. Powell and Paul J. DiMaggio. Chicago: University of Chicago Press.

DuBois, Ellen. 1978. *Feminism and Suffrage*. Ithaca, N.Y.: Cornell University Press.

———. 1991. "Woman Suffrage and the Left: An International Socialist-Feminist Perspective." *New Left Review* 186:20–45.

Echols, Alice. 1989. *Daring to Be Bad: Radical Feminism in America, 1967–75*. Minneapolis: University of Minnesota Press.

Eckstein, Susan, ed. 1989. *Power and Popular Protest: Latin American Social Movements*. Berkeley: University of California Press.

Economic and Political Weekly (EPW). 1979. "Maharashtra-II: Lessons in Flexibility." *Economic and Political Weekly* (Bombay) 14 (36): 1532–33.

———. 1980. "Maharashtra: Two Birthdays." *Economic and Political Weekly* 15 (33): 1383–84.

———. 1987. "Maharashtra: Long Wait." *Economic and Political Weekly* 22 (52): 2235.

———. 1988. "Pawar's Political Tasks." *Economic and Political Weekly* 23 (35): 1774.

———. 1995a. "Non-Congress, Non-Maratha." *Economic and Political Weekly* 30 (11): 533–34.

———. 1995b. "Still Born Third Front." *Economic and Political Weekly* 30 (2): 64–65.

Eisenstein, Zillah. 1984. *Feminism and Sexual Equality: Crisis in Liberal America.* New York: Monthly Review Press.

Engels, Friedrich. 1891. *The Origins of the Family, Private Property, and the State.* Moscow.

Enloe, Cynthia. 1989. *Bananas, Beaches, and Bases: Making Feminist Sense of International Politics.* London: Pandora.

Esping-Anderson, Gosta. 1985. *Politics against Markets.* Princeton, N.J.: Princeton University Press.

Etzioni, Amitai. 1968. *The Active Society.* New York: Free Press.

Evans, Peter. 1979. *Dependent Development: The Alliance of Multinational, State, and Local Capital in Brazil.* Princeton, N.J.: Princeton University Press.

Evans, Sara. 1980. *Personal Politics.* New York: Vintage Books.

Everett, Jana Matson. 1979. *Women and Social Change in India.* New Delhi: Heritage.

Fantasia, Rick. 1988. *Cultures of Solidarity.* Berkeley: University of California Press.

Fantasia, Rick, and Eric Hirsch. 1995. "Culture in Rebellion: The Appropriation and Transformation of the Veil in the Algerian Transformation." In *Social Movements and Culture,* edited by Hank Johnston and Bert Klandermans. Social Movements, Protest, and Contention Series, vol. 4. Minneapolis: University of Minnesota Press.

Ferree, Myra Marx. 1995. "Patriarchies and Feminisms: The Two Women's Movements of Post-Unification Germany." *Social Politics* 2 (1): 10–24.

Ferree, Myra Marx, and Beth Hess. 1985. *Controversy and Coalition: The New Feminist Movement.* Boston: Twayne.

Ferree, Myra Marx, and Patricia Yancey Martin, eds. 1995. *Feminist Organizations: Harvest of the New Women's Movement.* Philadelphia: Temple University Press.

Ferree, Myra Marx, and Frederick Miller. 1985. "Mobilization and Meaning: Toward an Integration of Social Psychological and Resource Perspectives on Social Movements." *Sociological Inquiry* 55:38–51.

Fireman, Bruce, and William Gamson. 1979. "Utilitarian Logic in the Resource Mobilization Perspective." In *The Dynamics of Social Movements,* edited by Mayer N. Zald and John D. McCarthy. Cambridge, Mass.: Winthrop.

Flavia Agnes. 1994. "Women's Movement within a Secular Framework." *Economic and Political Weekly* 29(19):1123–28.

Fligstein, Neil, and McAdam, Doug. 1997. "A Political-Cultural Approach to the Problem of Strategic Action." Working paper. Center for Culture, Organization, and Politics, University of California, Berkeley.

Forbes, Geraldine. 1981. "The Indian Women's Movement: A Struggle for Women's Rights or National Liberation." In *The Extended Family: Women and Political Participation in India and Pakistan,* edited by Gail Minault. Delhi: Chanakya.

Franda, Marcus. 1971. *Radical Politics in West Bengal.* Cambridge, Mass.: MIT Press.

Frankel, Francine R. 1978. *India's Political Economy, 1947–1977: The Gradual Revolution.* Princeton, N.J.: Princeton University Press.

Fraser, Nancy. 1989. *Unruly Practices: Power, Discourse, and Gender in Contemporary Social Theory.* Minneapolis: University of Minnesota Press.

Fraser, Nancy, and Linda J. Nicholson. 1990. "Social Criticism without Philosophy: An Encounter between Feminism and Postmodernism." In *Feminism/Postmodernism*, edited by Linda J. Nicholson. New York: Routledge.

Freeman, Jo. 1973. "The Tyranny of Structurelessness." In *Radical Feminism*, edited by Anne Koedt, Ellen Levine, and Anita Rapone. New York: Quadrangle.

———. 1975. *The Politics of Women's Liberation*. New York: Longman.

———. 1979. "Resource Mobilization and Strategy: A Model for Analyzing Social Movement Organization Actions." In *The Dynamics of Social Movements*, edited by Mayer Zald and John McCarthy. Cambridge, Mass.: Winthrop.

Freire, Paolo. 1970. *Pedagogy of the Oppressed*. Translated by Myra Bergman Ramos. New York: Seabury Press.

Gamson, William. 1975. *The Strategy of Social Protest*. Homewood, Ill.: Dorsey Press.

———. 1988. "Political Discourse and Collective Action." *International Social Movement Research*, vol. 1. Greenwich: JAI Press.

Gamson, William A., and David S. Meyer. 1996. "Framing Political Opportunity." In *Comparative Perspectives on Social Movements*, edited by Doug McAdam, John D. McCarthy, and Mayer N. Zald. Cambridge: Cambridge University Press.

Gandhi, Nandita, and Nandita Shah. 1991. *The Issues at Stake: Theory and Practice in the Contemporary Women's Movement in India*. New Delhi: Kali for Women.

Gangadharan. 1970. "Anti-social Movement." *Mainstream* 8 (March 2): 19–20.

Garner, Roberta Ash, and Mayer N. Zald. 1985. "The Political Economy of Social Movement Sectors." In *Social Movements in an Organizational Society*, edited by Mayer N. Zald and John D. McCarthy. New Brunswick, N.J.: Transaction Books.

Gelb, Joyce. 1989. *Feminism and Politics: A Comparative Perspective*. Berkeley: University of California Press.

———. 1990. "Feminism and Political Action." In *Challenging the Political Order: New Social and Political Movements in Western Democracies*, edited by Russell J. Dalton and Manfred Kuechler. New York: Oxford University Press.

Gerlach, Luther, and Virginia Hine. 1970. *People, Power, and Change: Movements of Social Transformation*. Indianapolis: Bobbs-Merrill.

Ghosh, S. 1974. *The Naxalite Movement: A Maoist Experiment*. Calcutta: K. L. Mukhopadhyay.

Gilmartin, Christina. 1989. "Gender, Politics, and Patriarchy in China: The Experiences of Early Women Communists, 1920–27." In *Promissory Notes: Women in the Transition to Socialism*, edited by Sonia Kruks, Rayna Rapp, and Marilyn B. Young. New York: Monthly Review Press.

Gitlin, Todd. 1980. *The Whole World Is Watching*. Berkeley: University of California Press.

Gluck, Sherna Berger, and Daphne Patai. 1991. *Women's Words: The Feminist Practice of Oral History*. New York: Routledge.

Gogate, Sudha. "The Status of Women as Reflected in Marathi News Media (1930–70)." Unpublished monograph. Bombay, Centre for Education and Documentation.

Goody, Jack, and S. J. Tambiah. 1973. *Bridewealth and Dowry.* Cambridge: Cambridge Unversity Press.

Gornick, Vivian. 1977. *Romance of American Communism.* New York: Basic Books.

Gothoskar, Sujata, and Vibhuti Patel. 1982. "Documents from the Indian Women's Movement." *Feminist Review* 12:92–103.

Gothoskar, Sujata, Nandita Shah, and Nandita Gandhi. 1994. "Maharashtra's Policy on Women." *Economic and Political Weekly* 29 (48): 3019–22.

Government of India (GOI). 1975. Committee on the Status of Women in India. *Towards Equality.* New Delhi.

———. 1981a. *Calcutta Census Handbook.* Calcutta.

———. 1981b. *Census of India.* Primary Census Abstract. New Delhi.

———. 1981c. *Greater Bombay District Census Handbook.* New Delhi.

———. 1986. Ministry of Social Welfare. *Handbook on Social Welfare Statistics.* New Delhi.

———. 1988a. Department of Women and Child Development. *Shram Shakti: Report of the National Commission on Self Employed Women and Women in the Informal Sector.* New Delhi.

———. 1988b. Ministry of Home Affairs. National Crime Records Bureau. *Crime in India.* New Delhi.

———. 1988. Ministry of Labour. *Indian Labour Yearbook.* Simla.

———. 1989. Ministry of Industry. *Handbook of Industrial Statistics.* New Delhi.

———. 1991. *Census of India.* Provisional Tables. New Delhi.

Government of West Bengal. 1986. *Economic Review, 1985–86: Statistical Appendix.* Calcutta.

Gurr, Ted. 1970. *Why Men Rebel.* Princeton, N.J.: Princeton University Press.

Gutentag, Marcia, and Paul Secord. 1983. *Too Many Women? The Sex Ratio Question.* Beverly Hills, Calif.: Sage.

Haraway, Donna. 1990. "A Manifesto for Cyborgs: Science, Technology and Socialist Feminism in the 1980s." In *Feminism/Postmodernism,* edited by Linda J. Nicholson. New York: Routledge.

Harding, Sandra. 1987. *Feminism and Methodology.* Bloomington: University of Indiana Press.

Harriss, John. 1989. "Indian Industrialization and the State." In *Sociology of "Developing Societies": South Asia,* edited by Hamza Alavi and John Harriss. New York: Monthly Review Press.

Hartmann, Heidi. 1981. "The Unhappy Marriage of Marxism and Feminism: Towards a More Progressive Union." In *Women and Revolution,* edited by Lydia Sargeant. Boston: South End Press.

Hellman, Judith. 1987. *Journeys among Women: Feminism in Five Italian Cities.* New York: Oxford University Press.

Heng, Geraldine. 1996. "'A Great Way to Fly': Nationalism, the State, and Varieties of Third World Feminism." In *Feminist Genealogies, Colonial Legacies, Democratic*

Futures, edited by M. Jacqui Alexander and Chandra Talpade Mohanty. New York: Routledge.

Hirsch, Marianne, and Evelyn Fox Keller, eds. 1990. *Conflicts in Feminism.* New York: Routledge.

hooks, bell. 1984. *Feminist Theory: From Margin to Center.* Boston: South End Press.

Hutnyk, John. 1996. *The Rumour of Calcutta.* London: Zed Books.

Inglehart, Ronald. 1988. "The Rennaissance of Political Culture." *American Political Science Review* 82:1203–30.

Jacquette, Jane S., ed. 1989. *The Women's Movement in Latin America: Feminism and the Transition to Democracy.* Boston: Unwin Hyman.

Jaggar, Allison. 1983. *Feminist Politics and Human Nature.* Sussex: Harvester.

Jain, Devaki. 1980. *Women's Quest for Power.* Delhi: Vikas.

Jayawardena, Kumari. 1986. *Feminism and Nationalism in the Third World.* London: Zed Books.

———. 1988. "Comments on Feminism and the Left in South Asia." *South Asia Bulletin* 8:88–91.

Jayawardena, Kumari, and Govind Kelkar. 1989. "The Left and Feminism." *Economic and Political Weekly* 24 (38): 2123–26.

Jelin, Elizabeth, ed. 1990. *Women and Social Change in Latin America.* London: Zed Books.

Jenkins, J. Craig. 1983. "Resource Mobilization Theory and the Study of Social Movements." *American Review of Sociology* 9:527–53.

Jenkins, J. Craig, and Bert Klandermans, eds. 1995. *The Politics of Social Protest.* Minneapolis: University of Minnesota Press.

Jenson, Jane. 1987a. "Changing Discourse, Changing Ideas." In *The Women's Movements of the United States and Western Europe,* edited by Mary Fainsod Katzenstein and Carol McClurg Mueller. Philadelphia: Temple University Press.

———. 1987b. "Both Friend and Foe: Women and State Welfare." In *Becoming Visible: Women in European History,* 2nd ed., edited by Renate Bridenthal, Claudia Koonz, and Susan Stuard. Boston: Houghton Mifflin.

———. 1991. "Making Claims: Social Policy and Gender Relations in Postwar Sweden and France." Paper presented at the annual meeting of the Canadian Sociology and Anthropology Association, Ontario, June.

Johnston, Hank, and Bert Klandermans, eds. 1995. *Social Movements and Culture.* Minneapolis: University of Minnesota Press.

Kabeer, Naila. 1994. *Reversed Realities: Gender Hierarchies in Development Thought.* London: Verso.

Kamat, A. R. 1980. "Politico-Economic Developments in Maharashtra. A Review of the Post-Independence Period." *Economic and Political Weekly* 15 (40): 1627–30, 1669–78.

Kandiyoti, Deniz. 1988. "Bargaining with Patriarchy." *Gender and Society* 2 (3): 274–90.

Kannabiran, Vasanth, and Kalpana Kannabiran. 1996. "Looking at Ourselves: The

Women's Movement in Hyderabad." In *Feminist Genealogies, Colonial Legacies, Democratic Futures,* edited by M. Jacqui Alexander and Chandra Talpade Mohanty. New York: Routledge.

Kaplan, Gisela. 1992. *Contemporary Western European Feminism.* New York: New York University Press.

Kaplan, Temma. 1982. "Female Consciousness and Collective Action: The Case of Barcelona." *Signs* 7 (3): 545–66.

———. 1990. "Community and Resistance in Women's Political Cultures." *Dialectical Anthropology* 15:259–67.

Karat, Brinda. 1991. "On Birati, the CPI(M), and Tradition in Bengal." *Economic and Political Weekly* 26 (12): 1182–84.

Katzenstein, Mary Fainsod. 1989. "Organizing against Violence: Strategies of the Indian Women's Movement." *Pacific Affairs* 62 (1): 52–71.

Katzenstein, Mary Fainsod, and Carol McClurg Mueller. 1987. *The Women's Movements of the United States and Western Europe: Consciousness, Political Opportunity, and Public Policy.* Philadelphia: Temple University Press.

Kaur, Manmohan. 1985. *Women in India's Freedom Struggle.* New Delhi: Sterling.

Kishwar, Madhu. 1990. "Women's Organizations: The Pressure of Unrealistic Expectations." *Manushi* 59:11–14.

Klandermans, Bert. 1984. "Mobilization and Participation: Social-Psychological Expansions of Resource Mobilization Theory." *American Sociological Review* 49:583–600.

———. 1990. "Linking the 'Old' and 'New': Movement Networks in the Netherlands." In *Challenging the Political Order: New Social and Political Movements in Western Democracies,* edited by Russell J. Dalton and Manfred Kuechler. New York: Oxford University Press.

———. 1992. "The Social Construction of Protest and Multi-organizational Fields." In *Frontiers in Social Movement Theory,* edited by Aldon Morris and Carol McClurg Mueller. New Haven, Conn.: Yale University Press.

Klein, Ethel. 1984. *Gender Politics: From Consciousness to Mass Politics.* Cambridge: Harvard University Press.

Kohli, Atul. 1984. "Communist Reformers in West Bengal: Origins, Features, and Relations with New Delhi." In *State Politics in Contemporary India: Crisis or Continuity?* edited by John R. Woods. Boulder, Colo.: Westview Press.

———. 1990. *Democracy and Discontent: India's Growing Crisis of Governability.* Cambridge: Cambridge University Press.

Kosambi, Meera. 1991. "Images of Women and the Feminine in Maharashtra." *Economic and Political Weekly* 26 (25): 1519–24.

Kothari, Rajni. 1986. "Masses, Classes, and the State." *Economic and Political Weekly* 21 (5): 210–16.

Kriesi, Hanspeter. 1995. "The Political Opportunity Structure of New Social Movements: Its Impact on Their Mobilization." In *The Politics of Social Protest,* edited by J. Craig Jenkins and Bert Klandermans. Minneapolis: University of Minnesota Press.

Kriesi, Hanspeter, Ruud Koopmans, Jan Willem Duyvendak, and Marco G. Giugni. 1995. *New Social Movements in Western Europe: A Comparative Analysis.* Minneapolis: University of Minnesota Press.

Kruks, Sonia, Rayna Rapp, and Marilyn B. Young. 1989. *Promissory Notes: Women in the Transition to Socialism.* New York: Monthly Review Press.

Kumar, Radha. 1983. "Family and Factory: Women in the Bombay Textile Industry, 1919–1939." *Indian Economic and Social History Review* 20(1): 81–110.

————. 1989. "Contemporary Indian Feminism." *Feminist Review* 33:20–29.

————. 1993. *A History of Doing: An Illustrated Account of Movements for Women's Rights and Feminism in India, 1800–1990.* New Delhi: Kali for Women.

Lahiri, T. B. 1978. "Calcutta—a Million City with a Million Problems." In *Million Cities of India,* edited by R. P. Mishra. New Delhi: Vikas.

Landes, Joan. 1989. "Marxism and the Woman Question." In *Promissory Notes: Women in the Transition to Socialism,* edited by Sonia Kruks, Rayna Rapp, and Marilyn B. Young. New York: Monthly Review Press.

Laslett, Barbara, Johanna Brenner, and Yesim Arat. 1995. *Rethinking the Political: Gender, Resistance, and the State.* Chicago: University of Chicago Press.

Lele, Jayant. 1995. "Saffronization of the Shiv Sena: The Political Economy of City, State, and Nation." In *Bombay: Metaphor for Modern India,* edited by Sujata Patel and Alice Thorner. Bombay: Oxford University Press.

Lele, Medha K., Nirmala Sathe, Anjali Mahadeo, and Simrita Gopal Singh. N.d. "Stree Mukti Andolan Sanpark Samiti, Maharashtra: A Case Study." Pune: Aalochana, Centre for Documentation and Research on Women.

Lessing, Doris. 1962. *The Golden Notebook.* New York: Bantam.

Lieten, G. K. 1994. "For a New Debate on West Bengal." *Economic and Political Weekly* 29 (29): 1835–37.

Lo, Clarence Y. H. 1992. "Communities of Challengers in Social Movement Theory." In *Frontiers in Social Movement Theory,* edited by Aldon Morris and Carol McClurg Mueller. New Haven, Conn.: Yale University Press.

Lovenduski, Joni. 1986. *Women and European Politics: Contemporary Feminism and Public Policy.* Amherst: University of Massachusetts Press.

MacKinnon, Catharine A. 1983. "Feminism, Marxism, and the State: Toward a Feminist Jurisprudence." *Signs* 8 (4): 635–58.

Maguire, Diarmuid. 1995. "Opposition Movements and Opposition Parties: Equal Partners or Dependent Relations in the Struggle for Power and Reform?" In *The Politics of Social Protest,* edited by J. Craig Jenkins and Bert Klandermans. Minneapolis: University of Minnesota Press.

Mainwaring, Scott, and Eduardo S. Viola. 1984. "New Social Movements, Political Culture, and Democracy: Brazil and Argentina in the 1980s." *Telos* 17 (3): 17–52.

Mallick, Ross. 1993. *Development Policy of a Communist Government: West Bengal since 1977.* Cambridge: Cambridge University Press.

Mani, Lata. 1989. "Contentious Traditions: The Debate on Sati in Colonial India." In *Recasting Women,* edited by Kunkum Sanghari and Sudesh Vaid. New Delhi: Kali for Women.

McAdam, Doug. 1982. *Political Process and the Development of Black Insurgency, 1930–1970.* Chicago: University of Chicago Press.

———. 1994. "Culture and Social Movements." In *New Social Movements: From Ideology to Identity,* edited by Enrique Larana, Hank Johnston, and Joseph Gusfield. Philadelphia: Temple University Press.

McCarry, John. 1995. "Bombay: India's Capital of Hope." *National Geographic* 187 (3): 42–67.

McCarthy, John D., and Mayer N. Zald. 1977. "Resource Mobilization and Social Movements: A Partial Theory." *American Journal of Sociology* 82:1212–41.

———. 1979. *The Dynamics of Social Movements.* Cambridge, Mass.: Winthrop.

Melucci, Alberto. 1985. "The Symbolic Challenge of Contemporary Movements." *Social Research* 52:781–816.

———. 1988. "Getting Involved: Identity and Mobilization in Social Movements." In *International Social Movements Research,* vol. 1, edited by Bert Klandermans, Hanspeter Kriesi, and Sidney Tarrow. Greenwich, Conn.: JAI Press.

Meyer, David, and Suzanne Staggenborg. 1996. "Movements, Countermovements, and the Structure of Political Opportunity." *American Journal of Sociology* 101 (6): 1628–60.

Mies, Maria. 1986. *Patriarchy and Accumulation on a World Scale.* London: Zed Books.

Minault, Gail. 1981. *The Extended Family: Women and Political Participation in India and Pakistan.* Delhi: Chanakya.

Mishra, R. P. 1978. *Million Cities of India.* New Delhi: Vikas.

Mitter, Swasti. 1986. *Common Fate, Common Bond: Women in the Global Economy.* London: Pluto.

Moghadam, Valentine M. 1993. *Modernizing Women: Gender and Social Change in the Middle East.* Boulder, Colo.: Lynne Reinner.

———. 1994a. *Identity Politics and Women.* Boulder, Colo.: Westview.

———. 1994b. *Gender and National Identity: Women and Change in Muslim Societies.* London: Zed Books.

Mohanty, Chandra. 1991. "Under Western Eyes: Feminist Scholarship and Colonial Discourses." In *Third World Women and the Politics of Feminism,* edited by Chandra Mohanty, Ann Russo, and Lourdes Torres. Bloomington: University of Indiana Press.

Molyneux, Maxine. 1981. "Women in Socialist Societies: Problems of Theory and Practice." In *Of Marriage and the Market,* edited by Kate Young et al. London: LSE Books.

———. 1985. "Mobilization without Emancipation? Women's Interests, State, and Revolution in Nicaragua." *Feminist Studies* 11 (2): 227–53.

———. 1989. "Women's Role in the Nicaraguan Revolutionary Process: The Early Years." In *Promissory Notes: Women in the Transition to Socialism,* edited by Sonia Kruks, Rayna Rapp, and Marilyn B. Young. New York: Monthly Review Press.

————. 1996. "Women's Rights and the International Context in the Post-Communist States." In *Mapping the Women's Movement,* edited by Monica Threlfall. London: Verso.

Morris, Aldon. 1984. *The Origins of the Civil Rights Movement.* New York: Free Press.

Morris, Aldon, and Carol McClurg Mueller. 1992. *Frontiers in Social Movement Theory.* New Haven, Conn.: Yale University Press.

Mutatkar, L. K. 1990. "Whither Maharashtra?" *Mainstream* 28 (29): 39–41.

National Sample Survey Organization (NSSO). 1988. *Sarvekshana* 11. Calcutta.

————. 1990. *Sarvekshana* 15. Calcutta.

————. 1992. *Sarvekshana* 16. Calcutta.

Nicholson, Linda. 1990. *Feminism and Post-Modernism.* London: Routledge.

Nossiter, T. J. 1988. *Marxist State Governments in India.* New York: Pinter.

Offe, Claus. 1974. "Structural Problems of the Capitalist State: Class Rule and the Political System. On the Selectiveness of Political Institutions." In *German Political Studies,* vol. 1, edited by Klaus von Beyme. London: Sage.

————. 1981. "The Attribution of Public Status to Interest Groups: Observations on the West German Case." In *Organizing Interests in Western Europe,* edited by Suzanne Berger. Cambridge: Cambridge University Press.

————. 1990. "Reflections on the Institutional Self-transformation of Movement Politics: A Tentative Stage Model." In *Challenging the Political Order: New Social and Political Movements in Western Democracies,* edited by Russell J. Dalton and Manfred Kuechler. New York: Oxford University Press.

Offe, Claus, and Helmut Wiesenthal. 1980. "Two Logics of Collective Action: Theoretical Notes on Social Class and Organizational Form." In *Political Power and Social Theory,* vol. 1. Greenwich, Conn.: JAI Press.

Omvedt, Gail. 1979. *We Will Smash This Prison.* Bombay: Orient Longman.

————. 1986a. "Women's Movement: Some Ideological Debates." *Lokayan Bulletin* 4 (6): 35–43.

————. 1986b. *Women in Popular Movements: India and Thailand during the Decade of Women.* Geneva: United Nations Research Institute for Social Development.

————. 1987. "Feminism and the Women's Movement in India." Bombay: Research Centre for Women's Studies.

————. 1993. *Reinventing Revolution: New Social Movements and the Socialist Tradition in India.* Armonk, N.Y.: Sharpe.

Patel, Sujata, and Alice Thorner. 1995a. *Bombay: Metaphor for Modern India.* Bombay: Oxford University Press.

————. 1995b. *Bombay: Mosaic of Modern Culture.* Bombay: Oxford University Press.

Pathak, Zakia, and Rajeshwari Sunder Rajan. 1989. "Shahbano." *Signs* 14 (3): 558–82.

Pearson, Gail. 1981. "Nationalism, Universalization, and the Extended Female Space in Bombay City." In *The Extended Family: Women and Political Participation in India and Pakistan,* edited by Gail Minault. Delhi: Chanakya.

Pendse, Sandeep. 1980. "Managements on the Offensive." *Economic and Political Weekly* 15 (30): 1253.

————. 1981. "The Datta Samant Phenomenon–I." *Economic and Political Weekly* 16 (16): 695–97.

Perrow, Charles. 1979. "The Sixties Observed." In *The Dynamics of Social Movements,* edited by John D. McCarthy and Mayer N. Zald. Cambridge: Winthrop, 1979.

Phillips, Anne. 1991. *Engendering Democracy.* University Park: Pennsylvania State University Press.

Piven, Frances Fox. 1984. "Women and the State: Ideology, Power, and the Welfare State." *Socialist Review* 14 (2): 11–19.

Piven, Frances Fox, and Richard Cloward. 1977. *Poor People's Movements: Why They Succeed, How They Fail.* New York: Vintage.

Pore, Kumud. 1991. "Women at Work: A Secondary Line of Operation." In *Indian Women in a Changing Industrial Scenario,* edited by Nirmala Banerjee. New Delhi: Sage.

Powell, Walter W., and DiMaggio, Paul J. 1990. *The New Institutionalism in Organizational Analysis.* Chicago: University of Chicago Press.

Przeworski, Adam. 1980. "Material Interests, Class Compromise, and the Transition to Socialism." *Politics and Society* 10 (1): 125–53.

Pye, Lucien, and Sidney Verba, eds. 1965. *Political Culture and Political Development.* Princeton, N.J.: Princeton University Press.

Raichaudhuri, Srabani. 1985. *Dimensions of Political Communication: West Bengal, 1970s.* Calcutta: K. P. Bagchi.

Ramanamma, A., and Bambawale, U. 1987. *Women in Indian Industry.* New Delhi: Mittal.

Ramanna, Mridula. 1989. "Social Background of the Educated in Bombay City: 1824–58." *Economic and Political Weekly* 24 (4): 203–11.

Ramaswamy, E. A. 1988. *Worker Consciousness and Trade Union Response.* Delhi: Oxford University Press.

Randall, Vicky. 1987. *Women and Politics: An International Perspective.* 2nd ed. Chicago: University of Chicago Press.

Ray, Bharati. 1988. "Freedom Movement and Women's Awakening in Bengal, 1911–1929." *Indian Historical Review* 17 (1–2): 130–63.

Ray, Dalia. 1990. *The Bengal Revolutionaries and the Freedom Movement.* New Delhi: Cosmo.

Reinharz, Shulamit. 1992. *Feminist Methods in Social Research.* New York: Oxford University Press.

Riley, Denise. 1988. *Am I That Name?* Minneapolis: University of Minnesota Press.

Roberts, Helen. 1981. *Doing Feminist Research.* London: Routledge and Kegan Paul.

Rohini, P. R. S. V. Sujatha, and C. Neelam. 1983. *"My Life Is One Long Struggle": Women, Work Organisation, and Struggle.* Belgaum, India: Pratishabd.

Rossi, Alice, ed. 1988 [1973]. *The Feminist Papers: From Adams to de Beauvoir.* Boston: Northeastern University Press.

Rothschild-Whitt, Joyce. 1979. "The Collectivist Organization: An Alternative to Bureaucratic Models." *American Sociological Review* 44: 509–27.

Rowbotham, Sheila. 1974. *Women, Resistance, and Revolution.* New York: Vintage Books.

Rowbotham, Sheila, Lynne Segal, and Hilary Wainwright. 1979. *Beyond the Fragments: Feminism and the Making of Socialism.* London: Merlin Press.

Roy Choudhury, Profulla. 1985. *Left Experiment in West Bengal.* New Delhi: Patriot.

Rucht, Dieter. 1996. "The Impact of National Context on Social Movement Structures: A Cross-Movement and Cross-National Comparison." In *Comparative Perspectives on Social Movements,* edited by Doug McAdam, John D. McCarthy, and Mayer N. Zald. Cambridge: Cambridge University Press.

Rudolph, Lloyd I., and Susanne Hoeber Rudolph. 1987. In *Pursuit of Lakshmi: The Political Economy of the Indian State.* Chicago: University of Chicago Press.

Ruggie, Mary. 1984. *The State and Working Women: A Comparative Study of Britain and Sweden.* Princeton, N.J.: Princeton University Press.

Rupp, Leila J., and Verta Taylor. 1990. *Survival in the Doldrums: The American Women's Rights Movement, 1945 to the 1960s.* Columbus: Ohio State University Press.

Ryan, Barbara. 1989. "Ideological Purity and Feminism: The U.S. Women's Movement from 1966 to 1975." *Gender and Society* 3:239–57.

Safa, Helen. 1990. "Women's Social Movements in Latin America." *Gender and Society* 4:354–70.

Salaff, Janet. 1981. *Working Daughters of Hong Kong: Filial Piety in the Family?* Cambridge: Cambridge University Press.

Sargent, Lydia, ed. 1981. *Women and Revolution. A Discussion of the Unhappy Marriage of Marxism and Feminism.* Boston: South End Press.

Sarkar, Tanika. 1987. *Bengal, 1928–34.* Oxford: Oxford University Press.

——. 1991. "Reflections on Birati Rape Cases: Gender in Bengal Ideology." *Economic and Political Weekly* 26 (5): 215–18.

——. 1992. "The Hindu Wife and the Hindu Nation: Domesticity and Nationalism in Nineteenth-Century Bengal." *Studies in History* 8 (2): 213–35.

Sarkar, Tanika, and Urvashi Butalia, eds. 1995. *Women and Right Wing Movements: Indian Experiences.* London: Zed Books.

Sarti, Cynthia. 1989. "The Panorama of Feminism in Brazil." *New Left Review* 173:75–90.

Savara, Mira. 1986. *Changing Trends in Women's Employment: A Case Study of the Textile Industry in Bombay.* Bombay: Himalaya.

Segal, Lynne. 1991. "Whose Left? Socialism, Feminism, and the Future." *New Left Review* 185:81–91.

Seidman, Gay. 1995. " 'No Freedom without the Women': Mobilization and Gender in South Africa, 1970–1992." In *Rethinking the Political: Gender, Resistance, and the State,* edited by Barbara Laslett, Johanna Brenner, and Yesim Arat. Chicago: University of Chicago Press.

Sen, Gita, and Caren Grown. 1987. *Development, Crises, and Alternative Visions: Third World Women's Perspectives.* New York: Monthly Review Press.

Sen, Ilina. 1989. "Feminists, Women's Movement, and the Working Class." *Economic and Political Weekly* 24 (29): 1639–41.

———, ed. 1990. *A Space within the Struggle: Women's Participation in People's Movements.* New Delhi: Kali for Women.

Sen, Sunil. 1985. *The Working Women and Popular Movements in Bengal.* Calcutta: K. P. Bagchi.

Sengupta, Chandan. 1987. "Bombay versus Calcutta: Ideas and Reality." *Nagarlok* 19 (1).

Setalvad, Teesta. 1995. "The Woman Shiv Sainik and Her Sister Swayamsevika." In *Women and Right-Wing Movements: Indian Experiences,* edited by Tanika Sarkar and Urvashi Butalia. London: Zed Books.

Sharma, Kumud. 1984. "Women in Struggle: A Case Study of the Chipko Movement." *Samya Shakti* 1 (2): 55–62.

———. 1989. "Shared Aspirations, Fragmented Realities: Contemporary Women's Movement in India: Its Dialectics and Dilemmas." New Delhi: Centre for Women in Development Studies Occasional Paper no. 12.

Singh, Prabhash Prasad. 1991. *Women in India: A Statistical Panorama.* New Delhi: Inter-India Publications.

Skocpol, Theda. 1985. "Bringing the State Back In: Strategies of Analysis in Current Research." In *Bringing the State Back In,* edited by Peter B. Evans, Dietrich Rueschemeyer, and Theda Skocpol. New York: Cambridge University Press.

Smith, Dorothy. 1987. *The Everyday World as Problematic: A Feminist Sociology.* Boston: Northeastern University Press.

Snow, David A., and Robert D. Benford. 1988. "Ideology, Frame Resonance, and Participant Mobilization." In *From Structure to Action: Comparing Social Movement Research across Cultures,* edited by Bert Klandermans, Hanspeter Kriesi, and Sidney Tarrow. Greenwich, Conn.: JAI Press.

———. 1992. "Master Frames and Cycles of Protest." In *Frontiers in Social Movement Theory,* edited by Aldon D. Morris and Carol McClurg Mueller. New Haven, Conn.: Yale University Press.

Snow, David A., et al. 1986. "Frame Alignment Processes, Micromobilization, and Movement Participation." *American Sociological Review* 51:464–81.

Srinivas, M. N. 1984. *Some Reflections on Dowry.* Delhi: Centre for Women's Development Studies; New Delhi: Oxford University Press.

Stacey, Judith. 1983. *Patriarchy and Socialist Revolution in China.* Berkeley: University of California Press.

———. 1984. "Are Feminists Afraid to Leave Home? The Challenge of Conservative Pro-family Feminism." In *What Is Feminism?* edited by J. Mitchell and A. Oakley. New York: Pantheon.

Staggenborg, Suzanne. 1989. "Stability and Innovation in the Women's Movement: A Comparison of Two Movement Organizations." *Social Problems* 36 (1): 75–92.

———. 1991. *The Pro-choice Movement: Organization and Activism in the Abortion Conflict.* New York: Oxford University Press.

———. 1995. "Can Feminist Organizations Be Effective?" In *Feminist Organizations: Harvest of the New Women's Movement,* edited by Myra Marx Ferree and Patricia Yancey Martin. Philadelphia: Temple University Press.

Standing, Hilary. 1985. "Women's Employment and the Household: Some Findings from Calcutta." *Economic and Political Weekly* 20 (17): WS23–38.

———. 1991. *Dependence and Autonomy: Women's Employment and the Family in Calcutta.* New York: Routledge.

Stree Shakti Sanghatana. 1989. *"We Were Making History": Women and the Telengana Uprising.* London: Zed Books.

Swidler, Ann. 1995. "Cultural Power and Social Movements." In *Social Movements and Culture,* edited by Hank Johnston and Bert Klandermans. Minneapolis: University of Minnesota Press.

Talwalkar, Govind. 1990. "Silver Lining in Gloomy Scenario." *Mainstream* 28 (29): 37–38.

Tarrow, Sidney. 1988. "National Politics and Collective Action: Recent Theory and Research in Western Europe and the United States." *American Review of Sociology* 14: 421–40.

———. 1989. *Struggle, Politics, and Reform: Collective Action, Social Movements, and Cycles of Protest.* Western Societies Occasional Papers no.21, Center for International Studies. Ithaca, N.Y.: Cornell University.

———. 1990. "The Phantom at the Opera: Political Parties and Social Movements of the 1960s and 1970s in Italy." In *Challenging the Political Order: New Social and Political Movements in Western Democracies,* edited by Russell J. Dalton and Manfred Kuechler. New York: Oxford University Press.

———. 1992. "Mentalities, Political Cultures, and Collective Action Frames." In *Frontiers in Social Movement Theory,* edited by Aldon Morris and Carol McClurg Mueller. New Haven, Conn.: Yale University Press.

———. 1994. *Power in Movement: Social Movements, Collective Action, and Politics.* Cambridge: Cambridge University Press.

Taylor, Verta. 1996. *Rock-a-by Baby: Feminism, Self Help, and Postpartum Depression.* New York: Routledge.

Taylor, Verta, and Nancy Whittier. 1992. "Collective Action in Social Movement Communities: Lesbian Feminist Mobilization." In *Frontiers in Social Movement Theory,* edited by Aldon Morris and Carol McClurg Mueller. New Haven, Conn.: Yale University Press.

———. 1995. "Analytical Approaches to Social Movement Culture: The Culture of the Women's Movement." In *Social Movements and Culture,* edited by Hank Johnston and Bert Klandermans. Minneapolis: University of Minnesota Press.

Thorner, Alice. 1995. "Bombay: Diversity and Exchange." In *Bombay: Metaphor for Modern India,* edited by Sujata Patel and Alice Thorner. Bombay: Oxford University Press.

Threlfall, Monica, ed. 1996. *Mapping the Women's Movement: Feminist Politics and Social Transformation in the North.* London: Verso.

Tilly, Charles. 1978. *From Mobilization to Revolution.* Reading, Mass.: Addison-Wesley.

Touraine, Alain. 1981. *The Voice and the Eye: An Analysis of Social Movements.* Cambridge: Cambridge University Press.

Tucker, Robert, ed. 1975. *The Lenin Anthology.* New York: Norton.

United Nations. 1991. *The World's Women, 1970–1990: Trends and Statistics.* New York.

Vanaik, Achin. 1990. *The Painful Transition: Bourgeois Democracy in India.* London: Verso.

Velayudhan, Meera. 1991. "Gender Ideology in Bengal." *Economic and Political Weekly* 6 (19): 1243–44.

Vogel, Lise. 1983. *Marxism and the Oppression of Women: Toward a Unitary Theory.* London: Pluto Press.

Wadley, Susan. 1977. "Women and the Hindu Tradition." In *Women in India: Two Perspectives,* edited by Doranne Jacobson and Susan Wadley. Delhi: Manohar.

Weiner, Myron, and Mary Fainsod Katzenstein. 1981. *India's Preferential Policies: Migrants, the Middle Class, and Ethnic Equality.* Chicago: University of Chicago Press.

Whittier, Nancy. 1995. *Feminist Generations.* Philadelphia: Temple University Press.

Wieringa, Saskia. 1985. "The Perfumed Nightmare: Some Notes on the Indonesian Women's Movement." The Hague: Institute of Social Studies.

Wildavsky, Aaron. 1987. "Choosing Preferences by Constructing Institutions: A Cultural Theory of Preference Formation." *American Political Science Review* 81:3–22.

Williams, Raymond. 1977. *Marxism and Literature.* Oxford: Oxford University Press.

Wood, John R., ed. 1984. *State Politics in Contemporary India: Crisis or Continuity.* Boulder, Colo.: Westview Press.

World Bank. 1988. *World Development Report.* Washington, D.C.

Wright, Erik Olin. 1985. *Classes.* London: Verso Books.

Young, Iris Marion. 1995. "Gender as Seriality: Thinking about Women as a Social Collective." In *Rethinking the Political: Gender, Resistance, and the State,* edited by Barbara Laslett, Johanna Brenner, and Yesim Arat. Chicago: University of Chicago Press.

Zald, Mayer N., and John D. McCarthy, eds. 1987. *Social Movements in an Organizational Society: Collected Essays.* New Brunswick, N.J.: Transaction Books.

———. 1980. "Social Movement Industries: Competition and Conflict among SMOs." In *Social Movements in an Organized Society,* edited by John D. McCarthy and Mayer N. Zald. New Brunswick, N.J.: Transaction Books.

Newspapers

Ananda Bazaar Patrika (1980–90)
Ganashakti (1980–90)
Indian Express (1980–90)
Loksatta (1980–90)
Statesman (1980–90)

Sunday Observer (1986–87)
Times of India (1980–90)

Movement Documents

All India Co-ordinating Committee on Working Women (AICCW). *The Voice of the Working Woman.* New Delhi: All India Co-ordinating Committee on Working Women.

All India Democratic Women's Association (AIDWA). 1990. Annual Conference Proceedings. Calcutta: AIDWA.

————. 1988. *Women's Equality: Quarterly Bulletin of AIDWA.* New Delhi: AIDWA.

Bera, Chhaya. 1990. *Women and the Left Front Government of West Bengal.* Calcutta: National Book Agency.

Brahme, Sulabha, Rahani Desai, and Sharayu Mhatre-Purohit. 1987. "The Material Basis for Women's Liberation." Bombay: Research Unit for Political Economy.

Centre for Women in Development Studies (CWDS). 1986. *Women and Development: Promises and Realities.* New Delhi: CWDS.

————. 1991. *Development for Whom?* New Delhi: CWDS.

Communist Party of India (CPI). *Emergency and the Communist Party.* CPI Publications. Delhi.

Forum Against Oppression of Women (FAOW). 1990. *Moving . . . but Not Quite There.* Bombay: FAOW.

————. 1991. *A Presention to the Joint Parliamentary Committee on Prenatal Diagnostic Techniques (Regulation and Prevention of Misuse) Bill.*

Forum Against Sex Determination and Sex Pre-selection (FASDSP). 1989. "Campaign against Sex Determination and Sex Pre-selection in India—Our Experiences." Bombay: FASDSP.

————. 1991. *A Brief Presentation to the Joint Parliamentary Committee on Prenatal Diagnostic Techniques (Regulation and Prevention of Misuse) Bill.*

Flavia Agnes. 1990. *My Story . . . Our Story of Rebuilding Broken Lives.* Bombay: FAOW.

————. 1992. "The Struggle and the Setback: An Evaluation of the Anti-Rape Campaign of the Eighties." Centre for Education and Documentation. Unpublished document.

Joshi, Sharad. *On Women's Question.* Shetkari Sanghatana pamphlet. Bombay.

Mukherjee, Kanak. 1985. *Nari Andolan o Amaader Kaaj.* Calcutta: PBGMS.

————. 1989. *Women's Emancipation Movement in India: A Marxist View.* New Delhi: National Book Centre.

Namboodripad, E. M. S. "Perspectives of Women's Movement." *Social Scientist* 40–41, special issue on women.

Nari, Mukti Sangharsh. 1988. *Conference Report.* Pune.

National Conference on Women's Studies. 1981. *A Report.* April 20–24.

National Conference: Perspectives for the Autonomous Women's Movement in India. 1985. *A Report.* Bombay.

National Conference Perspectives for Women's Liberation Movement in India. 1980. *A Report*. Bombay.

Pal Choudhury, Aparna. 1990. *Nari Andolan: Smritikatha*. Calcutta: PBGMS Publications.

Paschim Banga Ganatantrik Mahila Samiti (PBGMS). *Sanghatan o Sangbad*. Calcutta.

———. *Eksathe*. Calcutta.

Patel, Vibhuti. 1986. "Emergence and Proliferation of Autonomous Women's Organizations in India." Bombay: Research Centre for Women's Studies.

Ranadive, Vimal. 1988. *Feminists and the Women's Movement*. New Delhi: AIDWA.

Sachetana. 1986– . *Sachetana*. Calcutta.

Sachetana. 1986. *Annual General Meeting Report*. Calcutta.

Society for the Promotion of Area Resource Centres (SPARC). 1987. "Working It Out: Profiles of Women in the Informal Sector." Bombay: Society for the Promotion of Area Resource Centres.

Stree Mukti Andolan. *Conference Report*. March 8, 1979.

Women's Centre. Newsletters. Bombay.

Index

economic liberalization, 142, 165
employment and economic issues, 28–30,
    35, 43–44, 73–74, 96–97, 133, 160,
    181 n. 1
"Eve teasing," 123, 188–89 n.1

family issues, 24, 43, 80–82, 130,
    134–35, 164, 181 n. 1; and marriage,
    26–28, 189 n. 3; and law, 33–34
family courts, 146–47
feminism: as imperialist threat, 77; and
    male domination, 77–78, 134–35
feminism in Bombay, 113, 114–15, 116;
    influence of national and international
    feminism, 148–49, 189 n. 2; and Shiv
    Sena, 158
Ferree, Myra Marx, 12, 16
Flavia Agnes, 34, 38, 127, 129, 146, 158
Forum against Oppression of Women,
    116, 117–19; amniocentesis campaign,
    102–9, 113, 147, 150; autonomy from
    the state, 135–36, 162; and coalition
    politics, 143; consciousness raising,
    131–32; contraceptive issues, 149;
    cultural resources and media access,
    144–45; as dominant group in Bom-
    bay, 117, 126–27, 140–41; and family
    courts, 146–47; family as site of wom-
    en's oppression, 134–35; and feminism,
    134–35, 148–49; history, 117–18; ide-
    ology, 126–38; and Janwadi Mahila
    Sanghatana, 155–56; membership,
    124–26; and national and international
    feminist network, 148–49; organiza-
    tional structure, 150–51; the personal
    and the political, 137–38; rape as a po-
    litical issue, 127–28, 146; sexual harass-
    ment, 133; and the state, 146–48, 163;
    strategies 143–51; work as a political
    issue, 133. See also Women's Centre;
    women's organizations
Forum against Rape, 118. See also Forum
    against Oppression of Women

Forum against Sex Determination and Sex
    Preselection, 102, 104–5, 113; forma-
    tion, 106. See also amniocentesis
Fourth International, 117, 124–25
framing processes, 9
fundamentalism: Hindu fundamentalism,
    113, 133, 137, 181 n. 1; religious fun-
    damentalism, 142, 181 n. 1. See also
    Shiv Sena

Gamson, William, 151
Gandhi, Indira, 2, 4, 39–40, 54, 111, 167
Gandhi, Mahatma, 36, 39, 49, 114
Gandhi, Nandita, 108, 128, 135
gender interests, 17, 23. See also women's
    interests
general strike, 54, 57
Gore, Mrinal, 105, 113, 149, 152,
    190 n. 5

Hellman, Judith, 180 n. 11
Hutnyk, John, 45

Indian National Congress (INC), 36, 109.
    See also Congress (I)
Indian People's Theatre Association, 75

Janata Dal, 38. See also Mahila Dakshata
    Samiti
Janata Party, 40
Janwadi Mahila Sanghatana (JMS), 116,
    119–20; affiliated subalternity,
    156–57; and All India Democratic
    Women's Association, 154; anti–price-
    rise agitations, 152; and Centre of
    Indian Trade Unions, 153, 154–55;
    and coalition politics, 143, 155; and
    Communist Party India (Marxist),
    119, 137, 152, 154–55; consciousness
    raising, 132–33; family as site of
    women's oppression, 135; and femi-
    nism, 134–35; and Forum, 129,
    155–56; Hindu fundamentalism, 137;

RAKA RAY is assistant professor in the Department of Sociology at the University of California, Berkeley. She grew up in Calcutta, India, and came to the United States as an undergraduate at Bryn Mawr College. She received her Ph.D. from the University of Wisconsin–Madison.